Books should be returned or renewed by the last date above. Renew by phone **03000 41 31 31** or online *www.kent.gov.uk/libs*

Libraries Registration & Archives

CUSTOMER
SERVICE
EXCELLENCE
CSE

Kent
County
Council
kent.gov.uk

THE STY'S THE LIMIT

Years ago, after a drunken misunderstanding, Simon Dawson gave up his job in the city, moved to the wilds of Exmoor and became an accidental self-sufficient smallholder surrounded by animals. But now his life is changing all over again: horror of horrors, he's getting older. Enlisting a cast of best friends — including Ziggy, a panicked soon-to-be father; Garth, an annoying teenager; and the General, a rather handsome pig — to work through their age-related angsts, a plan is hatched to help each other mature (or immature). Hilarity and heartfelt discoveries ensue — all with a fair dose of pigs, chickens, goats and animal madness along the way.

THE STY'S THE LIMIT

When Middle Age Gets Mucky

Simon Dawson

ISIS
LARGE
PRINT

First published in Great Britain 2015
by
Orion
an imprint of the Orion Publishing Group Ltd.

First Isis Edition
published 2016
by arrangement with
Orion Publishing Group Ltd.
An Hachette UK Company

A catalogue record for this book is available
from the British Library.

ISBN 978–1–78541–157–1 (hb)
ISBN 978–1–78541–163–2 (pb)

Published by
F. A. Thorpe (Publishing)
Anstey, Leicestershire

Set by Words & Graphics Ltd.
Anstey, Leicestershire
Printed and bound in Great Britain by
T. J. International Ltd., Padstow, Cornwall

This book is printed on acid-free paper

To Peter Dawson and Jack Jackson, two dads who never got to see the life we'd go on to live but would have been so proud, once they stopped laughing.

Contents

Rolling in the mud

I hadn't had a crisis for ages. Ages and ages and ages, except, well, I had just had a kind of near-death experience, but it was hardly my fault and I wasn't exactly going fast when I rolled the quad bike — again. I'd say that on the scale of near-death experiences it was pretty far down the list, certainly way below electrocuting my testicles, which, on a man's hit parade of close shaves is the marker by which all others are judged. Let's face it, compared with lowering your nuts onto an electric fence, a near-death experience by rolling a quad bike pales into "hardly-counts-at-all". It's more, you know, a lapse in concentration. Definitely not a crisis.

"Oh. My. God! Rolling the quad bike . . . *is not a lapse in concentration!*" Debbie yelled as, squelching into the kitchen, I explained why I looked a bit muddier than usual. "That's a . . . a . . . oh, *GOD!*"

"I know, sorry, I've had a lot on my mind. But, hey, no harm done," I said, trying not to drip too much on the kitchen floor.

My wife took a deep breath and I watched her battle her nerves down from DEFCON panic to mildly catatonic. I wanted to give her a hug but I didn't want to restart her hyperventilation, plus I didn't think she'd appreciate sharing my mud. So I stayed where I was.

After a while she said, "Did you hit your head?"

"No."

"Break anything?"

"'Course not," I said, waggling limbs to prove all my bones were intact and at the same time inadvertently splattering mud onto the floor.

"Hurt yourself in any way?"

"Well, I do ache a bit," I said, trying to choose my words very carefully.

She considered me for a few seconds before concluding, "Right, two Paracetamol and three ibuprofen — and no arguments."

The ability of a woman to assess at a glance the extent of a man's injuries and instantly prescribe the curative mix of over-the-counter meds gives me the willies.

"Two and three," I repeated, nodding in a "That's a good one" way.

She sighed. "You're not going to take them, are you?"

I smiled brightly. "Not a chance," I replied, before breaking into song, "*Cos, I'm too sexy for my shirt, too sexy for my shiirrrrrt! I'm a model, you know what I mean, and I show my little bum in the kitchen.*" I peeled off my mucky clothes and danced them over to the washing machine.

It's the truth. I had a whole list of things on my mind:

1. Move Winnie (mum) and newborn piglets out of field shelter into a pig house in the woods.

2. *BEFORE* doing above, must renovate pig house in the woods.
3. Mend holes in stable roof made by Curry the goat running across it with her sharp hooves and try to figure out how to stop her getting up there in the first place.
4. Trim goats' feet.
5. Re-roof the love shack (chicken house).
6. Collect turkeys to bring on for Christmas.
7. Work out where to house Senorita Small, the rescued micro pig who isn't a micro pig.
8. Think of something to say on my radio slot this week.
9. Chop wood for fire.
10. Debbie's 50th birthday!

Okay, so that doesn't look quite as bad as I thought it would.

Debbie and I live on a smallholding in the middle of nowhere because fourteen years ago I accidentally agreed to swap our London life for a self-sufficient smallholding on Exmoor. I was young and drunk and it seemed like a good idea at the time. In no longer than the timespan of a TV commercial break, here's what happened:

It was New Year's Eve. The Millennium. The night the nineties clicked over into the noughties. We were in a crowded, boisterous, busy bar and I couldn't hear a word of what Debbie was saying. Not a word. I was thirty-two years old.

"I'm burnt out, done in, can't do it anymore. I can't do the work-until-you-drop thing for a second longer. I want out — I want *us* out. I want us to quit work, leave our London home, our London friends, our London life, everything we know and understand, and move down to the wilds of Exmoor, buy a 20-acre smallholding, fill it with crazy animals and live a self-sufficient good life," Debbie yelled into the noise. At least, it was something like that.

"But we'll only do it if you're absolutely sure. Absolutely. Sure. Positive, in fact, that you're okay to leave London. Are you sure?" she said.

London — I could lip-read that! Whatever she was saying, if it included London in the sentence we had to be on safe ground.

"Oh, yes," I said, nodding into my beer.

And . . . *BANG*! That was the moment right there when everything changed. One minute I'm a Londoner with a career (okay, I was an estate agent, but that's still a career . . . well, ish), a swish trendy flat, fast car, sharp suits, expensive crisp white shirts, silk ties, money in my pocket — folding money in my pocket, no less! Then . . .

Then, the next minute, I'm not. I'm not and haven't got any of those things. Granted, in reality it probably didn't happen all at once in the space of that exact minute. We had to sell the flat and shift our lives out into a cottage on Exmoor, which took a couple of months at least. But in my memory, it did happen that fast. It really did.

BANG! And nothing would ever be the same again. Including me — *especially* me. By uttering those two words, "Oh, yes," into my beer, my safe, sensible townie world fell off its axis and rolled away into a muddy countryside puddle populated with happy pigs (they do like a muddy puddle when it's warm) and ridiculous chickens, where ducks are not always waterproof and geese have all the social skills of a friendly neighbourhood thug. I've got a dog with one eye and a cat with Tourette's syndrome, a horse that's smarter than me and Curry, the world's most annoying goat. There are bleating sheep, ping-about lambs, quail, turkeys, chutneys and jam. Where everything is self-sufficient and homemade from scratch and mud makes its way into every conversation.

Prior to this iffy turn of events the closest I'd come to the countryside was brushing past a bucket of cut flowers in a petrol-station forecourt. I hadn't even been to a petting farm or seen a chicken that wasn't on a supermarket shelf. The first time I met a lamb was in my own vestibule, where it promptly headbutted me in the crutch. For a number of years, life was not so much a steep learning curve as a learning cliff, and I spent a large chunk of it falling off. Perhaps the other thing you should know before I go any further is that my best friends are a 350-kg male pig called the General and a bloke called Ziggy — actually, as best friends go, Ziggy's pretty rubbish.

"Is the quad bike okay?" Debbie called as I bounded naked up the stairs for a shower. Last time I rolled it the handlebars went all wonky, which was really annoying.

"Yes, it's absolutely fine," I said, which was almost true. Actually, the other reason I'd rolled it was because I saw the General up in the woods and was calling and waving to him and not watching where I was going, so I ran up the bank. It's easily done.

As I stood under the spray of the shower, attempting to dislodge chunks of dirt from my body with a bar of my homemade soap and what was left of my fingernails, the adrenaline from the tumble began to seep away.

Clean, dry, changed and smelling oh-so-herby, Debbie thrust a glass of homemade wine into my hand as I reached the bottom of the stairs and edged me into the lounge.

"We need to talk. Having stuff on your mind is one thing, crashing the bike because of it is another."

Put like that, she had a point.

Whatever the relationship equivalent to the Geneva Convention is, Debbie flouts it . . .

I told her that I had been waving to the General.

"You were waving to a pig?"

I don't get out much. "Yes. He was up in the woods?"

"And that's why you rolled the quad bike, because you were waving to a pig in the woods?"

That sentence doesn't sound anywhere near as odd as it should.

6

"Well, mostly," I said. "Partly, anyway. I've also got things on my mind, you know?"

Sitting forwards and giving me a "go on" look, she said, "So, tell me what's worrying you."

I gave her the official list, the one above. But there may be more to it than that. Sure, the list is full of practical, urgent things that all need attending to, and on its own it would be enough to stress me out, especially as we have no money, no materials to work with and not enough daylight hours to do it all in, but I'm kind of used to that. Virtually the entire smallholding has been put together with a little of this and a little of that — hammered, screwed and botched together until it almost fits. If Heath Robinson had a country retreat, this would be it.

No, the worry I haven't mentioned — mainly because it's not fully formed as yet and is more of an awareness lurking in the shadows of my mind, just out of sight and just out of reach. But it is dark, and definitely present, and has something to do with age. I was thirty-two years old on the day I said, "Oh yes!" into my beer. Had my age made a difference then? Would I have been any less stupid if I had been older, or younger for that matter, at that time?

I'm forty-seven now, though I swear if I still had hair I wouldn't look a day over twenty-eight — twenty-nine, tops (this way of life is extremely good for the skin).

When I'd finished going through the list, Debbie said, "Okay, I understand all that. Now tell me what's really wrong."

There is a level at which all women are telepathic. Debbie's level is towards the upper end of the scale.

"What? As well as all the things I've just listed?"

She gave me the look. You know, "The Look". And she held it . . .

"You want more? You want, what? Other stuff? How much more?"

. . . and held it . . .

"Other than the long, in-depth list I've just given you?"

. . . and held it . . .

"I don't know what else you want me to say."

. . . and held it . . .

I raised a hand, "Okay, okay, although it probably won't make much sense."

"Try me."

For a minute I sat there, wondering how to start, and once I had, where the conversation would go. I sipped some wine. Despite crashing the quad I'd managed to carry on and finish the rounds of the animals before coming back up to the house. It was dark outside now, and Debbie had closed the curtains and lit the fire. Solly, our twelve-month-old Great Dane, was sprawled asleep on the sweet spot of the sofa, upside down with all his legs in the air. I was perched next to him on the sliver of sofa that was spare. Debbie had her own sliver on the other side of him.

How do you tell someone that you've become unnerved about life? I'm not unhappy, I'm not unhappy at all, in fact I'm very happy, and fulfilled, and content, and loved. Life is good, probably as good as it gets, which is normally a sign that I'm about to give it a sharp kick in the shin.

I guess the dark presence in the corner of my mind, the age thing, was unnerving to me because it had something to do with me growing up. You know . . . older.

I blurted out, "I'm growing older." There, I'd said it. Then I panicked and tried to unsay it, which is what happens when you confess something nobody else knows. "I'm not really old, not yet. I haven't started watching daytime TV or anything like that."

"Yes you have. You were watching *Come Dine With Me* the other day."

"Was I?" Oh God. "Well, for your information, I was watching it, er . . . *ironically*."

"No you weren't. You can't watch something ironically; it doesn't work that way."

"Are you sure?"

"Positive. You're feeling old, go on . . ."

"Which wine is this?" I said, swishing and peering into the murky contents like a botanist searching for life forms. We make most of our own wine with varying degrees of success — the varying degrees ranging from really, really bad all the way down to borderline evil.

"Potato peelings. Don't change the subject. So, you're feeling old . . ."

"Yes, I am."

"Simon!"

"Okay, don't rush me. I think I'm unnerved because I'm not sure I know how to grow older doing what we do. If I was in London, I'd know exactly how to do it.

There, I've got parents who've done it all before me. I'd just have to copy them. But out here, on Exmoor, living self-sufficiently on our smallholding, surrounded by animals, I've got nobody to copy. I feel like I'm trailblazing the age thing, and it's unnerving."

"What's brought this on?"

Shrugging, I gave her a "you know" face. Clearly she didn't, so I tried to verbalise it. "I'm not sure, though it might have had something to do with a call I had from the health centre. They want me to go and have one of these Well Man test things, because I've 'reached that age'." I carved inverted commas in the air with my fingers. There are very few sentences where you're legally allowed to do this; "reached that age" is one of them.

"Lucky you! You should try being a woman. I'd have loved to have reached 47 before being summoned for my first intimate examination!"

"I don't feel lucky. I feel old. So does the General. I was talking to him earlier today . . ."

"You have no idea how weird that sounds."

"Really? Anyway, I looked over and I saw just how grey the poor old sod is getting. He's been throwing some very small litters. He's getting on. In pig years he's probably in his sixties or seventies. He's still keen on the ladies, mind, but he's not as potent as he once was. At some point we'll have to look into getting a young lad to replace him."

Debbie nodded assent.

"Oh." I was kind of hoping she might disagree. "It's going to break his heart. I think his eyesight's a bit iffy too."

10

"That's probably a good thing. He won't be able to see his hunky replacement."

"Hunky?"

"Of course, would you rather get an ugly husband for the ladies? They've been spoilt with the General." This was true, of course, in his day he was the Robbie Williams of the porcine world. Debbie looked up at me. "You're not going to have a midlife crisis on me, are you?"

I assured her I wasn't.

What would a self-sufficient midlife crisis look like anyway? Would I start using black leather jam-pot covers? Maybe get some stick-on flames scooting off the tyres of my quad bike? Wear welly boots that are any colour other than green? (Even out here there are standards, don't you know.) No, that was definitely not me. But then again, neither was getting old. The only typical things I knew about people when they get older were that they collect display cushions, build racks full of interesting wines and hold candle-lit dinner parties with easy listening music playing in the background.

"The dog would eat the cushions," Debbie said.

"Just for once I'd like to have a private thought, if that's okay with you?!"

"Then don't speak it out loud."

There wasn't much I could think to that, so I didn't, in case it came out of my mouth.

"I'll turn the music up," she said. "It might help calm you. It's Barry Manilow, we like him. You light the oil lamps, and . . ."

It had never struck me before, but in her way Debbie's as fond of a list as I am. Okay, she's more of a rattle-them-off type of girl, but lists are lists. She was going through the things we should do in order to have a nice evening. I took some highlights, which, when you're a man facing a line of info being spoken to you at close range, is what you do. We can't help it, it's how we're programmed. All I could hope was that the highlights I managed to glean roughly matched hers.

Here's what it looked like from my side: "Light candles" . . . "stormy out there" . . . "dinner's nearly ready" . . . "wine" . . . "I know what I meant to tell you!" . . . "talk more later."

Not bad, not bad at all. Except for the "I know what I meant to tell you!" bit, which is all I got on that, even though I'd like to have heard more.

"Okay," I said, getting up. "I wonder if there's a *Come Dine With Me* on planner?" There wasn't. Embarrassingly, it seems I'd watched them all.

Dinner was vegetarian — you'd be amazed how many nights a week we eat vegetarian considering we rear all our own meat. After, Debbie snuggled up to one side of the dog and I snuggled the other, which is about as close as a Great Dane will let you get in the snogging department. As Barry Manilow kicked out "I Write the Songs", Debbie said, "I still worry about you."

"Still? What do you mean, still?"

"You used to want to go back to London all the time."

It was one of those sentences with an invisible question mark at the end, and wasn't set in the past tense at all but was very now.

"I know," I said, "but not anymore. Not for a long time. You don't need to worry about that. Everything's different now."

I looked down to make sure the dog was asleep and, without making a sound, reached over the top of him and kissed her.

She smiled her side of the kiss. "I could probably help you not to feel so tense," she whispered, without removing her lips from mine. "And then I can *really* get you to open up and tell me what's going on."

"You'll have to be careful, I'm recently crashed goods."

"Oh, I can be *so* careful."

With a Ninja's quiet so we wouldn't wake the dog — who can be a real party-pooper at moments like this — we both moved away from Solly, who remained oblivious, snoring. Holding hands, we tiptoed towards the stairs.

WERR-HUMPF!

The front door crashed open. We both jumped like teenagers about to be caught by parents while the dog did a Great Dane version of leaping up and defending his territory. This involved an extended period of unravelling limbs until they were all roughly in place so that he could ascend into a standing position, but he didn't make any further moves to investigate because clearly he deemed the situation had the potential to be quite scary, so decided it was better to stand on the sofa and bark.

"What the hell . . .?" I stammered.

"Sorry. Slipped. Damn. Whoops. Oh dear." The voice was a loud whisper we could hear from the lounge, slurred, and one we hadn't heard for months.

Ziggy.

A friend in need is a friend who turns up late, drunk and unexpected

If you're lucky, when life is at its darkest, planets will align and strong, bold, intelligent help will be summoned to enter your life and toss a protective arm around your shoulders, leading you safely through troubled times. But if life isn't dark but just a bit dim, and unnerving, and you're not so lucky, you'll get a Ziggy.

"I really think you should have a strong coffee," Debbie said as she fussed around our unexpected guest.

"What, and miss out on some of your gorgeous homegrown plonk? What is it?" Ziggy said, peering at my glass.

"Potato peelings," I said.

"You're right, coffee would be much — oh God, it's not homemade coffee, is it?"

"No," I said, smiling. "You're such an arse."

"Can I hide here for a few days?" he asked. Same old Ziggy, always hiding from someone, and nearly always a

14

someone he'd accidentally fallen in love with or, more likely, had fallen for him. As relationships go, tricky, difficult and inappropriate were his watchwords. The relationships seldom lasted longer than a night or two and frequently came with a suspicious other half who wanted to knock his block off just in case their suspicions were correct, which of course they were.

The crazy thing was it wasn't his fault. Women threw themselves at him. Literally. I've seen it happen loads of times. We'd be in a bar and he'd go to the loo and come back with a phone number in his hand and lipstick on his face. He wouldn't even have been gone more than two minutes! Whatever pheromone or smell he secretes, it drives women bonkers. It's so unfair.

"Depends," I said, though it didn't, he was always welcome and he knew it. "Who are you hiding from, do I know him?"

He shook his head. "Not a him, a her."

"You're hiding from a woman? Well, there's a first."

Debbie handed him the coffee and he dropped his bombshell. "I'm pregnant. I'm going to have a fucking baby."

I did the long blink thing that people do when they are given shocking news. For London's premier gigolo with more notches on his bedpost than a ram at tupping time, he'd never got a girlfriend pregnant. He was evidently good lover material, but nobody had ever looked at him with he'd-make-a-good-father-to-my-child eyes. Until, it seemed, now.

I blurted out, "Seriously?"

"Seriously."

"But, seriously?"

"*Simon*! Ziggy, that's wonderful news! I'm so pleased for you both. That's so exciting." Debbie crouched down in front of the spot where Ziggy sat and cupped her hands around his. They were both holding his coffee cup. "I know you must be scared, but you don't need to be. You'll make a fantastic dad. Ziggy, forgive me, but I need to know some details. Is she married?"

He shook his head.

She breathed out very loudly.

"Are you in a relationship with her?"

He nodded. She breathed out loudly again and I wondered if she was going to be able to do that for every answer — we are talking about Ziggy here!

"She's amazing. We've been together nearly three months," he said.

"Three months," she nodded. "Okkaaaayy . . . Did she do the test?"

"We both peed on six tests."

"You both peed on them?" I said. Maybe he wasn't kidding when he said "I'm going to have a baby".

"She wanted to make sure they were working properly."

"Does she know you're here?" Debbie asked.

"No, I'm hiding," he said.

"Why are you hiding, Ziggy?"

"It's . . . complicated."

For the umpteenth time tonight, she unleashed the number-one weapon in her arsenal, "The Look".

16

After a while, he said, "I'm not hiding from her — I mean, I am, but not because she's pregnant. Well, it is because she's pregnant, but not because she's pregnant, if you get what I mean."

Okay, I'm lost.

"It's because of what it all means. Between us. I'm excited about the baby as a little person and everything surrounding him or her, but it's everything else; me, and her, and us, the way we are together. It's all going to change, isn't it?"

"Have you both talked about how she feels?"

"Of course. She's excited — most of the time. Then other times she seems worried, but not about the baby, about me."

Debbie nodded. "Well, hiding from her is the last thing you should be doing. I think you should call her. And as much as you're always welcome, I think you need to go back tomorrow and talk to her. Ziggy, darling, it's time to grow up."

So, Ziggy was going to be a dad. How about that? I left them talking while I went and fixed up the spare room for him.

In the morning Ziggy spent an hour on the phone before emerging looking bright and sparkly and, sickeningly, not hungover.

"All okay?" Debbie asked, buttering some toast and handing it to him with a hot drink.

"Tickety-boo. Left in kind of a hurry and forgot my tweeds and flannels, though. Bit annoying. I do like to fit in when I'm down here," he said, biting into the toast.

17

"What did she say?"

"As you'd imagine; angry at first. *Really* angry. Luckily I'd already told her about down here and how I near single-handedly built the smallholding when you first moved in. I left nothing out! However, *despite* that, in the end she seemed to think it was a good idea I was here. Even said it was fine for me to stay for a few days to get my head straight. Crazy misguided girl seems to think it might be good for me. No idea where she got that notion."

"Appreciated," I said.

He lifted his toast in acknowledgement and said, "Welcome. Oh, usual kind of embargo on all things related until the first scan."

"Bugger, and I've just spent all morning Facebooking and tweeting it as breaking news."

"You're such an arse."

"That's my line! You're turning into me!"

He looked up in mock horror — at least I think it was mock horror . . . "Don't even joke about that."

"Boys, please . . . Ziggy, you're welcome to stay as long as you like, though I really do think you need to go back as soon as possible and be with her. Poor girl must be terrified and confused, and while she's trying to get her head around things, you decide now is an ideal time for a mini-break. Of course I want to support you, but I just think you need to be there for her right now."

"Yeah," he said, "I know. But to be honest, I'm *really* struggling with it. I mean, me, a dad! Look, I'm no good to her as I am, I'm really not. I just need a few days. If you guys are okay, she said she was fine with it."

Debbie went quiet before saying, "They were the words she used, that she's *fine* with it?" Emphasis on *fine*.

Crinkling his brow, he said, "Yes."

"And by saying she was fine with it, you deduced . . . ?"

"That she was fine with it?"

"No."

"She's not fine with it?"

"No."

"Then why didn't she say that?"

"She did."

"She said she was *not* fine with it by saying that she was fine with it?"

"Yeeess!"

"Then, she wants me to go back, like, now?"

Debbie paused, but it wasn't a considering pause. "Yes."

"Oh."

"Yes."

"Can I stay until tomorrow?"

"No."

"Oh."

You'd never believe he was a lawyer — or maybe you would. As it turned out there were no seats available on any trains back to London until mid-morning the following day.

"You can make yourself useful then," Debbie said. "Why don't you two go and do the animals together, and don't forget to collect the eggs while you're down there."

He grinned at me, "I remember when you used to get all huffy about collecting eggs."

"He still gets all huffy about collecting eggs!" Debbie blurted.

Laughing, he said, "Nothing changes. Lead on, big boy . . ."

Senorita the micro pig — so dainty, so feminine . . .

Outside in the nippy Exmoor morning I led Ziggy towards the barn at the back of the house.

My everyday *modus transportius* is the quad bike: fun in the sunshine, miserable when it's raining, easy to roll over when you forget to concentrate, and highly nickable. And therein lies the problem. I rely so heavily on the quad that if I lost it, working on the land would be almost impossible. So, to keep it safe I placed some cunning obstacles even the most determined thief would balk at.

"Cows," Ziggy said, not getting too close to the gate.

"Cows," I replied, beaming.

"That's your anti-theft device?"

"That's my anti-theft device!"

"Well it works for me."

Actually they were my neighbour's cows and it was her idea, but Ziggy didn't need to know that.

"Be careful, they're terrible for licking," I warned him, opening the gate and dragging him in behind me to yelps of, "Eeerr! Gerrof me! Can't you . . . keep your

20

. . . sandpaper . . . tongue . . . to, YOURSELF! *Yuck, YUCK, YUCK!*"

I started the quad bike and Ziggy climbed on behind me, saying, "I must have had a lot to drink last night, your handlebars look a bit wonky, and why is there mud and grass on them?" My gorgeous outdoor dog, Dex, jumped up beside him and together we drove back out through the cows and down onto the land.

Of course I'm proud of what Debbie and I have created. I love it, I really do — twenty acres of fields and woods and the happiest, most eccentric, crazy-mad animals alive. I'm often *by far* the sanest one down there! But the infrastructure, the houses in which everyone lives, are, well, cobbled together. And the more time that goes by, the more cobbled they become.

I tried to remember how long it had been since Ziggy was last down. Months, certainly. Years? Probably.

It's true he was here at the beginning when we first bought the land and everything was new and pristine and shiny, but it's not true that he did most of the work. In fact, he spent more time upsetting the professional contractors we employed, and I still have no idea why he did it, by pretending he was all hoity-toity, telling made-up stories of his non-existent school years at Eton. He couldn't even spell Eton!

It must be nearly a year since his last visit.

The thing is, animals are hard on their homes. Especially pigs. And then there was that one time I accidentally got all the pigs drunk by feeding them beer slops from a local pub — I thought it would be a good idea, I thought they'd like it! Turns out they did rather like it, they rather liked it a lot, even though they did get totally hammered and beat the hell out of their houses, which have never been the same since. You know those big wrecking balls that smash into the sides of houses to demolish them? Well, drunk sows are pretty much onto the same trick. But even if you disregard the booze-fuelled demolition, things still deteriorate and need mending, and there simply isn't any money. So I improvise.

Bumping along the unmade track on the quad bike, we passed the General's house up in the woods: a half-metal, half-wood construction with a patchwork back and a put-together front porch. A functional, warm, dry, cosy love-pad for a pig. Beautiful . . . Or, a peculiar hodgepodge slammed together with whatever was handy at the time. My vote's on the former. I'd guess that Ziggy, fresh out of London, would plump for the latter.

I hate it that when I look around the smallholding suddenly I can see everything through Ziggy's London eyes. It's *so annoying*. This is what I see: a scruffy, botched-together micro-world held up with farmer's string and an awful lot of hope, which is the bad bit. Filled with little furry and feather faces everywhere peering out of makeshift windows from makeshift dens, all eager for breakfast and desperate to be let out for the day, which is the good bit. Good and bad, yin and yang. I want to be pragmatic and adult and think that it is what it is, but to be honest I feel a bit, I don't know, ashamed, I guess.

I pulled up and turned off the bike. Dex, my collie dog, jumped down. Looking around, Ziggy said, "You've been busy."

"Yeah, well, I can only do what I can do," I shrugged, not making eye contact. "I know it's scruffy, but I can hardly let everything rot. So I do what I can with what I can find. It's not new and doesn't look great, but the animals are all warm and safe and happy, and that's the important thing." I didn't mean to sound so defensive, but I couldn't help it.

"Are they glass shower doors attached to that chicken run?" he said, peering over.

"Mmm, but not chickens, quail. They get cold easily."

"It all looks amazing. I'm not kidding, I love it."

Was he being sarcastic?

"What's the trailer doing in the middle of the field?" he said, pointing.

"That's for Senorita. The micro pig."

Number seven on the "list of things on my mind":

7. Work out where to house Senorita Small, the rescued micro pig who isn't a micro pig.

"Micro pig? That doesn't sound like your style."

Picking out a dry-ish line through the mud we walked over to he trailer. The ramp was left down so Senorita wouldn't feel isolated, the delicate little flower.

I reached in, opened the cage door that was her temporary bed-room and stood back.

There was no cute waddling, no feminine, graceful, controlled exit, just a series of grunting swear words (and probably something about not having had a fag yet) as she marched out like she had somewhere very important she had to be, and she was running late. Somewhere she could have a fight. Against boys.

Ziggy jumped back as she shouldered her way past him. "Bloody hell! *That's a micro pig?*"

Keeping geese (your very own psychopaths)

Word is that the council phoned the local animal rescue centre because a family were living in a suburban terraced house with a pet pig and they deemed the pig wasn't ideal tenant material. The rescue centre phoned me. Could I take it?

Senorita had arrived two days before Ziggy did, in a dirty cloud of bad mood — and who could blame her? I swear this is true, the rescue centre said that when they arrived at the house she was lounging on a sofa watching an episode of *Loose Women*. It didn't improve her mood that she never got to see the end of the show. Nice warm sofa to trailer-park living, no wonder she was cranky. I had to sort out a permanent house for her soon. I told Ziggy the story as we watched her stomp around the field.

"What's she doing?" he said.

I shook my head, "I don't know. She's very unsettled. She doesn't know she's a pig. When she got here I tried to put her in with a small, friendly group of other pigs and she freaked, running away from them, screaming, going hysterical and trying to clamber out to me. I thought she was going to have a heart attack."

24

"So what are you going to do with her?"

I knew what I was going to do with her, the only thing I could do with her: teach her how to be a pig. But there was no way I was going to tell Ziggy that.

"Build her a house and give her some time to adjust," I said.

We watched Senorita sneak up on Dex. The poor boy didn't stand a chance, he only has one eye and she came up to him on his blind side. As she approached, we watched her physically change, getting smaller, slimmer, slower so that she developed a wiggle, her entire posture softening. Even the noises she made went from a guttural oink to a kitteny purr.

"That's weird," Ziggy said.

I laughed. "She's been like that since she laid eyes on him. Fell head over heels the moment she saw him, though frankly I think the whole 'being an object of desire' has traumatised the life out of him."

Too late, Dex realised she was by his side. He tried to run for it, but for a wobble belly she was nimble on her feet.

"She's not really a micro pig, is she?"

"Yep, came with papers and everything." Papers or not, micro pigs are a moot point and more often than not they're just normal pigs selectively bred to be small and then sold for ten times the going price. But they still grow. And grow, and grow. Currently she was the size of a small Labrador but with shorter legs.

We watched them dash, Dex in front, petrified; Senorita close behind, besotted, all the way to the other side of the field.

"Maybe I'm misunderstanding the term micro here, how big will she get?" Ziggy asked.

I had no idea. I estimated she was about twenty weeks old and a mongrel, a mix of piggy breeds. It was anyone's guess as to her eventual size, so I gave Ziggy mine. "A touch under full size, I'd think, something around 200 kgs."

"No wonder the council decided she had to go, she wouldn't be long for the sofa at that size."

I left him watching the unusual courtship while I went and checked on the horses, Georgie Girl and Alfie, who were happily munching their heads off in the field.

When I returned we got stuck into the morning task of break-fasting and letting out the mob. Chickens first, all three houses of them (two houses with a cockerel in each, and one where the hens could go if they didn't want to be bothered by a randy boy at night, which was usually empty); then the quail fed, watered but left in as they're too stupid to come back and would end up as some predator's snack by lunchtime. Ducks, two girls and a boy *wack-wacking* and fast waddling it over to the stream for a morning dip. Geese next . . .

"Do you want me to let the geese out?" Ziggy asked.

Geese are . . . have you ever seen Australian rules football, where the idea, as far as I can tell, is for the players to punch anyone within reach and not worry too much about the ball? Well, a team of geese would be considered too violent to play and might even bring the game into disrepute. Geese are the hooligans of the chicken field. The mobsters. I wasn't convinced they weren't running a protection racket amongst the smaller poultry as it was. A little corn and I'll make sure nothing untoward happens to you during the day. You catch my drift, little chicken?" The thought of watching Ziggy run for it whilst being chased by killer geese held quite a lot of appeal. But I said, "It's okay, I'd better do it. They can be a bit temperamental."

In the interests of balance and good goose relations, it's fair to say that geese do have the odd redeeming feature, one of which is that they are monogamous and mate for life. Our two have been together for years. The gander's story is one of insecurity and jealousy, where anyone, regardless of species, is a threat to his love and must be chased off. Her story . . . actually, I'm not sure she has one, other than being a foul-mouthed fishwife who yells obscene abuse at him and makes his life hell. Honestly, you just can't choose who you fall in love with. The combined name of two of our geese (Honey-Bunny) came from the opening scenes of the film *Pulp Fiction*, where the couple are sitting in an American diner drinking coffee and calling each other honey-bunny, "*I love you honey-bunny,*" right before they stand up and rob the place at gunpoint, her screeching, "*Nobody move, or I'll shoot every last mother-fucking one of ya!*" One goose wasn't Honey and the other Bunny, they were just Honey-Bunny. Collectively.

"You sure you want to do it? I don't mind," Ziggy said.

Yeah, you might.

I told him to stand well back, unlatched the door to the goose house, yanked it all the way open, then legged

27

it. But I wasn't fast enough. The type of speed and dexterity needed to avoid bad-tempered geese takes years to develop. My speed and dexterity were still in development.

Both geese bolted, heads back, chests out, wings outstretched, hissing, spitting and chasing after the first thing they saw, which was my disappearing bum.

There are some parts of the morning rounds that no matter what way you look at it are simply not a spectator sport. Letting out the geese is top of that list. In a millisecond they were right up behind me, their beaks inches from my soft derrière, so much so that I had to kind of tuck my bum under myself by bowing my body outwards, running crotch first and doing a crazy high-stepping run like a man pretending to be a dressage horse.

You'd think the geese had been badly brought up, dragged up, even, but they haven't. I've known them since they were eggs.

Not a second too soon the geese got distracted with the time-chewing business of duffing up the chickens and wheeled away from my butt.

I made my way over to Ziggy, who, between heaves of laughter, said, "I have never been happier in all my life."

Ziggy's in love

"What's next?" Ziggy asked. "Any other little darlings want to rip our hides apart, or maul us, maybe?"

"Yep, mauling next," I said, leading him over to the goats. Actually, I wasn't entirely joking.

The goat house is part of a complicated structure that looks for all the world like an old tin shed from the outside, but inside it is a warren of rooms and resting places for different animals. Wooden sheets line the walls to keep it warm, which are painted white to keep it light, and each section is designed to have slatted sides, windows or plain old openings so that when it's full, everyone in there has a cosy sense of togetherness, yet at the same time a feeling of their own snug space.

The goats' compartment is a big cupboard-like section in the middle of the structure (goats hate draughts, so the middle is perfect for them) with a slatted side looking into Alfie's stable, a wire door into the logging area where I chop wood for the fire, and a shelf running along the back where Niko the cat sometimes sleeps.

Reaching the cupboard Ziggy ran his hand down the wire door and shouted, "Amber and Bee! I remember you guys, it's good to see you. How've you been? Have you missed me? Of course you have. Well I'm back, but don't get too excited, it's only for a day."

I want to say that the goats looked unimpressed, or worse, bored, but they didn't. Letting me down entirely they started going all coy, flirting with him, batting their long eyelashes. It's the pheromone thing — it even works on animals.

"And who's that I see in there, a third little lady I don't recognise? Simon, introduce us would you, mate?"

He really is the most annoying idiot.

The third goat was Curry, a rescue found shivering next to her dead mother. She was less than a day old when she was brought to us and we bottle-reared her along with some orphan lambs. "Curry, be wary of this man, he's a seducer and a philanderer, he'll break your heart. And he's an annoying idiot," I said, opening the door. Curry dashed out, but Amber and Bee, being older and wiser, knew there was credit to be gained in making a man wait, so they took their time.

"Harsh," Ziggy said, fussing over Curry and doing his best to avoid her horns. "Besides, my play-around days are at an end. Ouch! Steady girl!"

"How d'you feel about it all?"

"Well, I am going to miss the variety," he said, deliberately misinterpreting the question and looking at me with a stupid grin on his face.

I grabbed Amber's collar and jumped her onto an old recycled freezer that had been lain on its side with a rubber mat on the top to make a firm milking platform. When she was standing nicely, I took a clean bowl from a packet, placed it under her, and gently began to squeeze her udders until warm frothy milk squirted out.

I knew I wouldn't have to prompt him to tell me more; Ziggy's favourite subject is always Ziggy.

He blew out a long breath and said so softly that I only just caught it, "Simon, mate, I'm so scared. I don't know what I'm doing. I can't . . . I can't work it out. The thing is, the truth is, well, oh shit man, it wasn't an accident. Her falling pregnant, it wasn't an accident. We planned it. I thought it would be a good way of always being with her, but as soon as she saw the little blue line on the pregnancy test and we hugged, I looked into her eyes and knew, suddenly I knew that everything had changed."

He sat down in the straw, his back against the freezer, cuddling Curry while I milked and listened.

"I know we've only been together for three months, but I've never felt about anyone the way I feel about her. She's so perfect. I can't stop thinking about her. I can't concentrate at work. I almost crashed the car the other day. It's torture. I have to stop myself from texting her constantly and when I do I count the seconds it takes for her to respond. I've *never* been like this before."

Unlike a lot of men, Ziggy has no fear of telling everyone around him exactly how he's feeling in full-colour, explicit minutiae. It's one of the things I like about him.

It was obvious he was bang in love, and I grant you it does sound deeper than his usual "I'm-in-love's", of which there have been many, *but three months and he's already planned a baby?!* Is it just me or is that a bit quick?

"She knows you feel this way?"

"Of course. There's no way I could hide it."

"What does she say?"

"That she feels the same."

"Okay, so you're scared because you've only known her three months and now you're going to have a baby. I get it," I said, careful to sound upbeat and positive. "It is quicker than things traditionally go, but —"

"What? No, that's not it, that's not it at all!"

"It's not?"

Suddenly he stopped, his face and body turning into a statue while he mulled over the thought, giving Curry the excuse to give him lots of loving head butts. The tart.

"Do you think it's too quick? Really? I hadn't thought about that. No. I'm not frightened because of that, I'm frightened because she keeps telling me to act my age. She told me her only reservation is whether I'm mature enough to be a father. Even Debbie last night said it was time for me to grow up."

Hmm, I suddenly remembered number eight on my list: 8. Think of something to say on my radio slot this week.

"I have this friend who has a dilemma . . ."

No, you're right, I'm sorry, it was just a stupid thought. Ignore me.

"When we talked about having a baby, she'd get really excited, said it would make a man out of me. She kept telling me stories of how it would change me, and how great I'd be as a dad. I listened, but I didn't take much notice because all I could think was, if we did have a baby together, it would mean we'd always have that link and I'd always be in her life no matter what, which is all I want, you know?"

"Should have asked her to marry you."

"Tried that. She turned me down."

Oh, Ziggy.

Amber was getting bored of being milked and her udders were now empty. Fearful that she'd kick over the bowl of milk, I told her she could jump down.

"I need to pour this into a jug and give the animals some breakfast," I said to Ziggy.

"Sure," he said, scrambling up.

We were talking about his love life. "I can see how things are going to be different, but it needn't be bad. Maybe it will bring you closer — isn't having babies supposed to bring people closer together?" I said, walking out of the barn towards an old dilapidated caravan that was our feed store. Ziggy came with me. As did the goats — Amber, Bee and Curry. Dex had managed to escape from Senorita for the moment and so he joined us, as did a lamb that shouldn't have been there in the first place and half a dozen chickens. It was a family outing.

As we walked, Ziggy continued, "I'm not sure we could be closer, I'm not even sure that's possible. I just want everything to be as it is; I don't want anything to change. Ever."

Tall order.

"However," he said, "If our relationship *is* going to change now that she's pregnant, which clearly it is, then it's obvious I need to change with it, or risk getting left behind. Don't you think?"

"I guess. So, what does *that* look like? In what way do you think you've got to change?"

We reached the caravan. All of us. He shrugged. "Do what everyone's been telling me I should be doing anyway. It's time for me to grow up."

I went inside to fill a bucket with feed while Ziggy babysat outside.

How is it that when you finally confront a lurking fear, a best friend parachutes into your life looking for the exact opposite? How is that even fair? Just because I'm unnerved at the prospect of growing older doesn't mean I need a counterbalance. Look, it's not that I don't love Ziggy as a friend, I do. Or that I'm not worried about his relationship and the whole pregnancy thing, I am. And of course I want to be there for him and help, that too. I'm not a monster; it's just, the timing sucks with him arriving at this precise moment in my life when I'm having my own thing going on.

I poured the milk into a jug before stacking several feed scoops containing each animal's individual breakfast on top of each other, and placing them into a bucket for easy carrying. I left the milk in the caravan for now, grabbed the bucket of breakfasts and called out, "When I come out everyone's going to bundle me for the food, so I'm going to have to run back to the barn, okay?"

"Sure. What do you want me to do?" Ziggy shouted back.

"Actually, I've got an idea. If you walk in the opposite direction everyone will go with you. I'll wait until you're a few feet away and that'll give me a head start."

It was a good plan. I watched through the window as Ziggy pigeon-stepped off with all the animals surrounding him, none of whom were fully convinced that he wasn't either made of food —

"Will you stop biting me!"

— knew of a secret food store that he was about to bolt off to, and therefore should be kept *very* close —

"Give me some room, will you?"

— or in the event that he tripped over, food would spill out of him.

"Wooow! *Wooow!* Careful, if I fall, I'll fall on top of you!"

Textbook-*ish* military manoeuvre: make the enemy look one way while you do your real work in the other, and if there's collateral damage to your cannon fodder — in this case, Ziggy — so be it.

With everyone distracted I opened the door and dashed on tiptoe back towards the barn. I whizzed around, placing each scoop of breakfast in the corresponding animal's area.

Then I stood back, leaning against a wall. As breakfasting goes, it was the most well-behaved, organised and silent one I'd ever prepared. Mainly because I was the only one in there . . . I nipped back unnoticed, which is amazing — I'd expected to get a head start, but not to make it all the way.

I walked back towards the barn. Ziggy had made surprising progress and was some distance away. I could hear him calling, "Any time you're ready, Simon. Any time you're ready . . ."

"Okay, come and get it! Come and get your breakfast while it's hot! There's croissants and jam, crumpets, toasted bagels with smoked salmon and cream cheese . . ." There wasn't, it was all boring old dried animal feed.

Suddenly the dark smudge surrounding Ziggy scattered as all the animals realised at once what was happening, turned tail and bolted towards me.

"Woah, woah, woah," I called out, holding up a stop-right-here hand to the stampede, which took absolutely no notice and stampeded on regardless. So I changed tack and became the race controller, ushering each set of animals towards their own spot with the use of the universal arms-out-wide-you-can't-get-past-me-I'm-a-road-block method of traffic control.

"You're welcome, hope you enjoy your breakfast. If there's anything else I can get you, fresh coffee perhaps, orange juice, you know, to make your stay with us more pleasurable, please don't hesitate to ask," I said in my best maitre d' voice as they whooshed past me so fast that if I had any hair, it would have blown back.

"I thought you'd never call them," Ziggy panted, bringing up the rear.

As anyone who's ever frequented a greasy spoon café and looked around them will testify, breakfast is all about speed eating with little or no pause for breath between mouthfuls. All too soon, and to the annoyance of everyone, Ziggy and I gathered up the feed scoops and took them back to the caravan. This trip we made alone: we're just not that interesting when you've got a full stomach.

"Pigs next, then we're done for morning rounds," I said.

As I opened a new bag of pig nuts and began shovelling them into a yellow bucket, I said, "I think women always want men to grow up, but the danger is that by doing so you risk losing the very thing that made you attractive to them in the first place — if the woman you're with is into boyish sparks, that is — and then you become boring, and she goes off you."

"So growing up equals boring?" Ziggy said.

"No, not at all." Given the choice of reading *The Secret Life of a Teenager* or *The Secret Life of a Forty-Something*, I'm clearing a day and finding a comfortable spot next to a heap of homemade vegetable crisps and a glass of wine and diving headfirst into the secrets of the forty-something, which is going to be *way* more fun and *way, way, way* sexier. "I'm just saying be careful not to lose sight of yourself in all this, that's all."

Bucket full of pig nuts, we made our way back outside.

Okay, so feeding the pigs goes like this: General and Pru first; then Winnie and her babies in the field shelter; Pippa and her bruisers, and finally two separate groups of delinquent hooligan teenage oinkers, or yobs, for short. I threw a quick breakfast into each pen before going back around and clambering in, taking time to talk to and touch every single pig, which keeps them friendly and makes sure there's no chance of me missing any potential problem. In return, they talk back to me. They do! Some come over and tell me what's been going on by woof, woofing in my face (forget grunting or oinking, when pigs are really excited they woof and bark like dogs), while others prefer the subtle communication of body language. I'm getting better at speaking both, and I can get by, you know, order the water and ask directions kind of style, but I'm far from fluent.

"Done," I said, tossing the empty bucket to one side and flopping side-saddle onto the quad bike seat.

When cockerels want something or want to call some attention to themselves, they do this funny sort of dance, like a soft shoe shuffle. Ziggy started soft shoe shuffling, dragging one foot flat on the ground while lifting the other toe and heel in a tight circle, then he moonwalked a step or two, slowly spinning, his hands in his pockets, all the while looking down.

"Mate . . ." he started slowly, "I was thinking, we should go for a beer tonight, after we've done the animals, just the two of us. You know, a boy's night out for once. On me."

The words were fine, but it was the actions that made me pause. They were the actions of someone building up to something. Something important but uncomfortable.

"See, the thing is, I think it would really help me if I could sit down and talk to someone who's already mature."

Noooooo!

Nine tips on how to avoid the onset of middle age, written in a pub

Ziggy was laughing and shaking his head between sips of beer. "I told you, I didn't mean it like that. I thought you'd take it as compliment."

We were in the Blue Bull Inn later that evening, just the two of us. It's a nice place, comfortable, an old coaching inn right on the top of the moor with crackling open fires, wonky floors and great beer.

"How can calling me an old man be a compliment?" I said, laughing, though a little less heartily than Ziggy. "So what, did you do a recce of all your friends and think, who's the master? Who's the Yoda? Who do I know that's aged the most and can therefore teach me more than anyone else? *I know . . .*"

"I'm sorry," he said. "I didn't know you were going through a thing yourself. And it wasn't like that at all."

A thing? I was going through a thing? Was I? How did he even know about *my thing* anyway?

I guessed Debbie must have told him while I was getting ready. She probably asked him to go easy on me because of my new angst. I picked up my glass.

"You want to go first and talk about your thing?" Ziggy said, switching to a semi-serious face.

I thought back to last night, how I'd tried to evade telling Debbie because I didn't know how to start, where to go with it or even fully what it was that unnerved me. "I don't know," I said. "I'm not even sure I know what the thing is, other than it has something to do with feeling like I'm getting older, but other than that it's a bit hazy and confused."

He said, "I didn't want to say anything, but when I walked in last night you were listening to Barry Manilow."

"Yeah, but that's not what I'm worried about," I tell him. Mind you, we hadn't even been listening to it on Spotify, which would at least have dulled the concern.

"I think it should be," he said. Ziggy's one of those irritating music snobs who believes anything released more than half an hour ago is a relic and should be danced to in tank tops and flares.

"He did some great tunes," I said.

"*Tunes*? Since when did you start using the word *tunes* rather than tracks?" he spluttered, putting his head in his hands — he can be so over-dramatic at times. Irritating Music Snobs *never* refer to music as tunes. For them it's always tracks.

"This is bad. I've seen it happen before. I know what's wrong. I know what's wrong with you. You're getting old before your time."

"'Copacabana', 'I Write the Songs', they're nice to have on in the background —" Don't say easy listening, don't say easy listening . . . "— plus they're good tracks."

Is that it? Is that what's bothering me? Is that what I'm unnerved about, that I'm growing old before my time?

"Oh my God, you might be right." I sank my head into my hands too — yeah, I know, we were both overdoing the drama and in danger of landing lead roles in *EastEnders*. There followed a silence between us that was built of no words, though was anything but quiet. It was full of other stuff — bar chatter, laughter, people moving about, glasses clinking, a dog barking somewhere upstairs.

Time passed.

"Have you still got your head in your hands?" I asked, not looking up.

40

"Mmm. You?"

"Mmm."

More minutes slipped by.

"We must look odd," I said.

"Probably."

I peeked between my fingers, he really had still got his head in his hands.

"It's not that bad, is it?" I said, feeling awkward, but not quite awkward enough to sit up properly.

"'S'okay, I've moved on to my own problems," he said, his face still covered.

"Appreciated."

"Welcome."

There has only ever been one other occasion when I've sat in a pub with my head in my hands, and that was the day Debbie convinced me to go and look at a pig, just because I'd never seen one before. This was before we had the land, in the days when my only contact with animals was on TV or through books, and I was still commuting back and forth to London for work. I was grumpy — what did I want to go and look at a stinky, dirty, poxy pig for?

I was taken over to a make-do-and-mend pig pen and inside was the biggest girly pig in the world. She was huge! Lined up against her soft belly was a line of tiny baby piglets all feeding from her.

I was struck, absolutely struck. It was the most beautiful thing I had ever seen.

I bought two piglets. Not Debbie, me. I bought them. On the spot. Spur of the moment, "Yep, that's for me, I'll have two please guv'nor," and called them

Black Bum and Spotty Bum before I'd even left the barn.

It was only when I got outside that I started feeling wobbly.

"I think we need to find a pub," I said to Debbie. "I think I need a drink."

We found an out-of-the-way place on the way home and sat at a corner table.

"I thought it was going to be a real battle to get you to agree to buy a couple of piglets, but you just jumped in. I can't believe you did that," Debbie said, but through a smile.

"Neither can I. I don't know what's happening to me anymore. We never used to make decisions independently of one another. I don't know if I like it. I don't know if it's healthy."

"Well, you did it."

"I know."

Her voice softened, and she said, "I have never seen love at first sight happen before. It was beautiful, you really fell for those pigs."

"It was awful," I said. "I think I feel sick. I think I want my mum. Oh my God, what have I done?" and raised both hands to cover my face as the full force of my stupidity hit me.

Now here I was, fifteen years later, in a pub and once more covering my face with my hands.

Had it really been fifteen years?

"I've got it!" Ziggy announced way too loudly, causing a couple of dogs in the bar to sit up and boggle at us.

42

With beautiful synchronisation, we both reached for our beers. Hiding can be thirsty work. Ziggy looked happy, which I took as a worrying sign.

"What you need is some help. You need mentoring. Someone young to set you back on the right path. Someone like —"

"You." I finished for him.

His smile widened.

"Let me guess," I carried on. "You need mentoring too. Someone older to set you on the right path to maturity. Someone like —" He didn't finish my sentence. He didn't need to.

"I'll have you down with the kids in no time, and I'm, like, not even joking."

Oh God.

He sat forward. "Hear me out . . ." He was thinking on his feet. You can always tell when he's doing that because he sticks out a thoughtful tongue between sentences. It probably helps to air-cool his brain. "Two best friends find themselves together right at the very moment when the other is experienced in the very details we each need. It's almost cosmic. You want to feel younger —"

"No I don't. I just don't want to get old before my time."

He waved a hand. "Same thing. While I absolutely want to feel older and wiser, more mature as befitting my imminent status change into fatherhood." Tongue out. "It's perfect," he said, holding his hand out for me to shake. "You help me, I'll help you!"

It's going to end in tears, I know it's going to end in tears.

"What do you think?" he encouraged, reaching his hand further towards me.

What do I think? I think Debbie's going to kill me. I gripped his hand and we shook on it. It was a deal. He looked pleased while I knew I looked terrified, and if I didn't, I ought to have done.

"No time like the present," he said, rubbing his hands together. "So, where to start . . ."

Not only was his tongue out but he had scrunched his face closed. He was either in very deep thought or he needed the toilet . . .

"What to include? What to leave out? Nothing too complicated . . . Keep it simple . . . What's young anyway? Clothes are a must. That's number one right there. Music — the staple of anyone young at heart. Television — what else are you going to be doing but here in the back of beyond? Internet — obviously, goes without saying. Social media — anyone under the age of thirty without a social media presence is probably in prison. What else . . .? You're sickeningly happily married so chasing the opposite sex is probably out. Attitude? And outlook? Very little between them so we'll lump those two together. Very important to have a healthy attitude and outlook when trying to stay young. What else? Style . . ."

He looked across at me, but it wasn't a look that called for a reply, so I drank some beer and tried to give off a young person's vibe, but instead managed to slosh the drink onto the table when I put the glass down a little more nonchalantly than normal.

He continued. "Yeah. Keep it simple. Style can come later. Hair! The sign of virility and youth. Hair must be on the list. How many's that?" He counted in his head with his lips moving. "Seven. Uummmumum . . . what else? Food. That's good. And one more . . . one more . . . Oh! Of course! Language!"

Summarising like only a lawyer can, which is brief but very expensive, he spouted off the list of things I had to follow *to the letter* to stave off early middle-age. I jotted them down on a beer mat. Clothes, music, television, internet, social media, attitude and outlook, hair, food and language.

"Okay," I said. "Got it. So . . ." I held up a hand and prepared to count off the fingers as I repeated his list, "One: clothes. Homemade garments are out, is that the gist of it?" He's always had a thing about me making some of our clothes.

"If you take nothing else away from tonight other than that, it will still all be worth it, but no, that's not the gist of it, it's the start of it."

"I've made some cool things, smart t-shirts and tops. They look good."

"Fashion. Trust me, what you make is not fashion."

Moving on I grasped another finger. "Two: Music . . ."

"Absolutely. Other than lounge crooners, who do you listen to?" he said.

My goodness, where to start? "Well . . ."

I thought through the contents of my phone. There were podcasts — heaps of podcasts — audio books, and some music that definitely marked me out as a forty-something, but in my defence, when you need some oomph to muck out a stable you want something 80s. I've tried all sorts, but 80s is the only music that can knock twenty minutes off mucking out a stable: Dexy's Midnight Runners, Madness, UB40, Kool and the Gang, George Benson, Blondie, Adam and the Ants — they all work. "The thing is . . ."

He held up a stop-right-there hand. Unlike goats, sheep, Senorita the not-micro pig and chickens, I took notice.

"If you're going to start with excuses, I'm guessing there's nothing very recent?"

"Depends what you mean by recent."

"Got any Drenge or Royal Blood?" He sipped his beer.

"No, no Drenge or Royal Blood."

"White Denim, they've been around for a while."

I shook my head, feeling like the oldest granddad at a grunge, garage, rave thingamajig.

"Woman's Hour?"

"Are you kidding me?" I sat up, suddenly completely engaged and animated. "I've got loads of Woman's Hour. I mean, I don't completely get all of it, some of it is quite girly, but I love Jenni Murray and download the Radio 4 podcast all the time."

"What are you talking about? Woman's Hour — the band?"

Oh. "Of course. Sorry. No, no Woman's Hour."

He sat forwards. Locked eyes with me. "Okay, forget all that. I think you'd love all those, but for now forget them. Just do one thing for me. Simon, promise me you will get some Kwabs."

It just sounded so funny. "Is that like an antacid, or something?" I said.

"You have no idea who I'm talking about, do you?"

"Not a clue," I admitted, gripping number three finger in the hope that we could move on.

"Hang on, hang on" he said, slumping back. "I'm not sure this is working. Perhaps we're doing this the wrong way around. Maybe doing it another way would be better."

"Like me telling you why I'm feeling old rather than you telling me what I need to do to avoid it?"

He sipped his beer and shrugged.

"Or would be if I knew what it was," I said, which I didn't. I still couldn't fully identify the fear yet, this unnerving awareness lurking in the shadows of my mind. It didn't feel as though I'd progressed much past establishing it had something to do with growing older, and possibly, and much more relevantly, growing older out here, doing what we were doing, smallholding and all of that malarkey. Knocking-on-a-bit smallholders have their own set of challenges, and none of the books on self-sufficiency talk about fitting in an afternoon nap between looking after the animals, or how to cope when you're out chopping wood and gasping for a nice cuppa at the same time.

Having said that, it did feel right that if I could avoid slipping into early middle age this age-related thing would go away. Surely you only begin to feel old when you start getting older? So if you don't start *getting* older, you won't start *feeling* older, and then the unease that surrounds it disappears, doesn't it? It sounded logical to me — even through the beer.

Ziggy was fiddling with his phone and saying, "And this kind of works for both of us, so tell me, in your opinion what marks someone out as having hit middle age?"

I did the display cushions, wine rack, candle-lit dinner parties and easy listening music bit.

"Ever fancied going on a cruise?" he said, nodding and swishing his fingers across the face of his phone.

"No."

"Good. Um, bought any travel sweets for the car recently?"

"Not unless you count buying chocolate and stashing it in the cubbyhole compartment of the quad bike."

He looked up. "Sorry, yep, that counts."

"Rubbish, eating chocolate on a quad bike is not a symptom of getting older!"

"Yes it is. Judge, jury and executioner, I have the final say. When was the last time you misplaced your glasses or your keys?"

"Where are you getting all of these?" I asked.

"Does everyday technology such as tablets and smart phones scare you?" he continued, without answering my question.

"This is stupid. Can we go back to your list?"

"Do you know what a selfie is?"

"Yes, a selfie is when someone goes up to the bar and doesn't get a drink for his friend because his friend's being an annoying arse."

He looked up sharply. "Tell me you know what a selfie is?"

"I was joking."

"Mmm, interesting. Do you find yourself complaining a lot of the time, especially about the rubbish on TV?"

"Ziggy!"

"Do you groan when you bend down and sometimes unexpectedly pass wind? Have you started sprouting hair from unusual places?"

I got up and would have gone to the bar but I didn't have any money, so I went to the gents instead. By the time I got back there was a fresh drink on the table in front of my chair. I went to say thanks, but Ziggy cut me off by saying, "I should come down here more often, you know." Then he added, "You're right. That didn't work. So, back to my list it is. We've covered numbers one and two: clothes and music. Go on, number three, television . . ."

I took a quick drink before putting the glass down and gripping finger number three and rattling off the third of Ziggy's How To Avoid The Onset Of Early Middle Age commandments.

"Okay, three: TV. I must make a point of watching at least one reality show a week that does not involve cooking or antiques, right?"

"And watch something on iPlayer," he added. "If your broadband speed can take it."

Nodding, I said, "Four: Internet. What's that, like an hour a day surfing the net?"

"Nobody says surfing the net anymore."

"Five: social media — I'm already on Twitter and Facebook. Six: adopt a younger attitude and outlook. Seven, and I guess this is sarcastic: hair. Eight: food. Nine: how to speak like a lad — I'm really not sure about that one. Actually I'm not sure about any of them."

"Don't give up so easily. How's it feel?"

"Like I want to book a cruise."

"That's the spirit, old boy! Tickety-boo. So, that settled, now I need your list of what I need to do to grow up and mature."

He held up a hand, gripped a number one finger and looked expectantly at me before prompting: "One: . . . ?"

With Ziggy having done all the heavy lifting, all I had to do was view his list from a different angle to encourage a more mature, considered outlook.

Here we go . . . "Clothes, anything homemade is good, and despite your reservations you absolutely can make your own clothes and keep stylish." I didn't even bother waiting for him to move onto finger number two before zipping on. "Two: music, The Clash, The Jam, Abba, Madness, *Barry Manilow!*, early Stones, Radiohead — obviously — hard rock and anything from the 80s are all to be encouraged."

It was easier than it looked.

"Internet and social media: I'd say it should be used to look up lots of news, culture and world events. Television's an interesting one; cooking programmes, antiques and lifestyle, building homes and sheds and hard-boiled late-night American TV series, along with, you know, nature, grow-your-own and gardening. What's next?" I studied the beer mat. "Attitude and outlook: Inquisitive, balanced and compassionate, with some sort of animal contact. Hair: bald's a good look! Food: homemade, home-produced or foraged. Language: well, it probably pays to get a head start and begin learning the technical terms for ailments and maladies as the older you get the more they seem to enter your vocabulary."

I scanned the beer mat, making sure I hadn't missed anything. Okay, my list wasn't perfect, but then neither was Ziggy's. But it wasn't bad either, so I said, "and that, cats, is what you need to do in order to grow up!" with a finishing flourish, and sat back.

A moment passed before he said, "God, that sounds boring. You sound like my father."

"Appreciated."

"Welcome."

We both sipped beer.

"Will it work?" he said. "If I follow the list, will I mature and grow up?"

"Guaranteed. And me? My list. Will I stave off early middle age?"

"Without a doubt."

Of course by giving guarantees we were both lying through our teeth, but what was the alternative? To hitch up our metaphorical skirts and skip giggling in a direction of life that neither of us wanted to head? The lists, though far from flawless, did at least represent a real effort to change, and maybe that in itself would be enough. I guessed only time will tell. For now, they would have to do. The nine commandments to halt/encourage middle age and maturity: clothes, music, television, internet, social media, attitude and outlook, hair, food and language. What could possibly go wrong with that?

The Well Man test

"Excuse me. Sorry. Move over, I'm coming in." I squirmed into the homemade pigsty until my head was all the way up level with the General's. I had itchy straw down the back of my jeans, which I find is the main hazard of scrambling in to be with my best friend, other than, you know, the other hazard that a 350-kg pig might accidentally roll over and squash the life out of me, but what friend doesn't come with the odd caveat?

It was early in the morning. I was first up, leaving Debbie and Solly in bed, and although I hadn't exactly sneaked out of the house, I hadn't knocked on Ziggy's door either.

I yanked a handful of straw out from the back of my jeans. It smelt nice in there with the General, kind of fresh and earthy at the same time, but not at all piggy or dirty — pigs really are super-clean animals. Noticing the General had some sleep in his eyes, I reached over and rubbed it away with my thumb. He didn't even flinch, just lay there looking at me. His face was wiry and a bit grey. I wondered if he had any conception that he was getting older. I wondered if he ever felt uneasy about his life?

"You up for a chat?" I asked him.

Bit by bit I told him about last night and Ziggy's nine commandments, rattling them off so he knew what I was talking about: "Clothes, music, TV, internet, social media, attitude and outlook, hair, food, language." Good, now the General was as fully up to speed as I was.

"You know what strikes me about the list?" I said, stretching out with one of my arms draped buddy-style over the General's shoulder. "It's very Ziggy. Very visual and on the outside; nothing much that's internal. But then maybe that's what getting older is all about? You stay the same on the inside as you were when you were a teenager, it's the wrapping that ages. My mum's seventy — you've met my mum, General, remember? — and she often says she feels like a little girl until she looks in the mirror. I thought it was just her, but maybe that's how everyone feels?"

Which begged the question: how old do I feel? I don't feel like a teenager, that's for sure. I feel like a forty-something. But maybe that's part of my problem? Maybe I *should* feel like a little boy on the inside trapped in this old codger's body?

Then again, I'm not at all sure I want to feel like a little boy again, I was never very good at adolescence the first time around, and I can't see I'd fare any better having another crack at it now. Besides, my body doesn't feel codger-like, it just feels a bit worn and achy.

On the subject of achy, I switched topic. That's one of the good things about talking to a pig, they don't mind you going off on a tangent. "I can't believe I rolled the quad bike again the other night. Not that I can remember much about it, just that I was driving along waving at you one second and the next I had this lifting sensation as the bike stopped and I didn't. That's a really weird feeling, it's like this moment of absolute clarity where all the noise and chatter in your head goes quiet, and wandering thoughts cease. It's almost euphoric. Until you hit the ground, and then that moment of clarity kind of shatters into a bazillion pieces as your brain sends out frantic 'are you hurt?' messages to every corner of the body, and the body replies, 'are you kidding me? *Of course I'm hurt, I've just crashed!*' While another corner of the mind helpfully screams, 'OhShitOhShitOhShit', over and over again."

There was a farting noise from the General. It's what happens when he concentrates really hard.

"I can't be that old if I survived the crash without even a bruise, can I?" I moved my buddy arm from his shoulder and put both hands behind my head, looking up at the tin roof of the make-do-and-mend pigsty.

Without the benefit of a crash in progress to calm my thoughts, my chaotic mind did its usual trick of whizzing all over the place as ideas and memories and exaggerations and insecurities and imaginations all flitted about. One of them was Ziggy's list. In the morning light it seemed even more questionable than it had last night in the pub, and last night it looked pretty iffy. But I did feel as though I had got to do *something*.

Let's be honest, I'm either writing, which is a one-man show, or I'm on the land, which is a one-man-and-his-animals show. Either way, I'm on my own much of the time. So if you remove social influence from a man, is his natural bias to wander early into middle age? Or is it just me? And if I have wandered early into middle age, do I simply need to replace social influence in order to halt the progress, maybe even put it into reverse? If that's the case, then embracing Ziggy's list is *exactly* what I need to do.

Nodding off next to me the General started to snore. It began as a gentle rumble but soon built into something maddening. It's hard to think when you feel like you're lying next to a machine that digs up tarmac on roads, so I gave up, crawled out and went to start morning rounds.

The weather was everything you would expect from a British late-summer morn, but at least I'd thought to put on a coat, base-ball cap, gloves, wellies and an extra jumper. Still, the thought that I might actually be onto something with Ziggy's list put a strut into my step as I did the animals, to the point that even the geese thought twice about chasing me. Sadly, after thinking twice they came up with the same thought as usual and pelted after me, but my strut had given me a head start and I managed to escape the near-fatal bum-nipping for another day.

Animals done, I zoomed up the hill on the quad. Walking into the house my first thought was that I must have been out for longer than I realised because the kitchen was a hive of activity with bread fresh from the oven cooling on a rack, a tea towel draped over the bowl of the food processor (which could only mean butter churning underneath — it makes a heck of a splashy mess if you don't use a tea towel to cover it), a pan on the hob with what looked to be the top of a ham visible, and in the middle a frazzled-looking queen bee in the shape of Debbie.

The divvy-up of jobs has evolved over the years so that we could both remain sane. Debbie adores the creativity that self-sufficiency brings out in her within the kitchen — she loves to cook and feed people really good, healthy food (and I'm very good at eating); while I predominantly focus on the land and the animals, though there's plenty of cross-over. It's never "her job" or "mine", it's more a case of this list of things needs doing, so what's the best way to go about it?

"What time is it?" I asked, stripping off my outerwear and hanging it up to dry.

"About eight, I think. How are all the animals? Did you get my telepathic messages to get eggs?"

Sighing, I said, "Normal human beings would have picked up the phone. I did have my mobile on me, you know."

"Too busy," she said, clearly flustered.

"So you sent telepathic messages instead?"

She looked up grinning, and with a big exaggerated nod said, "Yeah! Did you get them?"

I really, really, really wanted to say no — who wants to give the slightest hint of encouragement to their wife that she can dip into your head and plant a message there whenever she wants to? So I said, "No, of course I didn't," but produced nine eggs anyway before launching into a long and complicated monologue on how telepathy was impossible and pure science fiction, and that it was utterly my own intuition that had prompted me to collect the eggs.

Bustling past me she planted a kiss on my cheek and whispered, "I know," winked, then bustled on by.

I hate it when she does that.

"Where's Ziggy?" I said.

"Still in his room, I guess. I've not seen him. I think he's on his phone, to . . . did he tell you her name? I don't even know her name yet."

"No, he's being very coy about it. He hasn't really said much about her at all, other than the fact that she's completely captivated him."

"Can you wash the butter, please? It's lovely to see him, but arriving unannounced didn't give me any time to prepare and I can't send him on a long journey back to London without something to eat, so I've been getting some ham sandwiches ready for him."

"How long have you been at it?"

"Couple of hours. Butter, please . . ."

I washed my hands then lifted the tea towel. A blob of yellow butter clung to the blade of the food processor above the bowl. I peeled the butter off, took it over to the sink and ran it under the cold tap.

"I thought we had butter and bread," I said, nudging my shoulder towards the loaf that she'd obviously just made.

"Yeah, we did," she said, then changed her voice to a loud whisper, "Have you seen how much he eats?!"

When the water falling from the butter ran clear I took it over to the side and started patting it with a wooden spoon to get rid of any liquid that might be trapped inside.

"When he leaves for his train I'll do you ham, egg and toast," Debbie said.

"Not today, I've got to starve myself for my Well Man test, remember? Debbie, do I look old to you?"

"Oh, not now. I've still got stacks to do."

"That's a yes, then. I do look old to you."

"No, that's not a yes, that's a 'I've still got stacks to do', okay? Do you think Ziggy'll be all right with runner bean chutney on his sandwiches?"

Definitely a yes. "Of course he will," I said.

"You're really worried about this doctor's appointment, aren't you?" She came over and put her arms around me. "You'll be fine. Besides, it will be interesting to see how healthy you are. I've been running this body . . ." she stepped back and poked me in the belly, " . . . on nothing but homemade, home-produced food for yonks now, and I'm keen to see how it's doing."

Not at all sure I was in love with the idea of being someone's lab rat, even if that someone was my wife and the experiment involved lots of gorgeous food that would make a two-starred Michelin chef salivate — which of course made it impossible for me to moan — I wandered off for a shower. Traipsing upstairs I met Ziggy coming down. We swapped pleasantries; I called him a lazy good-for-nothing oaf, while he offered condolences over my continuing hair loss.

I shaved slowly, showered slowly, dried myself slowly and dressed even slower, all under the childhood illusion that it was actually possible to slow time when faced with something you didn't want to do. Confident that I'd removed every last hint of possible pig pong from my early morning chat with the General, I made my way back downstairs. Slowly.

Ziggy and Debbie were drinking coffee in the kitchen. Over to one side was a packed lunch the equivalent size and shape recommended for teams trekking the Himalayas. I felt my stomach rumble and said, "I've got to go."

Ziggy stood up and came over to me. We embraced like brothers, which is to say close and sincere, whilst the words that came out of our mouths were also like those of brothers — stupid and jocular and meaning nothing. Then I breached the man code for goodbyes by saying, "You look after yourself Ziggy. Everything's going to be fine, you'll see."

He nodded and stepped back.

"Don't forget to tell them about your diet," Debbie said, moving in, "And how everything you eat is homemade from scratch, and that you never have any additives or E numbers, and that you have hours of exercise every day, and if they say your weight is too high, remind them that it's mostly all muscle, and that . . ."

"It's okay," I assured her, and with a kiss turned to leave.

If you think that because I have a small farm and need to transport animals and huge bags of feed and bales of hay and straw about, I should have a big posh 4x4 truck, you'd be absolutely right — that's exactly what I should have. However, what I actually drive is a tiny, old, on-its-last-legs hatchback, which is fine, but I do kind of have to fold Solly up to get him in the back, unless it's a nice day in which case I can open the sunroof and he can poke his head out like a periscope. If we need to do any farm stuff, we borrow a neighbour's truck. Today, however, all I needed to transport was me.

I parked outside the doctor's surgery and walked in. The downside to living in a small rural community is that everybody knows everybody else. I smiled at the receptionist, who smiled back. Her smile was slightly different in texture to the one she uses on the days when she isn't a doctor's receptionist and instead works in the local café, where she does a roaring trade in hot drinks, toasted sandwiches and friendly gossip.

"Hiya, who are you in to see?" she said, looking down at her notes.

I told her and took a seat, ready to bury my head in a book, but didn't even get the chance to open it before I was called in. That's the upside to living in a small rural community where everybody knows everybody else.

"Take a seat, I'll be with you in one second," said a teenager in a white coat several sizes too large for her, clearly there on work experience. Probably one of the doctor's daughters, I reasoned. Well, good for her, it

60

was cheering to see the youth of today getting out there and experiencing what life's really like in the workplace.

When she turned towards me I gave her a big, warm smile.

"Would you take your top off, please, Mr Dawson."

"No probs." Should I strike up a conversation about Justin Bieber, I wondered? Or who her favourite One Directioner was?

"Now, I just need to take some blood . . ."

"You mean . . . Um, you mean . . ."

She shrugged. "You're here for the Well Man test, right?"

I nodded.

"Have you followed all the recommendations of dos and don'ts?"

"Sure."

"Okay then, so I just need to take a sample of your blood to send off for analysis."

My goodness they *really* let work experiences get involved these days. Didn't she have homework she should be doing instead?

She rested a tray on the arm of the chair next to me. There were needles and syringes and everything in there.

"So, hahaha, you've done this before, right?" What I wanted to say was, do your parents know what you're up to?

She looked at me for a long minute, then said, "Not on an actual live person, not for real, but I did spend a long time last night reading the principles in a book, and they did make it sound very easy." She fitted a needle onto a barrel and held it up for us both to see. Then she met my eyes and said, "I'm the senior doctor here, I've done this a thousand times, okay?"

Some of the blood made its way back into my face. "Of course. Look, um . . ."

"It's okay," she said, "Lots of older guys think I look young, which is a compliment, right?" before she dug the needle in, smiling to indicate she was joking as she began pulling off my blood. That or she really enjoyed this bit of her job.

"You're back early!" Debbie exclaimed as I walked into the kitchen. "How'd it go?"

"Not completely brilliantly, if I'm honest." I told her what happened, finishing with, ". . . and I'm still not convinced she wouldn't spend her lunch hour playing with Sindy dolls. *And* she said I was old!"

"What am I going to do with you?"

"Well, if you wouldn't mind budging out of the way you can watch me drink a gallon of coffee and woof my own body weight in toast."

"Sit down. I'll do it. What about the rest of the test, what did she say?"

"Nothing, there was no rest of the test. I have to go back in a week's time for that. I get the results of the blood test then, too."

"They didn't ask you any lifestyle questions?"

"Nope. All that's done on results day. How was Ziggy, did he leave okay?"

"He left you a present. Apparently you'd understand. Said it was on your computer, and told me to tell you to plug in your phone to collect it. You know how he is."

I did, and when it connected to iTunes, I found a new track had been downloaded to My Music. It was Kwabs.

Never work with animals, especially on a rickety old tin roof

I awoke the next morning feeling bad. It had been several days since I'd done anything more meaningful on the land than the bare minimum of feeding, watering and bedding down the animals, so I resolved to spend the entire day making up for it. Ziggy's list aside, I still had my own "list of things on my mind" to contend with.

Having restored my caffeine level to something nearing optimal working levels by speed-chasing several cups of strong coffee, I braved the cows. "Coming through, no licking, barging, kicking or stamping, or I swear I'm going to McDonald's for lunch to eat one of your cousins." Next I collected a very-happy-to-see-me Dex and drove the quad bike down onto the land.

I did the morning rounds without so much as nearly killing myself or anyone else, which is always nice to report. Then I sat back on the quad, Dex chivvying for fusses under one arm, Curry the goat chivvying for the same under the other, and tried to work out which job was most pressing.

Winnie and her piglets were quite happy in the field shelter, so I knew I had a week or so before moving her became urgent. However, the holes in the stable roof were getting worse by the day, especially as I still couldn't work out how to stop Curry getting up there and charging across it like a hooligan, her sharp little hooves piercing tiny and not-so-tiny holes in the rusty metal. Fixing the roof would also give me time to think about Ziggy's list, although, as important as that felt, in the spirit of hitting the crocodile closest to this crazy boat I knew I should probably try to figure out something to say on the radio this week *and* think about Debbie's birthday, both of which were also urgent.

Precision tools selected from the caravan (precision tools are anything with less than fifty per cent rust on them), and some old recycled sheets of corrugated iron salvaged from a pig house that was no longer in use, I hitched the trailer to the quad and backed it up to one side of the stable, as I don't have a ladder and so needed the trailer to boost myself up onto the roof.

I managed to clamber up. I'm not great with heights; I looked out across the expanse of dirty brown and heavily rusted metal. The roof looked horribly unsafe. But what choice did I have? It had to be mended. As long as I was careful, it should be fine, which, let's face it, are words that are not meant to be spoken with any confidence — and they weren't. Knowing that the more spread out a weight is, the less pressure it puts on an unstable surface, I slithered flat on my tummy out onto the expanse.

Crawling onto the roof I made my way out very slowly, concentrating, listening, ready to scramble back to safety at the first sound of cracking.

Carefully, oh so carefully, I inched forwards, bit, by bit, by careful bit.

Odd noise.

I stopped. Braced myself. Preparing to dash back, I braved a look.

So close that I could reach out and grab them were four hairy brown legs. I looked higher, knowing what the legs were connected to, but hoping I was wrong. I wasn't wrong. They were connected to Curry, who was so overjoyed to find me up there (obviously to play, why else would anyone go up there?) that she started pinging about like an agricultural Tigger. The noise of her hooves hitting the tin surface was deafening.

"No! Curry, please, no. Don't jump about. Please don't jump about."

She didn't listen to me and pinged around even more. However, she didn't go crashing through the roof either. Maybe it wasn't in as bad a shape as it looked?

I sat up. In front of me the world's most annoying goat stopped leaping about and came over for fusses. "If we fall through because of your leaping I will grab you and use you as a cushion to land on, you know that, don't you?" I said, fully aware that the opposite was the truth and I was much more likely to cradle her on the way down, but there's an odd comfort in threatening a good squashing on the perpetrator of your impending demise.

Curry's pratting about did make me feel a little less petrified, though I was anything but comfortable with the situation. Still, silver linings and all that; there was no need to worry any longer about a story to tell on the radio this week, as meeting Curry on a rickety old roof would do nicely.

Placing the sheets of corrugated iron over the holes and securing them, all the while with Curry dancing around and giving me frequent "come on, let's play" headbutts, I distracted myself by thinking about Debbie's birthday. It was a biggie; she was going to be 50.

If we had been living in London with a regular life and a regular income, it would have been easy. I'd have whisked her away on a romantic weekend to Rome, or Paris, and we would have spent the entire time eating, drinking bubbly and necking like teenagers in the backs of late-night taxis. But we don't and we haven't, and somehow recreating that sexy atmosphere along the North Devon Link Road didn't have the same appeal.

So what do you give someone when you have no money but you still want to make their birthday really special?

I decided to do the only thing I could, which was to make something. It was a good decision based on the sound principle that there really was no other option. However, it wasn't until I started thinking about it that I realised how tough it would be to pull off. Sentiment is fine, but the primary job of a homemade present is to look good. Gathering a couple of sheets of coloured cardboard together, some glue, something sparkly, a button and a handful of paper clips and then doing a *Blue Peter* special on them is fine when you're a kid, but it's a struggle to wow people with the same technique when you're 47.

I had been mulling over ideas for a couple of weeks but I still had no firm thought on what to do. I'd discounted planting a tree her, because, although romantic, it's not exactly fun. A soft toy was a bit twee. A wooden box a bit boring. For a couple of days a hand-crafted oak spoon and spatula set made all the running, but in the end it was hard to see her on the morning of her birthday getting excited about kitchen utensils.

I could always make her a "This is Your Life" book, with pictures and snippets of things that meant something to her? Would she like that? Probably. But it didn't seem very exciting. After all, all I'd really be doing was collating the memorabilia she already had. Where was the wow in that?

No, it had to be something new.

But something linked to special moments in her life.

No, not special moments, special *people* in her life.

I sat up. The roof had become rather busy. In addition to Curry there were now three chickens and Niko, the feral cat. How the hell was I ever going to stop them all getting up here? For a while I watched them play merry-go-round together with the goat chasing the cat, the cat chasing the chickens and the chickens chasing the goat. It was fun until one of them collided with my bucket of nails and the whole lot went skidding everywhere.

"Enough!" I yelled. Honestly, it was worse than having kids.

Scooping the nails back into the bucket I thought, what could I get all the people in Debbie's life to donate, first of all that they wouldn't mind parting with, and secondly that I could put together and make into a thing?

From my rooftop vantage point I watched Senorita the not-so-micro micro pig disappear into a chicken house in search of food, and an indignant chicken — that was not going to be turfed out without having a hissy fit — tumble, squawking loudly, out.

I don't know, what do women like?

I was a whiz with a sewing machine. What if I made her a coat, like Joseph's Technicolor Dreamcoat, only this one made from fifty bits of material, each section sent to me from a friend?

Too complicated, and she'd never wear it out.

Joseph's Technicolor Dressing-gown was an idea, but it didn't have the same gravitas.

Unless . . .

Same theme, but a little more basic; how about a patchwork quilt? A *friendship* patchwork quilt. Fifty squares obviously as it was going to be her fiftieth birthday, each one sent to me from someone special in her life that I could stitch together. A quilt is practical. She could put it on the bed or even over the back of the sofa. If she was feeling low or unwell she could wrap herself up in it. I like it. I like it a lot. It has wow *and* "husband of the year" written all over it.

All I had to do was email her friends and ask them all to send me a piece of material without her finding out. What could be simpler?

With that I took a final swish with the hammer and my hat trick of problem solving: stable roof, story for the radio and Debbie's birthday was complete.

Gathering up the precision tools I clambered down from the roof onto the trailer, and from there onto *terra firma* where I was mobbed by a crowd of animals so hungry you'd think they hadn't been fed for a year rather than just the few hours it had been since breakfast.

It's crazy how motivated by food my animals are.

I checked the time. One forty-five. Compared with mornings, evening rounds are considerably more chaotic and take anywhere between two and three hours — sometimes longer, sometimes a lot longer — and because there is no electricity on the land, at this time of year when the leaves are falling from the trees and the nights are drawing in I have to start the rounds in the early afternoon to ensure I'm not fumbling around in the dark to finish.

Okay, even with that in mind I knew I was still a touch early, but by the raucous screeching of the mob they seemed unlikely to make it much longer before fainting with starvation anyway, so I thought I might as well get started.

"Okay, okay, I get the message! Just don't blame me if the BBC turn up with the *Britain's Most Overweight Creatures* film crew to do a documentary on you lot. None of you ever heard of portion control? Saving yourself? *Dieting?* Not mentioning any names, but, hey guys, it's been a while since some of you could get anywhere near a bikini!"

I parked the trailer (Senorita's temporary bedroom — yes, I know, maybe that should have been top of the list today) back in the centre of the chicken field and walked very slowly towards the caravan feed store. By the time I had reached halfway, I was moving more slowly still, taking miniscule steps so that from a distance you'd have had to watch me for some considerable time to think I wasn't stationary.

The reason for my halting progress was because we were moving as a squad. Early or not, it was obvious where I was heading, and it was equally obvious that I couldn't be trusted to make the trip by myself, so I was accompanied by the three goats, several ducks, Senorita, killer geese, Dex, a dozen sheep and a good-sized clutch of kamikaze chickens who, presumably because their hunger had become too much to bear, were trying to fling themselves under my feet in what could only be described as assisted suicide. I'd already almost trodden on two, both of whom were now walking with a distinct wonk.

There's an art to shuffling on mass. You've got to move slow enough not to leave a trail of spatchcock chickens in your wake, but fast enough to avoid the painful humiliation of getting duffed-up by sheep and goats, who, if I slowed too much, would thrust the tip of an encouraging horn deep into one of my buttocks.

"*Orff! That hurt!* Okay, okay, I'm speeding up, I'm speeding up!"

At the caravan I opened the door and squeezed in, slamming it shut behind me. The noise reached a crescendo outside as each set of animals tried to outdo the others and thereby lay claim to being most-in-need-of-being-fed-first by sheer screechy volume alone. In an effort to shut them up as fast as possible I quickly shovelled some pig feed into a yellow bucket and dashed back outside. The wall of noise that greeted me was like watching a rock band returning to the stage for an encore.

Right, this all had to happen fast. Forget shuffling, forget tiptoeing, speed was now of the essence. Sprinting through the middle of them, I ran flat out to the trailer. I was there seconds ahead of the mob. Tipping the bucket of feed into the trailer, I spun around. They were there, right behind me, pushing, shoving, slipping and sliding in a race to get up the ramp. Flicking chickens out of her way with her nose, Senorita bundled up the gangplank and in. I shut the door behind her.

One down, loads to go.

Goats next. There had to be an easier way to do it. After a quick sprint back to the caravan, I grabbed some goat feed and bombed back outside. I know that to an onlooker feeding time seems like bedlam, and it kind of is, but it's organised bedlam. When all the animals are out free-ranging together during the day, this is the reality of putting them to bed.

I headed straight for the goats' cupboard and filled their bowl with nuts. No sooner had I put it down than they were there, noses in. Door shut behind them, *bang*.

I grabbed some hay for the sheep to keep them quiet while I braved the geese, who are a little less aggressive of an evening, and when they were in and done, I moved onto the chickens.

The yard was much calmer now.

I put feed into each of the chicken houses and stood back. As long as there's only one cockerel in each house I'm usually happy for the hens to pick and choose where they want to sleep. As each house filled, I closed and locked the doors behind them.

Stupid the cockerel is always the last one to bed.

"I'm not messing around tonight, Stupid. Come on, in!"

Normally when he realises he's the last one out he'll become all panicky and rush over to his house, but tonight he didn't do that. Odd, because that wasn't like him at all.

"Anything out of the ordinary is always a cause for concern. Are you all right, boy?" I walked over towards him. He seemed agitated. On edge. It was kicking off in one of the other chicken houses too. What was going on tonight?

With Stupid still wandering about, I went back to the chicken house where all the noise was coming from. One of the hens was frantic to get out, flapping and going nuts at the door. I didn't get it, had she found herself in the wrong place? I knew she normally slept in there.

She was flinging herself against the sides in her desperation to get out. Worried that there might be something seriously wrong, I let her out. As soon as she was free she bolted over to Stupid who jumped on her back for a quickie before bed.

"Are you for real? That's what all this is about?"

You kind of get used to moments like this where everything stops for a sex break.

Fortunately it was over pretty fast, which was good for me as the last thing I wanted to do was hang around while they made a night of it. He got off. Head up, chest out and a serious strut to his step, Stupid marched around her in a chicken's equivalent of a lap of honour, while she fluffed herself up and had a good shake. Then he ran off without even a "I'll call ya!", leaving her all alone. She watched him go. She didn't go after him, just watched him go. She didn't move, just sank down into a sitting position. I walked over and picked her up.

I kind of felt sorry for her. She looked forlorn. "Oh sweetheart, men are shits. I'm so sorry, they are. Walking talking penises, every last one of them." I took her back and popped her into her own house. She didn't take her eyes off the door that Stupid disappeared into.

Ducks next, then quail — both are always really easy to do.

The problem with pigs, though, is they all want to be done *right now*! So, with them next on the list, I ran between the pens, scooping nuts out of the bucket and flinging them into each enclosure. That's the easy bit.

The hard work is the water. Back and forth I trudged from the edge of our land where the river runs through it to the pig pens, filling all the drinkers. It took about half an hour. That done, I made sure their beds were plump with fresh straw, and left them to their evening.

The horses live out until the weather gets bad, so all they needed was a quick flick over with a dandy brush, their feet picked out to remove any mud or stones that may have become lodged during the day, a scoot through with a hairbrush on their manes and tails, followed by dinner. While they were eating I took in two wedges of hay for pudding, checked their water and threw a rug over each of them. Done.

Finally I put something out for Niko the cat, and did one last walk around, to check that I hadn't missed anything or anyone. You can get quite OCD about life when you have lots of different animals to worry about. I walked around twice, checking and rechecking everyone was safe for the night. Then I went off to chop wood.

Our sole form of heating in the home is a log fire. There's nothing else. No central heating, no storage heaters, nothing. Just the log fire. So having enough wood to keep it blazing is a big part of my day in the colder months.

I should just steam into the logs with the axe, but I never do. Without all the animals running around everywhere the place was quiet and felt . . . tidy. Organised. It was nice, I liked it. There was no chaos, no stress, no noise! Everyone was fine, everything was done. I could relax.

My phone was in my pocket. I took it out, untangled the ear buds wrapped around it and put them in, then scrolled through My Music. Bottom of the list was Kwabs. I tapped play.

Of my twenty acres, ten are made up of forest. A lot of it is too dense and desperately needs thinning out. I do what I can, and whatever comes down gets piled up for the fire. Having selected a few logs, I picked up the axe and started splitting them into manageable chunks.

The music was mellow and had a good feel to it. I liked it, even if I couldn't make out all the words. I wasn't sure I'd like to muck out a stable to it, but for chopping wood it was pretty perfect. However, any thoughts that listening to Kwabs might make me feel younger were outweighed by the effort of axing the logs, which just made me feel old and knackered.

Back up at the house I unloaded the logs, parked the bike, then kissed and fed Dex before closing the barn door behind him. We keep several farm dogs in there and they've all grown up together, so they're like brothers. Daytimes for Dex are all about protecting the poultry, while evenings are a time for him to let his canine hair down.

"How's everything?" Debbie said as I peeled off my dirty clothes.

"All good. Senorita's still a right little madam. Horses are fine, yeah, everyone's happy. I've had a thought about your birthday and I know what I'm going to do for you. It's going to be a surprise. You're going to love it. But I need to ask you not to read my emails for a while." There's only one laptop in the house, so we share.

She looked up and said, "Reading your emails has nothing to do with my birthday. I don't see why you have to get all secretive all of the sudden."

"Don't be like that, it's for your birthday, okay?" I flicked off my wellies. Then, in an attempt to change the subject and because I knew it would make her go aaahhhhh, I told her the story of the hen and Stupid. "He went back into his house and left her there, all on her own. She looked really sad."

"You've got to stop putting human emotions into the animals. They don't think like that. They're animals, they don't think like humans," she said.

With those words, one of the biggest components of my world smashed into bits right there in front of me.

So I make sense of the world around me the only way I know how

Look, I know I sometimes put human emotions onto the animals, but it's how I make sense of this crazy world. This self-sufficient living isn't natural to me; I wasn't brought up with it. I'm a London lad. That is, until I was 32 years old and nodded "Oh, yes" into my beer and my world went . . . *BANG*, I knew nothing about animals. I was an estate agent. I was street-smart, not field-savvy. I understood people. I understood what motivated them. I understood what made them tick. So plucking me out of that environment and plonking me down in the middle of an alien world in the form of a smallholding full of animals, I made sense of it the only way I knew how — by giving the animals feelings and motivations that I recognised.

Is that wrong?

From this side of the fence it didn't feel it.

Had I damaged the animals?

Had I caused them distress?

No. Of course I hadn't.

Had it meant that I'd found a way to bond with them?

Yes.

Again, is that wrong?

Take that away from me and suddenly I have absolutely no connection to the animals. I'm lost. I walked out of the kitchen and went upstairs. Sat on the bed. Stared at my hands.

See, while I still feel as though I'm fumbling along trying to make sense of this self-sufficient smallholding life, Debbie isn't. She pretty much grew up with animals around her. She knows her stuff inside out — which is good, because that means at least one of us does. It also makes her my go-to.

She'd never said anything like that before. Never even hinted that that was what she thought. I knew I should go down and talk to her, find out if she was just being snappy and reacting because I asked her not to look at my emails. That was possible . . . Recently her mood swings had been more mood hairpin bends, but that didn't make it any easier to understand. I needed to know if she really believed what she said, so I headed back downstairs.

In the kitchen I filled two glasses with wine. Debbie was talking, chatting, oblivious, but I wasn't listening.

"Debbie, we need to talk."

With a tiny shake of her head she said, "What's up?"

"What you said; that I shouldn't put human emotions onto the animals. Everything aside, I need to know if you really believe that. Or if you were just being arsey because I asked you not to look at my emails." I closed my eyes. "This is really important to me. My whole world view, my understanding of this mad way of life, everything, the writing, the farm, my entire universe is all for shit if I'm doing it wrong with the animals."

"No, you're not doing it wrong with the animals!" She came close and tried to hug me but I didn't respond and so she backed away. She sighed. "Sometimes you do go over the top. But not all the time. Most of the time you're more perceptive than anyone. It's like you read their minds. It's gorgeous to watch."

"But not all the time? Sometimes I get it wrong?"

"Maybe. Just occasionally. Oh, sweetheart, that hen wouldn't have felt betrayed by Stupid the way you made it sound. They just don't think like that."

"She looked forlorn, I swear she did."

Debbie put her hand on my arm and squeezed it. She didn't say anything, which was far worse than if she had because I filled in the blank with what I assumed was going on in her mind, which was something along the lines of: it's a chicken with a brain the size of a pea.

They don't think the way we do. They don't have the same complex array of emotions that we have. Their emotions are basic, to do with food, and survival, and procreation. Not love and loss and disappointment.

She put her fingers underneath my chin and lifted it. "Don't change what you're doing. You're doing beautifully. Just, try not to go too far with it. Keep it real, you know?"

"I do!" I blurted out like a four-year-old.

"I know."

For the rest of the night we didn't say anything more about it. I pretended to read; I went over the same page twenty times and still couldn't tell you what was written on it. I drank too much wine. That didn't help — not the way it should have done. That's what getting pissed does for you, it makes your thoughts soggy and difficult to grasp. Even the important ones.

The main problem was I thought she might have had a point. In the kitchen when Debbie went quiet, her side of the argument popped up so sharp and clear in my head that it was hard not to accept that part of me agreed with it. So where did *that* leave me?

My head was a mush. I wished I hadn't drunk so much . . .

The next morning, that thought was still predominant in my head. "I wish I hadn't drunk so much last night," I said between gulps of water in the kitchen.

"You did go for it. But then you were in a bit of a bad place. How'd you feel now — not about drinking too much, about the other stuff?"

I shook my head. "Confused. I think you were right, but I also think I was right, too. Only I'm not sure we can both be right, which means someone must be wrong, but I can't work out which of us is wrong when I think we're both right. Does that make sense?"

"Not in the slightest."

"No, I'm not sure it does to me either."

We both went quiet. Then she said, "We need to discuss my birthday."

The quilt. "You can't look at my emails." Not that I'd done anything about it yet.

"That's not what we need to discuss, though I'm not happy with you hiding things from me. I want to cancel my birthday. I don't want to be 50. So we're just going to ignore it, okay?"

I was too hungover for it, so I said, "I think that's a great idea. I need to go and do the animals," then got ready and left.

The cold air helped my mood a lot more than the wine had the night before. That was something to remember. I took Dex through the cows but decided I was probably still a bit too winesoaked to drive, so I left the quad bike parked where it was and walked the rest of the way. By the time I had made it down on to the land two things had happened. One, I'd sobered up, and two, the drizzle that had been evident when I'd left had stopped and it had started to rain properly. The two, quite possibly, were linked.

"Coming in. Make room for a little one." I crawled in with the General. He didn't stir much, just opened one eye in acknowledgement and closed it again.

"I might be in trouble, real trouble this time," I said. "This isn't about Ziggy's list, or even *my thing*, this is something new. Something that happened last night."

I settled myself next to him, scrunched my eyes shut and said, "When the hell did life get so complicated? I'm sure this isn't how things are supposed to be. I'm sure when you get to my age things are supposed to make a lot more sense than it does. So why is everything so confusing all of a sudden? Even the things I thought I understood are starting to look shaky. This time last week I didn't even know I had *a thing*, whatever the hell *that* is, and now I learn that you guys are animals." I looked over at him. As bad as I felt he still made me smile. "Did you know that? That you're animals?"

Of everything that was going on in my head, this, I felt, needed sorting out most urgently. So come on, I told myself, sort it out . . .

Okay, they're animals, I get it. They're not human. They don't have feelings like us, BUT, *they do have feelings*. They might not be *our* feelings, but they do have them. So I exaggerate them and build stories around them, so what? It's how I make sense of what's going on around me. And what if I do go over the top every now and again? So my interpretation of their actions is off the mark occasionally, so what? It's not affecting anyone other than me. The animals don't know what I'm thinking. I don't treat them any differently.

We're mates.

Good mates.

I don't want to lose that, and I'm scared that if I do change the way I make sense of the world and the animals it will dilute. So do I just ignore what Debbie said, even though part of me agrees with her? Or is the real problem that she thinks I'm a bit of a dick for talking to them all as if they're human? Or, worse, is this the start of me losing my marbles?

In the distance I can hear the cockerels' *cock-a-doodle-dooing*. "I've got to go and start the rounds," I told the General and crawled out.

I let everyone out, breakfasted them, and stood in the middle of them all while they wandered about — pecking, nosing, drinking from the spring, running after one another, shagging, touching, squawking and fighting. I watched it all and tried hard not to interpret their actions with human emotions, I really did, but I found that it meant it lost all the fun, all the juice. So instead I did what I normally did and read emotions into their morning activities: arguing, befriending, hating, loving, teasing, feeling good, feeling bad, falling in love, falling out of love — generally filling their lives with the everyday intricacies that, for me, make it worthwhile getting out of bed.

Even if I had got it wrong, I didn't want to do it differently.

Over by the stables one of the goats was down on her knees. She looked like she was praying. I went over to her. "Bee, pretty girl, are you okay?" Catching her unawares I lifted one of her feet — she *hates* her feet being touched — and looked between the pleats. The skin there was gooey and smelly; Bee had come to us with bad feet and despite trying everything I could think of, including getting a vet to look at them, I'd never been able to get them right and they had a tendency to flare up from time to time.

Summoning my very smiliest bedside manner I declared, "You're a tart," because that's what a bedside manner is all about, putting your patient's mind at rest. "I've only just given you breakfast and you were fine. Between then and now, your foot's going to fall off. I'm sorry, you are a tart." I should have been a doctor.

However, underneath my rather excellent patient care, I was a little worried and knew I had to treat her foot straight away to avoid it escalating into something far worse. Only, I was out of antibiotic spray. Getting some had been on my to-do list for months. It had been on both Debbie's and my lists, and we'd both been avoiding it.

I finished off and wandered back up to the house.

"Milk and eggs?" Debbie asked as I walked through the door.

I shook my head on the egg front, "I'll get them tonight," but I did produce a container of fresh warm goat's milk and slid it onto the table.

"How'd you feel?"

"You know . . ." I shrugged. "Everyone's fine down there, but, um, Bee's feet are bad. She was fine yesterday, fine when I gave her breakfast this morning. Then suddenly she just went completely lame. You know what a tart she is. Anyway, I need to treat it."

"Of course. Antibiotic sprraaayyyyy . . ." she tailed off. "We're out, aren't we?"

I nodded.

She blew out a long breath and said, "Oh."

We both knew it meant a trip to the vet to collect a can of antibiotic spray. That's what we'd been avoiding, that's why we hadn't picked up a can before, even though we both knew we needed one, because it meant going to the vet. We had a bad time there last year. We took one of the animals in and it all went wrong. It was traumatic, really traumatic, and returning to the practice would bring back all those painful memories. So we'd been avoiding it, until we could avoid it no longer. Until today.

Offering to go on my own, as it seemed pointless both of us getting upset, Debbie insisted we do it together because, she said, "It's not just the good times we have to share." I folded Solly into the car — it had started raining again so I couldn't open the sunroof for him, which made him moan and whinge and keep nudging the roof lining with his nose.

I hadn't even pulled away when Debbie blurted out, "Tell me about Ziggy's list."

She didn't want to know about Ziggy's list, she just wanted me to fill the silence so she didn't have to think.

It was a bad sign.

"Is the prospect of going *that* bad?" I said.

She didn't answer.

"Look, why don't you stay here," I said, adding the see-through lie of "I don't want you to come with me anyway. Girls smell. And all they talk about is underwear and pretty frocks and, and, *feelings*! Besides, me and Solly want to talk about football and war and the price of tractor tyres."

She smiled, reached out and squeezed my hand. "You know nothing about football."

Indignant, I said, "I do so know about football!" I don't. I don't even have a working pub-knowledge of it. Truth be told, I don't know much about war or tractor tyres either.

"Come on, drive before I change my mind."

"You sure?"

She nodded, "I want to be with you," she said quietly. "Do you want me to talk about my underwear?"

"Hell, yeah!" First gear, clutch out, on our way . . .

Laughing, she said, "Come on, seriously, tell me about Ziggy's list."

"Spoilsport." As we drove I outlined Ziggy's key points: Clothes, music, TV, internet, social media, attitude and outlook, hair, food and language.

"Hair? In case you haven't noticed —"

"Yes, thank you, I have noticed. We do have mirrors you know."

"And this list of Ziggy's is supposed to do what, exactly?"

"I'm not entirely sure. I mean, I know it's supposed to make me feel younger and less like I'm hurtling into middle age . . ." Pause. Long pause. The type of pause where the pauser is waiting for the pausee to jump in and say something, and gives the pausee plenty . . . of . . . room . . . to . . . do . . . the . . . jumping . . .

Come on . . .

Eventually: "You're not middle aged," she said.

About time!

"Oh, you don't need to say that. I wasn't fishing." I forced myself not to look at her because I knew she was watching me and smiling, and if I looked, I'd have to acknowledge it. So I didn't, and carried on.

"The thing is, if it's true that I'm uneasy about growing older in this self-sufficient, smallholding world we've created, which I think it is — at least mostly — then the answer must be not to grow older in the first place, and for that Ziggy's list is the perfect antidote to all things middle-aged."

"Mmm, I'm not convinced that's what you need." Any hint of a smile in her voice was now completely gone. "I thought what you were worried about was growing older without family around you, which I understand. But listening to music you're not into, or wearing clothes that make you look sad and desperate isn't going to change that."

"I don't wear clothes that make me look sad or desperate!"

"Not yet, but it's on Ziggy's list. What was the music like that he gave you?"

"Fantastic, you'd love it!"

"How many times have you listened to it?"

I laughed. "Shut up."

She laughed too. It was a good moment.

"You haven't listened to it at all, have you?" she said.

"I have. Once. But I've been busy."

"I hope Ziggy's okay. I do worry about him — have you heard from him?"

86

I told her I hadn't.

We were around the corner from the vet's. I could feel Debbie go quiet and I wanted to say something to fill the gap and make it better, but I couldn't find anything that wasn't related, as if my entire head had given itself over to what happened a year ago.

I feel that this is a story I need to tell here. It feels colossal inside me, like it's taking up all the room. It also feels important, and relevant, and somehow connected to what's going on at this point in the book. I'm not sure how or why, but that's just how it feels. It's not a story I've told before, even to myself. After it happened I just packaged up the memory and shoved it over to one side of my mind, hoping never to have to unwrap it again. Weirdly, until right now, until this very second, I didn't even realise how big and heavy it felt, and how much space it was taking up. I'm sorry, I know you'll have guessed it doesn't have a happy ending, but I'll be as quick as I can.

Debbie and I have had Great Dane dogs for more than twenty years. We just clicked with them. There was Baloo, then Deacon, then Darcy — all boys — then we had Brodie, a girl. And now we have Solomon.

Brodie was stunning, a brindle with orange and black tiger stripes. She was beautiful, and there were no two ways about it, I was hers, she was mine and we were inseparable. Man and his best friend, and all of that.

She was eight months old when we got her, and after her first season when we had to buy dog knickers for her so we could use a sanitary towel, it was obvious she had to be spayed. After her second season, it was *really* obvious!

We booked her in. Took her to the vet. Took her into the waiting room. Handed over her lead, and she walked off, not looking back, happy and wagging her tail. We were told to phone several hours later. We did. The operation was successful, the vet was happy. No problems. We could come and get her. We drove back to the vet.

"She's quite a sleeper, isn't she?" the vet joked. "We've had trouble keeping her awake long enough to go out for a pee."

We started the paperwork and paid while they went and got her.

"She really must be tired, they're taking ages," I said, reading the notice board for the third time.

The doors opened. The vet was alone. "There's a problem," she said, ashen-faced. "Brodie's collapsed. We've restarted her heart, but we need to go back in and open her up again. I'm sorry . . . I'm sorry, but her chances aren't good. I'll do what I can."

Debbie and I sat in the waiting room, holding hands and drinking disgusting tea.

After half an hour, the doors opened again. The vet walked out slowly. "I'm so sorry," she said.

Fuck, that hurts. I mean . . . *fuck*. I wanted to be angry, but there was nobody to be angry at, not even myself. Clutching each other, we walked out and went back to an empty home, with the small chicken-and-rice dinner we'd made for Brodie still cooling on the side. When you're used to having a dog, a house without them just feels cavernous.

Bludgeoned half to death while performing a pedicure on a cantankerous goat

I parked the car just a little way down from the vet's. "I'll go and get the antibiotic spray, you stay here," I said to Debbie.

"Will you be okay?"

"Me? Are you kidding? Heart as tough as an old saddle." I whacked my chest a little too hard and brought on a coughing fit.

In reception, while I waited for someone to get the antibiotic spray, I read the notice board. Not much had changed in a year. There were still dog-walking groups looking for members, as well as agility classes and puppy training, along with lots of info on teeth, ticks and fleas.

Although I was reading the words and looking at the pictures, resting one foot on the other, arms crossed, head on one side, shoulders soft, it was all a physical lie designed to hide the internal war that was going on, where every scrap of mental power not taken up with life support was working to a white-hot frenzy in an effort not to think about Brodie. The fact was, the memory was being boosted by the sights, smells and tastes in the air as I stood in the vet's again. It was her smell I remembered most, and those huge paws. It made me believe that maybe there was something to be said for spending time with sad emotions around the time they hit and not doing the stupid man thing of taking a raw, painful, emotional wound and tossing a rug over it in the hope that it heals itself. It never does. It just gets infected and putrefies. Sure, out of sight out of mind has its place, but it's no long-term fix.

They all affect you, you know, every single loss. They all change you in some way.

Unpacking Brodie's story leaves me with mixed emotions. Sadness, but also guilt at not having thought about her for so long because it just feels too painful. But there's something else I can't quite work out; it's connected to her death, and all I know is it's really relevant. It's frustrating that I can't work it out.

Unless . . . unless it's her death itself?

She was too young to die, that's the phrase that runs on a loop inside my head. She was too young to die. So does that mean when you're older it's okay to die?

I don't like that thought.

As a little boy, from the age of about four or five, I was terrified of dying, and I mean cry-myself-to-sleep terrified. I don't know where it started. I have no recollection of what brought it on, only that it was a big thing throughout the whole of my childhood and deep into adolescence. As an adult it went away. I haven't thought about it in ages because I found a way to block it out of my consciousness.

One thing's for sure, if that was the connection here, if that was what was nagging me about Brodie's story, there was no way I was ready to unpack that, and I

90

certainly wasn't ready to let it back into my consciousness — 47 years old or not.

Antibiotic spray in hand, I returned to the car. It had stopped raining and the sunroof was open. Solly's head was out, his chin resting on the part of the roof where it meets the top of the windscreen. It made me and several passers-by laugh, until he barked and they all scattered.

"How was it?" Debbie said.

"Sad but fine — not as bad as it could have been," I told her honestly, battling my way in as the dog did an I'm-so-pleased-to-see-you run around the back of the tiny car. "It's been a year. That's a long time — will you calm down, *Solomon!*"

"He's happy to see you," Debbie exclaimed, as he switched from running to resting his chin on my shoulder and drooling down my neck. Given the choice I preferred the running.

The return journey was easier, the conversation lighter and friendlier. Once back home we went straight down onto the land in search of the patient, who seemed to have become bored with hanging around and had begun to entertain herself by eating the innards of my chainsaw helmet.

"Well you shouldn't have left it lying around," Debbie said when we saw the helmet in tatters.

"I didn't!" Actually, I might have. "Let's just get her foot done, okay?"

Debbie took hold of Bee's collar while I removed my glasses and placed them on the side — we've done battle over feet before; ever since she came to us she's been funny about a pedicure. I reached down for her leg. The second I touched it, Bee went ballistic.

"You're hurting her," Debbie said, holding on while Bee flipped around like a rodeo horse.

"I'm not, I'm only at her ankle, I haven't even got to her foot yet!"

"Why's she going crazy, then?"

"I don't know, it's Bee, she hates her feet being done. Calm down pretty girl — *yaowl*!" I screamed as she slammed her knee into my eye.

"Hurry up, I can't hold her for much longer."

"I can't see. She's got me in the eye."

"Spray the foot."

"I can't see the foot!"

Our little party was starting to draw attention. Amber and Curry, the other two goats, were the first on the scene and decided a few well-placed headbutts were in order.

"Will you stop nutting me!"

Dex added some volume with some quality barking.

"Dex, go quiet . . . *go quiet*!"

Not to be left out, Senorita wobble-bellied it over and, in the excitement, jumped to the reasonable conclusion that we were eating Bee, only she couldn't quite reach for her own portion so instead she took a chunk out of the next best thing, which was my leg.

"*My leg*!" I screamed. "What the hell was that?"

"Hang on . . . It's okay, it's Senorita."

"Okay? It's not okay, she just bit me!"

"Have you still got Bee's leg?"

I knew I had something in my hand but I wasn't at all sure if it was Bee or someone else. I looked down with my one good eye. "Yes, hang on . . ."

Actually, because the scrum had become quite compact, I found her foot in the ideal position — squashed between me and one of the other goats — so I could open the pleat and direct the spray right at the sore spot. Then I let her go.

I slumped down like a soldier in the field, debating whether to call for a medic. Debbie slumped next to me. We were both breathing hard.

"We should have taken her somewhere away from everyone else, somewhere on her own," Debbie wheezed.

"I thought she'd be calmer and less stressed being outside and not shut in. I think I might have been wrong."

Dex came over and did a Fosby-flop into my lap.

"How's your eye?" Debbie asked after a while.

I touched the wound and looked at my fingers. There was no blood.

"Is this going down as another near-death experience?" she said, knowing my obsession with collecting stories of all my accidents and relating them to anyone who would stand still long enough to listen. I gave this incident a title:

"Bludgeoned Half to Death by a Goat's Foot"

There was a ring to it, but the lack of spilled blood prevented it reaching the upper echelons and warranting anything more than a memorable mention.

"It's not quite up there," I said.

"Stiff competition?" she laughed.

She'd heard all the tales many times and particularly appreciated the ones where my testicles came into serious jeopardy — you've no idea how dangerous learning to ride a horse in loose-fitting underwear can be to a man's dangly bits! Oh, and the one where I all but drowned myself on a gate by accidentally tipping a bucket of water into my face and breathing in. Or the time I was savaged by a pussy cat. Or when I ran myself over with my own quad bike. Sadly, there were just too many classics for bludgeoning half to death by a goat's foot to fit anywhere near the top of the list.

"I'm going up to the house," Debbie said. "Coming?"

"I should stay down here and work. I've got stacks to do."

"Anything urgent?"

"It's all urgent."

"Anything that can't wait until after lunch?"

"No," I said, and we made our way across to the quad bike.

Picking out the celebrities in the story of someone else's life is fraught with danger

Up at the house, fire alight and slices of bread balanced on forks toasting in front of the flames while Debbie scrambled eggs, I settled down with the computer on my lap and wrote an email to all her friends:

Dear all,

Please forgive the global email.

The thing is, it's Debbie's birthday in November and it's a biggie — the big five-oh!

I've decided to make her a few gifts, but the main one is going to be a quilt, a sort of friendship quilt.

So I'm asking the 50 most important people in Debbie's life, both family and friends, if they'd be kind enough to send me a piece of material and I'll sew all 50 together to make the quilt. I'm hoping to get a piece from all the people she loves and who love her.

To that end, I was hoping you might be able to send me something and be part of it?

The material. It needs to be at least 7 inches square. Other than that, it could be anything. Cut out from an old pair of jeans, or a t-shirt, a top, shirt, skirt or trousers, or a dress — something that you're no longer going to wear, obviously, haha. Just something that means something to you. Or it could be a snippet from an old pair of curtains, or a tablecloth, or even something new where the colour has significance. You could also embellish it, if you wanted to — jazz it up, bedazzle it or give it a touch of bling, just as long as it represents the person it's from. New, old, plain or jazzed up, it's entirely up to you.

Obviously please don't mention any of this to Debbie. Oh, and I'll need it in the next few weeks,

if that's okay, to give me time to put my tailoring
skills to the test:-)

Thank you, thank you, thank you.
Simon x

Then I wrote in the subject bar: *Debbie's birthday* and
sent it to her immediate family and current closest
friends. I counted how many it had gone out to. It came
to 26, more than half, which was pretty good going for
an initial sortie. Then I sat back and considered who
else had been an important part of her life.

It was a good question. Picking out the celebrities in
the story of someone else's life is a tricky business, even
if you are married to them. Old school friends, for
instance. There were stock names she brought up each
time school was mentioned, so should they be included
even though she hasn't seen them in 35 years? Then
there were workmates from early jobs. Old friends she
no longer had regular contact with but clearly was very
fond of. New friends who'd just arrived in our lives.
Where do you draw the line? If I included everyone I'd
go way over the 50 squares for a fiftieth birthday. What
about the animals, they needed to be included too,
didn't they?

So I worked backwards. Giving priority to the
animals — as I knew that's what Debbie would want —
I made a note of those who could donate a corner of a
blanket, or coat, or bed, and then from the number of
squares left tried to work out who were the important

96

human characters in her life and fired off emails to them too.

After lunch I went back down onto the land and soon after my mobile rang.

"I can't get into your emails," Debbie complained.

"I changed the password," I told her. I was trudging along the path ferrying what ice-cold water wasn't sloshing down the inside of my boot to the pigs. "Besides, we agreed you weren't going to check them."

She replied with a "Mmm" and was gone.

I carried on, one foot squelching. I had Kwabs on again, the music Ziggy left me. As Ziggy was on my mind I emptied what remained of the water from the bucket into one of the pig's drinkers and dialled his number. It wasn't often I had money on my phone, but when I did it was bloody lovely. He answered on the first ring.

"I was just thinking about you," he said.

"Where are you?" I said.

"The office, working on fish files."

Fish files, he'd told me before, was the term used by solicitors for problem cases that were so stinky they avoided touching them.

"Anything juicy?"

"Not really. So how're you getting on? Thanks for putting me up. And tell Debbie she was right, she did expect me back even though she clearly said it was fine for me to stay."

Turning to go back to the river for another refill of the bucket I said, "How is she?"

"We're still working things out," he said. "Maybe taking off like that wasn't one of my best ideas."

"Hindsight. I got the music, thanks. This Kwabs fella's pretty good, isn't he?"

"You like him? Great! How're you getting on with the list?"

"You know."

"No, so why don't you tell me?"

He knows me too well.

"Well, it is a load of rubbish, and has absolutely no relevance to my life out here, and I'm not even certain it's the right approach for what I need."

"So are you going for it or what?"

"Of course I am. How about you?" I asked.

"I haven't made any of my own clothes yet, if that's what you mean. I think it's easier for someone to adopt a younger attitude than the other way around because younger is fun, whereas trying to be mature just looks like a world full of toffee sweets, which I hate, brown clothes, which I hate even more, and reading books, and I haven't read a book since I was at school — I haven't even read yours!"

I did say he was a rubbish best friend.

"You do have a knack for negativity, you know," I pointed out.

He laughed, "Well, having spent most of my life hanging out at parties, nightclubs, bars and restaurants, all in the arms of beautiful women, growing up just looks dull."

"You're going to be a dad. That trumps everything, doesn't it? Besides, don't you think it might be fun to

98

have a real relationship with someone that lasts more than twenty-four hours?"

"I know."

"So, you going for my list?" I asked.

"Of course," he said. "I'm that desperate I'll try anything. Mind you, I am adapting it a bit, there's only so much foraging you can do in London so I'm widening the meaning to take in shopping, which I thought was a good compromise, and as for animal husbandry I'm making a conscious effort to stroke more cats. Where are you?"

"Hang on —" I'd made it back to one of the pigs' drinkers with the bucket and tipped in the water. Then I climbed over to Pru, who was up in the woods eating dinner, and crouched down beside her, fussing her head. "I'm in with Pru."

"Say hi from me. Listen, mate, I've got to go. Laters."

Laters? What the hell is that supposed to mean?

I carried on filling the pigs' drinkers until they were all full. Then I drove the quad bike over to check on the sheep, one of whom, I noticed, had a rather mucky bum, and reluctant to leave it, I nipped off to gather some equipment to take care of it. Then I went back and caught her.

Stuffing her between my knees and gripping, I bent over her rump and started shaving her back end with huge electric clippers that draw their power from the quad bike. Known as dagging, this particular smidgen of animal husbandry sits right up there on my fun-o-meter with such classics as stubbing my toe and drinking on-the-turn milk. In fact, the only thing that could possibly make it worse was if it started raining, which of course it did, and within a few minutes it was tipping down.

Sheep are rubbish at looking after themselves, and if left unattended will develop a terribly dirty bottom, which is revolting, unless you're a fly who wants to lay its eggs in the tastiest morsel it can find, in which case a bum covered in poo has all the appeal of a bacon sandwich.

So the mucky bum has to come off, but in true sheep fashion you can't just trim it neatly and quickly, oh no, you have to get properly stuck in and shear it.

Unhappy about my downstairs hairdressing, and quite possibly experiencing a tiny bit of justifiable fear over her nether regions getting closer to electric equipment in the soggy wet weather than is entirely comfortable, she tried to sit down. I couldn't stop her. All I could do was follow, which meant leaning so far over in an attempt to see what I was doing that my face was nearly upside down, and my glasses swung away from my nose and came to rest on my forehead. Blind, but committed, I carried on shearing, my nose now inches from her stinky backside.

Meanwhile the rain had softened the chunks of poo attached to her to such a degree that every time the clippers ran into one it exploded, which isn't great when you're inches away. By the time I finished my face looked like the number plate of a car that had been driven at high speed through a fly storm it had so many splatters of poo on it. I let the sheep go and she bounded two feet away before kicking her back feet out at me.

My back ached and I smelled so bad I had to stop breathing through my nose. When I joined Dex on the quad bike he sneezed and turned his head away. Fine. I drove back up to the house and for a while the breeze meant we both enjoyed a brief respite from the stench of sheep ablutions.

"I really need a shower," I announced at the house. Not daring to go in, I announced it through the kitchen window.

"Well you'll have to wait for the hot water," Debbie said.

Dex and I shared a look, and then man's best friend became a distant acquaintance and he left me, probably to go and find some sweet-smelling ammonia to inhale and clear his sinuses.

I felt awful. The day had been horrible. I'd had to re-live what happened to Brodie, been smashed in the eye by Bee's leg, sloshed cold water down one boot and to round it off I now had a face covered in splatters of sheep poo. Sitting on the back step I became as philosophical as a man can get when he stinks to high heaven, so I started writing a mental list of all the injustices that only I, out of everyone in the world, suffered. However, just as I reached the end of my first virtual A4 sheet from the imaginary pile of blank paper beside it like a stack of poppadoms, I did something really stupid and licked my lips.

The link between taste buds and brain was instant.

"Waugh! Whahoo!" I shouted. The only way I can describe it is if you have ever eaten really strong goat's cheese and all you can taste is goat. Well, it's the same if you lick sheep poo. Without letting my tongue back into my mouth, I said, "Ho! hease hell he hi hidn't hust ho hat."

"What are you saying?" Debbie shouted from the kitchen.

"Hothing. Hi heed ha hink heally, heally hickly." Oh sod it. "I need a drink really, really quickly," I repeated. "Like, NOW!"

"Okay — shall I make you a coffee?"

"No time. Faster! Water!"

"Are you okay?"

Quite possibly I would never be the same again.

The ~~sheer terror~~ fun of live radio

I survived the night. Just. Delighted to have made it to the morning without catastrophic sheep-poo poisoning setting in, I was up and out before dawn because it was my radio day, when I was due to appear on the breakfast show, which meant I had to be in town early.

Dashing about trying to get the morning rounds finished, including checking on Bee's bad foot — which looked a lot better already — I left a bucket full of water in the middle of the field. When I turned my back, one of the ducks went over and sat in it, bobbing and moving slightly where she must have been waggling her feet under the surface. Her companion squatted on the ground beside her, doing that thing that ducks do by turning their head backwards and nestling it under a wing to fall asleep, while two feet away from them a spring washed down the centre of the field.

I have no idea why she had chosen to sit in a bucket rather than the spring, or the pond. Maybe it was warmer, or less muddy, or maybe she just liked the elevated position — who knows what goes through the mind of a duck?

What goes through the mind of a goose, however, is easier to recognise. Mobsters of the chicken field, nothing goes on without their say-so, and nobody is allowed to have more fun than them.

I watched the geese make their way over to the ducks. Sensing danger, the duck on the ground didn't need any encouragement to skedaddle and was up on his feet and waddling away almost before he had a chance to wake up and face forwards.

The bucket-swimmer thought about defending her position, then decided better of it and splashed and flapped herself over the side, plopping onto the ground and doing the duck version of hurtling headlong after her friend.

With no more need for confrontation than a simple show of their presence, which is pretty much how they live their lives, the geese ambled up to their prize. Together they studied the bucket, tried to eat it, walked around it one way, then the other, dipped their heads inside all the way to the bottom just in case the duck had been sitting on a stash of food, found nothing, spread their wings, squawked in victory, and then very slowly the female raised herself up and climbed into the bucket as elegantly as any lady has ever stepped into a bath.

Only she was too big and didn't fit. She didn't even nearly fit. But there was no way she was going to give up either. If the ducks could do it, she could do it. With a little work she got her bum in and most of one leg, but that was about it for a while until she wriggled and jiggled and somehow managed to get the other leg in, along with a bit more of her belly, by shifting slightly to allow some of the water to spill out.

She sat still for no more than a few seconds before she twisted and glanced over one shoulder in the direction of the ducks — not at them, definitely not at them, because she was way too superior to care a jot about how they felt and she didn't mind in the slightest if they were watching her or not, but just in their general direction. You know, in case they were looking over. And they were. *Obviously* they were. They were glued to the performance. We all were.

Reluctantly I carried on with whatever I was doing. Then I turned back to the geese. She was still there, in the bucket, and it was evident she was stuck.

What do you do with a goose stuck in a bucket? Call the vet? Call the fire brigade? I've heard of chicken in a basket, but goose in a bucket?

Carefully, I got close and, with an outstretched foot, tipped the bucket over. It rolled over onto its side. She was still stuck. I had to get hold of it and shake the bucket upside down to get her loose. The ducks watched from a distance, which was probably wise because when she did slosh out with the remaining water, she was as angry as a dragon.

The ducks were happy, though.

You see, *YOU SEE*! How is it even possible to make sense of situations like that if you can't give them human emotions like pride, envy and jealousy?

Back at the house I cleaned up and left for town to do my radio thing.

Let me tell you, live radio is the scariest thing anyone can do. There is nothing more terrifying than knowing that everything you say is being broadcast for thousands of people to hear.

The first time is the worst. For me, that was on BBC Radio Devon.

". . . so, we have Simon Dawson with us this morning. Hello, Simon!"

All I had to say was hello. Simple as that: hello. But no, suddenly all the other options crept into my head: Hi; Good morning; Good to be here. How can there be so many greetings? And then there's the tone of voice: Bubbly and happy; Serious and mature; Relaxed and confident. In a moment of sheer panic, I did the only thing that seemed sensible and opted for everything. "HelloHiGoodMorningToBeHere." I even managed to squash all the tones of voice in there, which wasn't easy. To anyone listening it must have sounded like a minor human explosion and I imagined people staring dumbfounded at their radios.

Arriving in the town centre I parked and wandered down the high street towards the radio studio. I was early, so I took my time. The contrast to being on the smallholding was nice, and I liked the fact that nobody was trying to bite me, stamp on me or chase me, and not one person screamed out demanding food. And nobody, not a single, solitary soul, needed their bottom shearing.

I love the way you can become invisible in a high-street crowd. Walking past the market I ducked down a side path and round the back of the shops. Compared with their fronts, the backs of the shops were surprisingly uninviting and all bore notices informing visitors that if they were hoping to pinch some money, they would be disappointed because there wasn't any. The bell for the studio next to one for a medium who promises to contact the dead for price. If the two notices are to be believed, the medium can't be doing very well.

I pressed the bell and waited.

It was a few minutes before I heard footsteps running down the stairs, then the door flung open and the friendliest face in all of Devon beamed out at me.

"Simon!"

I read somewhere that if you could harness all the energy from a single bolt of lightning it would produce enough power to run a city for a month. Quite why nobody has ever thought of putting a similar calculation on radio breakfast-show presenters is beyond me.

"Hopps!" It's impossible to greet him without smiling and getting a sense that everything is all right in the world.

"How you doing buddy?" he said. I told him I was fine.

I followed him up two flights of stairs and into the studio.

Banners everywhere told you that you were in The Voice FM — local radio for North Devon. Good, I thought, I'm in the right place.

Hopps rushed around to his side of the desk while I threw my coat over the arm of a handy chair and took a seat opposite on the guest/contributor's side. There was music playing through the speakers, Michael Jackson's zombie epic "Thriller".

If you live in North Devon or have ever visited it you will have heard of Paul Hopper — better known as Hopps. He's the breakfast show guy here. You'd hear his voice and go, "Oh, he's *that* guy," and you'd smile because that's what a good radio presenter makes you do.

I'll tell you what it's like sitting in the studio, I'll tell you exactly what it's like. Remember the last time you came home unexpectedly and walked into your fourteen-year-old son's room, and he's there in the middle of this chaotic melodrama of technology, with several computers on the go, a smartphone, the house phone, music blaring, the TV on and a game station in the corner playing the latest game, and part of you (the part that wasn't about to blow a head-gasket over the electricity bill) thought, how the hell does he do all of that at once? Well, walk into a radio studio — which, let's face it, is geek-city central with monitors and buttons every where — and it's exactly the same feeling.

"How's life on the farm?" Hopps asked, looking down to see how much time there was left of "Thriller" before the manic laugh of Vincent Price brought it to a finish. There was a monitor my side too. One minute twenty seconds still to go. It's a long track.

I have rarely spoken to Hopps outside of the studio, so my entire friendship with him is built around snippets of conversation off-air while songs are playing, or on-air when I do my bit, which means that everything we know about one another has been communicated in three-minute bursts. I find it very hard not to come across as completely wacky and eccentric in anything less than eight minutes.

"Oh, everything is great," I said, wondering if I should tell him about the sheep poo incident of last night or whether it would take too much explaining and have to be left half-told, which might make me look a bit odd rather than simply a victim of circumstance, which is what I am. As I said, eight minutes, nothing less.

"Good," he said, reaching for his headphones and putting them on, "I'll play one more track and then it's you, okay?"

I nodded and gave a thumbs up as the red "on-air" light blinked and the music faded out.

Into the microphone he said, "Love that song, though it's given me the permanent willies for walking through graveyards after midnight. Imagine getting confronted by all those dancers and all that choreography in the middle of the night! Okay, so coming up we've got the smallholding legend that is Simon Dawson, and he'll be with you right after this . . ."

Red light out. Music faded up.

"Busy week?" he asked, taking off the headphones and putting them to one side. The music for the entire show is pre-programmed on a computer so at least he didn't have to flit about between songs searching for the next track.

"Kind of. Senorita the not-so-micro micro pig's settling okay, though I've still not managed to get her to accept that she can't have daytime TV, or that she's got to integrate with the other pigs at some point." Senorita's arrival was last week's story.

He laughed. "What are you going to do with her?"

I didn't say teach her how to be a pig, not even eight minutes could de-weird that one. "See how she goes, I guess," I said, which was almost true. "How are things with you?"

He sat back and smiled and talked about the station and the scheduling of presenters and promotional appearances, and didn't like to say that's not what I meant. I meant, how *are* you? With an emphasis on the, *are*. But I guess he's aware of the three-minute time slot too.

The song was coming to an end. I knew this because, one: Hopps reached for his headphones, and two: my inner ear ranked up the volume of my heart so loud I might have been forgiven for thinking a tiny drummer had crawled inside my head and was smashing sticks against my eardrum. Quite why the human body feels the need to alert you that you're scared by turning up the noise on its internal workings, I have no idea. It's very off putting.

"Ready?" Hopps asked, sliding on his headphones.

I nodded, moved the microphone in front of me and over the soundtrack of my heart smashing away in my ears, and began the mantra used by everyone who's about to go live on air: Don't swear, don't swear, whatever you do, *don't swear!*

Red "on-air" light on. Music faded out.

My mouth was so dry I'd have sold my soul for a lozenge.

"That was Simply Red and 'Money's Too Tight to Mention'. Coming up we've got the biggest dance-floor hit of the 1990s that's going to get your toes-a-tappin'. But first, it's Simon Dawson! How are you, Simon?"

In a split second all bodily functions returned to normal, which was handy. I could no longer hear my heart and my mouth felt as though I could actually use it to speak.

Laughing out loud, I said, "I'm really good."

"Now last week you were telling us about Senorita the micro pig who isn't a micro pig. How is she?"

"Oh, she's a hooligan, and an ever-increasing-in-size hooligan, at that. Her micro days, it's fair to say, are pretty far behind her now, and her wobble-belly days lie ahead just like the rest of us."

Both laughing, he said, "So other than Senorita, what's been happening on the farm this week?"

"Well, what happened was . . ." and I launched into my story about meeting Curry on the rickety old stable roof. The most stupid thing you can do, while talking on radio, is to act out the story as you speak because nobody can see you. But that's what I did. I couldn't

110

help it. I had arms and legs going everywhere, and when I reached the bit about Curry wanting to play and I was hanging onto the roof for dear life, my body was going through the motions of acting it out in the studio. I glanced at Hopps over the top of the microphone and saw that he was with me in the story, but he did raise his eyebrows and a look of worry flitted cross his face as my re-enactment called for me to fling my arms around wildly and I narrowly missed the mic.

"How did the goat get up on the roof?" he asked as the anecdote wound down.

"There's a tree to one side of the barn and she climbs up that," I said.

"I had no idea goats could climb trees."

"Unfortunately, oh yes, they're really good at it."

"So what's in store for you this week?"

No idea. Quick, think of something, "Surviving," wrong thing to say, think of something else . . . "and, er, I really must sort out a permanent home for Senorita rather than the temporary accommodation she's in at the moment." Good recovery.

"Somewhere with a television?"

"A girl's got to have her daily fix of *Loose Women*."

Laughing, he said, "That's great, thanks Simon, see you next week. Now, that dance-floor hit of the nineties, it's Rozalla, and everybody's free to feel good."

Music up, red light off.

I felt elated. Absolutely elated. And a teenager. I felt like a teenager again. Sod Ziggy's list, do this all day and I'd be, like, props young.

"That was so funny," Hopps said, taking off his headphones. "I really had no idea goats could climb like that."

"The other two don't, but Curry's into everything."

"Did you get the roof fixed in the end?"

I nodded. "Yes. All patched up."

Outside I switched my phone back on and immediately it rang. It was Debbie.

"Hiya," I said.

"How was it?"

"Just got out. It was great, loved it, loved it, loved it."

"Good. Are you on your way back?"

"Yeah, why, what's up?"

"I've been talking to Steph." Steph's a neighbour. "She wants us to go to her for lunch. She wants to ask you something."

A to-do over lipsticks

Whenever anybody invites you to lunch in order to ask you something, it's never going to be good. Nobody in the history of luncheon invitations has ever said, "Now, while you tuck into that sandwich — and don't hold back on the chocolate cake afterwards — I wanted to ask if it would be okay if I were to lend you a hundred pounds?"

Steph owns an adult riding centre on the moor just up the hill. When we first arrived in Devon from London, Steph was the first person we met, and for a while Debbie worked for her as a chef cooking for the guests. I had no idea what she might want to ask me.

I stopped at Waterstones on the way back from the radio studio because they have free Wi-Fi. I checked emails on my phone. I had eleven, all in response to the message I sent out about Debbie's birthday.

What a lovely idea, I'll get something to you asap.
Laura x

Mate, you're going to sew it yourself??!!!! This I've got to see — will speak to Carol and put something in the post to you tomorrow.
Damian

I've got the perfect thing, and don't worry, it's a fake!
DC x

This made me cry, I wish my husband would do something like that for me.
Leslie xxx

And so on.

So it looked as though my idea was a hit after all. I wasn't sure how it would go down. Asking someone to send a bit of old material was somewhat strange, but so far everyone seemed ennthusiastic. I drove home with the radio blaring and a huge grin fixed on my face that you couldn't have knocked off, even with a goat's leg.

Indoors I said to Debbie, "Do you know what Steph wants?"

"I think she wants to offer you a job."

I laughed. "You're kidding?"

"No."

"But I don't want a job. I haven't got time for another job. I've got too much on as it is. No. Absolutely not a chance. No, no, no, and that's final. No." I could hear the hysteria in my voice. It was hysterical.

"You don't even know what it is yet."

"I don't want to know."

"Okay. But you might be interested in what she's offering to pay"

"No. No, I'm not. I'm not interested at all. Honestly, I'm really not" My backside didn't touch a seat from morning to night. Where did she think I was going to get the time for a weekend job no matter what the wages?

"She's willing to pay you in hay and straw."

Oh.

"Look," she said, "I know there's a lot on right now, but just for a second imagine not having to stress all the time over the pigs' bedding or the horses' hay?"

Oh.

"Could we at least think about it? That's a chunk of stress and money we don't have to worry about. And it probably wouldn't take you that long."

"What wouldn't? What does she want me to do?"

"Muck out her horses."

"*All of them*? How many has she got?"

"Seventeen, but —"

"*Seventeen!*"

114

"It's not as bad as it sounds. They're all out in a yard, so it's just going round with a wheel barrow and shovelling up the droppings."

"I don't care, I'm not shovelling shit for seventeen horses! Have you seen how much they produce? I'll be there all day!"

She came over to me, put her arms around my waist and nestled into my neck.

I said, "If you're going to tell me that you think I'll be really good at it, a natural, I will murder you and bury you in the garden."

"We haven't got a garden. I know it's not a perfect job —"

"Oh I don't know, after fourteen years as an estate agent I'd consider it a step up."

"Don't be like that. Money's so tight that the prospect of one less thing to worry about is just so appealing. At least will you come up and talk to Steph with me? Please?"

What could I say? No? The lifestyle we had created came with an awful lot of benefits, but money wasn't one of them. After the animals were fed and most of the bills were taken care of, there was never anything left over for us. Luckily we could feed ourselves from the land, but anything else we wanted or needed we had to build, create, stitch, glue, make or mix together. Or do without.

The idea that we could eliminate both hay and straw stresses by working was very appealing, even if I did have to shovel shit for it. Anyway, I agreed to go up and talk to her.

"I'm going to look at the horses," I said, as we wandered onto Steph's place a while later. Debbie and Solly headed towards the house, but I wanted to see what seventeen horses looked like, and try to gauge how active their bums were. Which was very . . . Judging by the evidence, you'd think there was no more effective laxative in the world than grass. Mucking out my two horses when they were in took about twenty minutes each stable if accompanied by some decent 80s sounds. Times that by seventeen and this mob would take . . . well, ages!

After watching them poo for several minutes, which is exactly as much fun as it sounds, I followed Debbie into the house and overheard her saying to Steph, "My friend Paula works in a pharmacy and sent me some lipsticks, and I now wear three different colours, a daytime one, an evening one and a fun one."

I didn't know she had three different lipsticks, and I certainly never knew about a fun one! Kicking off my welly boots and with Steph distracted, I looked a question at Debbie.

"What?" she mouthed.

I didn't bother to reply quietly, "I never knew you had three different-coloured lipsticks."

In the seconds that followed there was one of those horrible moments in a relationship where time gets sticky and slows down. I watched her shoulders sag and her eyes close in an exaggerated blink. When they opened, the look she gave me was of utter disappointment.

116

Right at the wrong time Steph came back in, so I said, "The horses' bums are all in fine working order," because that was the only thing I could think of saying.

"Did Debbie tell you about the weekend job?" Steph asked, not commenting on the energy in the room.

I told her she had.

"It will only take two or three hours each day, if that," she said. "In return, you can take hay and straw for your animals."

I told her I'd do it and instantly regretted the decision. I was to start the following Saturday.

The rest of the day was taken up and it wasn't until much later that I was finally able to speak to Debbie. "It came out wrong," I explained. "Of course I know you have three lipsticks. I was just surprised at the fun one, that's all."

"Yeah? Name them."

"Pardon?"

"If you know all about them, what colours are they?"

I'd done a little private investigative work when she wasn't looking. "Ah, you think I don't know. Well I do. Lipsticks don't come in colours, you little monkey, trying to trip me up like that. They come in numbers. Your three shades are slight variations on the same colour, so they all have the same number."

"Which is?"

I started grinning at how clever I was. "Number seven!"

"That's the brand."

"Is it?"

"Yes."

"It's not the colour?"

"No, it's not the colour."

"Are you sure?" I said.

She didn't bother to answer.

"So I still need to tell you the colour?" I said.

"Colours. Yes."

"Well, it's . . ."

"Here's a clue, *I'm wearing one of them!*"

"Is that the fun one?"

"No it bloody well isn't."

Unfortunately Debbie isn't a stormer-out-of-rooms type of girl, so she just stood there, staring at me. It was very uncomfortable.

"I'm sorry. I'm a bit distracted."

"I know. Ziggy's list." The look on her face was the same look she reserves for clearing up vomit.

"It's not just that," I protested.

"I know."

"Remember I told you about the list of farm things on my mind? Well, they're still on my mind."

She shifted so she was standing, arms crossed, one foot and one hip thrust forwards. "I know."

I hate this part of a row, the "I know" part. It's really irritating. "Besides, you're the one who made me uncover my unease in the first place. I was happy not knowing what it was," I said.

"You rolled the quad bike. You could have been killed. Don't you think that was an indication that it was building into something you could no longer ignore?"

118

I sat down on the sofa. "I guess. Look, I'm really sorry I didn't know about your lipsticks."

She dropped the folded arms and adjusted her leg until it kind of slouched next to the other one. "It's really hard to look nice when you're being self-sufficient and living without money," she said. "Do you know what my beauty regime is? 'Course you don't, because I haven't got one. You have to be able to afford a beauty regime, and I can't. I'm not complaining, it's just a fact. BUT, I do try so, so hard, and when you don't even pick up on the littlest thing I manage to do . . ."

She was looking at her feet. I got up and put my arms around her. I felt like seventeen horses' worth of poo. I told her she looked lovely and she pushed me away. She dabbed at her nose and said, "And I don't like Ziggy's list."

"Why ever not?"

Burst tears coated her eyes. She sniffed a tiny sniff as she walked over to where she'd pushed me and placed the flat of one hand on my solar plexus. When she spoke, she spoke in a whisper. "Because I'm scared it might work. What if it does make you younger? Simon, I'm going to be fifty in a couple of months."

I hugged her tight and said, "No you're not. We agreed you weren't going to have a birthday this year."

She laughed.

I said, "I'm the one who's getting older and having a non-crisis over it, remember? Can't you find your own unease?"

"It's not the same thing," she said into my chest. "You're worried about getting older, but you're not worried about being older right now. I feel old right now. I feel like an ancient artefact that's just been dug up and everyone's walking gingerly around it in case something falls off."

"Oh sweetheart, that's not true at all, you're young and beautiful."

"Huh." She put me down in favour of a wine glass that she cradled in her hands.

"Ziggy's list isn't supposed to make me *actually* younger," I explained. "It's just supposed to help me have a younger outlook that'll stop me slipping into middle age."

"That's exactly what frightens me."

Hot water and towels, she's about to give birth!

In future all dinner-party conversations will go like this: "So, Simon, do you have an actual proper job as well as the smallholding and the writing?"

"Yes, yes I do — would you mind terribly passing me the salad? Oh, and perhaps just one more glass of the Châteauneuf-du-Pape, thank you so much. Yes, my job. It's nothing in the city, I'm afraid. It's nothing very grand. I shovel shit for seventeen horses. Mummy's *so proud*."

Oh God.

I got up early the next day without waking Debbie, my spot on the bed instantly taken by Solly, who stretched out, his head on my pillow, his back squirming tightly into my wife, giving me a look of, "Don't slam the door on the way out, old boy." Love him to bits but, bloody dog!

My aim was to go straight down onto the land. I needed to talk to the General about last night's conversation with Debbie and try to work out what it all meant, but I didn't get the chance. Having messed about checking emails, tweeting, Facebooking and having a Google, all the while feeling rather pleased with myself that I'd covered both internet and social media topics from Ziggy's list and it was hardly daylight yet, then faffing about trying to get through the cows, that by the time I drove out with Dex riding shotgun behind me on the quad, Debbie was walking up towards us.

"You were fast asleep cuddling Solly when I got up," I said, pulling over next to her.

"You woke me when you slammed the door on the way out. Fancy some company?"

Making space I said, "Of course!"

It's difficult to speak over the sound of the engine, so we pootled down the hill in silence. It's unusual for Debbie to come down first thing — her "me" time is the evening and she hates mornings, whereas I'm the other way around. As soon as we reached the land, Debbie asked, "Have you already been down?"

I told her I hadn't.

"Then why are the geese out?"

Looking up I saw them, and in sheer panic hurdled the gate without bothering to open it and ran over. They were, they were out, the door to their house pinned back the way I secure it open during the day. I must have forgotten to shut it last night.

"Are they okay?" Debbie said, coming up behind me.

"Yeah, they're fine. I must have left the door open last night." Blimey, was I that distracted? Oh God, I'm losing my mind, aren't I? "That's really bad. Really bad. I've never done that before. Christ, they could have been eaten by a fox or anything."

"They look fine," she reassured.

"Yeah."

"But it is a bit worrying that you left it open."

"It is. Very."

Resting her head lightly on my shoulder, she said, "What would you have said if they had been taken?"

"Oh, I'd have lied." I assured her.

"You mean you wouldn't have told me?"

"I'd have told you they'd been taken. I just would have made up a story about how it happened."

While we were talking the geese wandered back inside the shed where the gander stood guard over his wife. He kept tapping the top of her head with his beak, sort of pacifying her: "It's okay, love, keep your head down, I've got it all under control," then he'd turn to us in the doorway and, taking a deep breath, hiss and spit a string of expletives so profound it would have made a late-night stand-up comedian blush.

"It would have been a brave fox. Not exactly friendly, are they?" I said.

122

"He's being attentive and looking after her," Debbie said. "He's lovely."

"Actually he's preparing to charge us, we'd better step back."

I couldn't believe I'd forgotten to shut their shed door.

"I can't believe you would have lied to me," Debbie said.

"No. You're probably right." I smiled nicely. I'm an ex-estate agent, a writer *and* a man. Given the choice between voluntary suicide by telling the truth or a little porky-pie, I'll be the one with my head in the cupboard searching for the chutney.

"I wouldn't have been happy," Debbie said.

Yeah, I kind of worked that one out.

"I need to get the rest done," I said, feeling depressed and terrible that I could have missed something like not shutting the geese away, thereby endangering their lives. The one most important thing above all else is in our life of self-sufficiency is that the animals are safe and happy.

"Bloody hell, how pregnant is Pru?" Debbie shouted a few moments later from over by the pigs.

My feet felt heavy as I walked over. That's what dread does, it gives you heavy feet. Pru is in with the General. She's his wife-of-right-now. Debbie had already clambered in with them.

"Christ, she's uddering up and producing milk, it's spilling out of her! She's imminent. We've got to get her moved, like, NOW!"

I hitched the trailer to the back of the quad and reversed it to the gate.

"Don't go all introspective on me now, I need you with me, Simon," Debbie said over the engine noise of the quad.

Dropping the ramp I said, "Yep, I'm fine."

"Okay, do your stuff," and she stepped back.

I grabbed a bucket of feed and moved into the pen, leaving the gate open behind me. The General came over. "Hey Big Man," I said, fussing his head. "Not you today, it's your missus I need."

Before he had a chance to barge past me and go down to the trailer — the trailer to the General either means sex or food, and on a good day, both — I threw a handful of pig nuts on the floor. That caught his attention.

It also caught the attention of Pru, who came barrelling over too.

The sight of her made me wince. It wasn't just slightly obvious she was pregnant, it was about as clear as watching a woman struggle from a taxi outside a maternity unit holding her huge bump with her husband on one side and a midwife on the other both yelling, "Breathe, phff, phff, phff, breathe . . ." There's no "is she or isn't she?" debate.

How the hell had I missed it? I mean, I knew she was pregnant. I knew it was due soon, but not to have spotted that it was nearly here, that's unforgivable.

"Pretty girl, Pru. Oh little one, I'm so sorry, I should have moved you a week ago." I shook the bucket. That made her look up. "Come on, come with me, let's get you somewhere nice and quiet where you can have your babies. I thought you might like one of the stables? I've fixed the roof so it's even dry now. I know! Luxury!" Thank goodness I had fixed the roof.

She followed me out, waddled down and into the trailer. I closed the ramp behind her then dashed up to shut the gate on the General. "If you can do without a woman until lunchtime, I'll get one for you then, okay?" I called. He does like company.

I dropped Pru off at the stable, then filled it with clean, fresh straw. She nuzzled about, then plonked herself down in the middle.

"Penny for them?" Debbie said, coming up beside me so that we were both leaning over the stable door watching Pru doze. She looked very comfortable.

"Oh, you know, patting myself on the back for being such an attentive farmer."

She patted me on the back. "There, I'll join you."

"Thanks."

Banging her hip against mine, she said, "Don't be so hard on yourself. Everyone's fine. Pru will either give birth tonight or early tomorrow, and the geese — would you really have lied to me if they'd have been taken?"

Thinking yes, I said, "No, 'course not."

She banged against me again, only this time harder. "Liar, liar pants on fire."

"So mature."

Smiling she said, "Yeah, well."

I felt a bump on my shin and looked down. It was Senorita using my leg as a scratching post. I let her get on with it.

Inside the stable Pru suddenly went rigid, all four feet stuffed out in front of her then slowly drawn back and down as though she was practising for the world's slowest doggy paddle.

"Contractions. Blimey, we really did only just move her in time," Debbie said.

"I'm not paying enough attention down here. I'm missing things," I said, not shooting for any awards in the category of "this'll shock ya."

"Didn't you see it? It's when she goes all stiff and groans in pain."

"I didn't mean the contractions. I meant . . ."

She turned to look at me. "Simon, I know. And while I agree, I'm not beating up on you. I'm worried about you. And I'm worried about us. Maybe pushing you to face your insecurity was the wrong thing to do."

Since when did it get the upgrade to insecurity? I must have missed that memo.

"You don't need to worry. I've a feeling after this I might be fixed."

She stared at me for a while, then said, "I need to get on — are you going to stay down here with her?"

I said I was.

"Okay then. I'll stay in touch and phone you regularly. As soon as she starts I'll be straight down."

With Pru imminent I pottered about, doing stuff but not tasks. Tasks take commitment and time and I didn't want to invest in either at that moment, so I did housework on the chicken houses, cleaning, tidying, plumping up the cushions. I nipped back to Pru every few minutes, who kept herself busy by building a nest with a neat line down the centre that she lay along, and when her contractions were much closer together, I disinfected my hands, put my phone on silent and went in.

I took hold of her trotter and told her how clever she was. She didn't get up, just snorted once between gasps. I told her to shush, be quiet, save her strength. She buried her face in the straw and gasped some more.

It was ages before anything happened and for a while we both catnapped in the straw between contractions. Then, the miracle of life was loaded, aimed and fired, and the tiniest little piglet shot out the back.

"That's it! That's it!" I encouraged. "Go girl!"

The piglet was slimy and shattered, you've no idea how exhausting the journey out is, so I had to help her poke her head out of the milky sack they're delivered in and point her in the right direction for the milk bar.

I stroked Pru's cheek and held a cool wet wipe on her brow. "It's a little girl," I told her. "You've had a little girl. She's beautiful and perfect. Little face. Little nose, all crinkled up. Ears all pinned back. Actually, she doesn't look entirely pleased at being out. She looks a bit grumpy. You might have trouble with that one. Can you feel her feeding? Does it hurt?"

It was ages before the next one was born. I filled in the time by gently tugging bits of dried embryonic sack off the piglet's back that had gone all crispy. It's just like peeling holiday burnt skin. Hours of fun.

With the next one, the complications started. It was well over an hour between the first and the second, a little boy, and when he was born he also was completely encased and too tired to work his way out. I had to work fast to free him, but it was just so slippery. I ripped the bag, grabbed his head and pulled it through. I opened his mouth and cleared the airway, then rubbed his sides to stimulate breathing. Nothing. I rubbed harder, got up, took hold of him with his head pointing down and swung him back between my legs and out again — once, twice, three times. I carefully put him on the straw and felt for life. Still nothing.

Then he coughed and took his first breath. I breathed too, synchronising my puffing and panting in a "this is how you do it" kind of way. I cleaned him up and laid him next to his sister with a teat in front of him, but it was all he could do to raise his head. I knelt beside him and forced both my hands under my knees. The urge to help is almost overwhelming, but the trick is to let them do as much as possible themselves. After a while I could see his strength building, and soon after that he started feeding.

The next in line had similar trouble and was even weaker. Even though I want them to do as much for themselves as they can, there does come a point when you have to get involved. A baby girl, I cleaned her up and plugged her onto a teat but she showed no interest in sucking, so I gently held her mouth open and milked Mum by hand straight into her mouth. I alternated cuddling her, trying to get her to feed, keeping her warm, jiggling her to keep her stimulated, everything I could think of, but if they are not going to make it, there is little you can do. After about ten minutes she closed her eyes and didn't open them again.

Fuck! Fuck! Fuck! "Oh, no you don't!" I shouted, "Don't you give up on me, don't you dare!"

She had.

I slumped down, cradled her close and put the little head under my chin. Rocked her back and forth for a while, then I hid the body in a bag.

If there's a problem, the golden rule is not to let Mum know. She's got enough on her plate. "You're SO clever," I told Pru in a singsong voice. "You're amazing. That's two. Go girl, oh yeah, go girl . . ." I was banking on the fact that she couldn't count.

My phone buzzed in my pocket. It was Debbie. I moved to the other end of the stable and answered it.

"How's Pru?" Debbie asked.

"Three born, and two of them are just so gorgeous."

"One dead," she guessed.

"U-huh."

"Poor Pru. Do you want me to come down?"

I told her it was fine, that I could deal with it, but to stay in touch.

Peeling the dried membrane from the back of the second born, I waited for more. The last litter Pru had was eight; the one before that was ten. They can have up to twelve.

I waited . . .

And waited . . .

And waited . . .

Debbie phoned again. "Still only two?" she asked.

"Yep."

And waited . . .

Another phone call. "Any more?"

"Not yet."

And waited . . .

Hours went by.

Pru slept. The piglets crawled up by her face and zonked out too. I stayed awake, watching her back end for signs of action. There wasn't any.

When daylight turned the world from black to greyscale and morning arrived, I stumbled through the rounds before checking on Pru and her two sprogs one last time. She'd woken up now and came barrelling over to greet me, snorting manically in my face as though she were saying, "Did you see what happened to me last night?!"

I fussed her, pulled her ears and gave her a huge breakfast and a big drink, telling her over and over, "You're amazing, Mum. You're so amazing." Then I went home.

I walked in, desperate for a shower, a gallon of coffee and some serious sleep. I kicked off my boots, wandered into the kitchen and stopped dead. It was dark. Silent. The table had been moved into the middle of the room and set for dinner, but not just any dinner, a special romantic dinner, with candles, and wine, and placemats and knives and forks all laid out beautifully. There were flowers in the centre. At one setting was a card. My name was written neatly on the outside. I opened it. It said: *I want you to be happy, so I think you should follow Ziggy's list and I'll try and support you all I can. I love you. D x*

130

Debbie came down brushing her bed-hair with her fingers and leant against the door jamb. She had a powder-blue dressing gown wrapped around her. "How's Pru?"

"Fine. Two babies." I waved a hand around the kitchen, trying to encompass the table, the half-cooked meal on the side. "I'm sorry."

"It was for last night. I thought Pru was closer and it would be all over quickly. I wanted us to talk the way we should have done the night Ziggy arrived. The way we should have done every night since. But it's okay, we'll try again tonight. Oh, by the way, you had some post. Several parcels arrived for you." She handed me three packages.

"Well, aren't you going to open them?"

"Later . . ."

So go on, talk . . .

It was later.

I was on my own. Upstairs. In the bedroom.

I undid the three packages and laid the contents out on the bed text to the wrapping. A skirt and two tops. Ladies' tops. Frilly, flowery, pretty tops. I thought everyone would just send me a square of material, but here were whole garments. Where was I going to hide a skirt and two tops? And this was just the start. I had fifty pieces coming to make the quilt. Fifty pieces of clothing — that's very nearly a wardrobe! How would I hide it all where it couldn't be found, and if it was found, how would I explain all the women's clothing squirreled away? I don't exactly have the figure for cross-dressing so Debbie was more likely to jump to the other conclusion, the one that involves girls hot-footing it out of our bedroom having forgotten to dress both halves of their body, and that conclusion runs a far greater risk of Debbie deciding to separate me from my testicles. We teach butchery. I've seen her wield a meat cleaver.

Working on the basis that the best place to hide something was in plain sight, I reached up and pulled a suitcase down from the top of the wardrobe. There was a thin layer of dust coating the lid and inside it was full of summer clothes from a time in the past when we used to go on holidays. Bikinis, sarongs and coconut suntan lotion for her, swim shorts for me. There was even sand in the bottom. I stuffed the skirt and tops down the side and put the suitcase back. Then I went downstairs.

"Do you miss holidays? I said, walking into the kitchen. I'd showered, slept, dressed in clean clothes and felt okay, but my day recovering from last night came at a price. I was late for evening rounds. I had to rush.

My question made her freeze where she was, which was bending over the oven with something half in and half out. "Oohhhh, what I wouldn't give for a little break. You know, it's been seven years since we last went away on holiday. Seven years!"

I pulled my boots on.

"What made you think of that?" she said.

"Oh, you know, nothing really. Look, I've got to go."
Quick kiss and I was out of the door.

Late, late, late. Halfway through the rounds and it's dark. Not just a bit dark, but really dark. Winter dark.

Winter dark is completely different from summer dark. Winter dark is full of shadows and menace and sounds that are all too close to shuffling. Only the undead shuffle. The word was invented for the way they move, all . . . shuffly.

Now I do accept that there are different schools of thought regarding ghosts, but the people I like best are the ones who say, "Oh, I don't believe in ghosts, utter rubbish! But if I did meet one . . ." which is hedging at its best.

If I met one, you would not see my bum for dust. I've read too many Stephen King and James Herbert novels to hang around for a cosy chat — or go looking for them. Why would you do that? On Saturday nights they rerun all the old black-and-white horror films on TV where there's a ghostly scream in the middle of the night and one person jumps up out of bed to go investigating, on their own! NO! Pull the covers over your head and hide until morning like any normal coward.

Cats are notorious for staring into blank corners as though they can see someone there, but equally gifted in this regime of terror are piglets. I was merrily feeding my way around the animals. It was dark but I was quite happy. I had my iPhone playing a podcast in one ear; Mark Kermode and Simon Mayo's Wittertainment

133

(hello to Jason Isaacs), when suddenly all the piglets, as one, stopped eating and stared over my shoulder.

Very slowly I tugged out the ear bud and listened for shuffling. Then I turned, oh . . . so . . . slowly . . . Every follicle on my skin was on end. I had goose pimples on goose pimples. I decided I was turning too quickly and slowed it down, giving me plenty of time to allow whatever was there to move or vanish or whatever they do. I considered coughing, just so they'd definitely know I was coming.

I'd never seen a thing, but from that moment on, I was spooked. As I drove back through the smallholding the headlights of the quad bike cut through the dark ahead of me, but it wasn't the *ahead* that I was worried about, it was the *behind*. Ghosts love grabbing shoulders from behind.

So I sped up, until I was going hell for leather across the field, gripping on for all I was worth, and still I felt like there was something behind me. I scrunched further forward towards the handlebars, ducking my head a little lower. But it was no good, the cold, rotting Scooby-Doo-like ghost hand was still there, hovering just above my shoulder. The fact that I was doing 40km/h and this thing behind me was supposed to be shuffling at the same speed was neither here nor there. As far as I was concerned, I was in imminent danger of being grabbed by the undead.

In front of me a gateway yawned wide open. Luckily all the ghosts on my land understand that gateways are out of bounds, and we all slowed down. For a second I was tempted to leave the gate as it was because I know

134

they're there, the ghostly goolies, in the shadows, making noises and shuffling and reaching out for me, but after everything I messed up the other night, I knew I couldn't do that. So I stopped.

I could still hear the podcast in one ear, the hosts bickering over the fact that Mr-flappy-hands-Kermode hadn't seen one of the films in this week's top ten. I tried to concentrate on it. Block everything else out. I got off the bike. Turned. Took a step towards the open gate.

Suddenly there was movement out of the corner of my eye. Short, sharp movement. I tensed, my body taking over, Mother Nature's autopilot kicking in, and, *pow*, adrenaline and instinct combined and I clenched my fist and punched out with all my might . . . and hit . . . a branch.

My heart was *pounding*. "Brave," I murmured. "So brave."

"You look pale, are you okay?" Debbie asked, looking concerned as I walked into the house after my close encounter of the spooky kind.

"Me? Are you kidding? Never better."

Her concern deepened. "Tell me."

Nope. "*Mmm, hum, hum.*" Bit of dust on my lapel, just . . . there. Hate it when that happens.

"*Simon*! Tell me. Are Pru and her babies okay?"

"Fine. Really, it's all fine. Just cold out, that's all."

"After the geese debacle and because I now know you'd lie to me, I'm not sure what to believe. Promise me everyone's okay."

I promised.

She handed me a glass of wine and held up her own and chinked it. "Okay, tonight it's time for that chat. It's time to open up and talk. Sit." She pushed me over towards the table that had been refreshed but was basically the romantic spread from last light. I sat.

"Okay, so talk. Don't filter, don't worry if it doesn't make sense, I'm not going to judge you or anything like that, I just need to get to the bottom of what's going on. So, go . . . Talk . . ."

"How can I after you've said that?"

She tutted, but not unkindly.

Okay, so let's do this. I scrambled around inside my untidy brain for a starting point but found it was like delving into a ball of string that had been unravelled and scrunched untidily back together. If I had had time I'd have rummaged for a beginning, but I didn't. So sod it, I thought I'd just grab hold of a middle piece and follow it, and see if I could get to an end that way.

"I think I suddenly feel as though I'm about to be old. Not really, really old, at least not yet. I could still play rugby for England if they asked me very nicely. But just — you know the saying, over the hill? Well, I feel as though I'm on the brow. I feel as though this is the highest point of my life and I'm about to start the drop down the other side into old age and, if I'm honest, I want to hang round up here for as long as I can."

"Keep talking, I'm still listening," she said, moving away to shake some saucepans.

"Well, that bit's fine. Standard. I guess we all feel something similar at some point. Ziggy's list is a way of

136

stopping gravity grabbing hold of me and yanking me down the other side. That much is obvious."

"Uhuh. And . . ."

I shrugged, "And this is where it gets a bit hazy. It's got something to do with — I've said all this before —"

"Doesn't matter, say it again."

"It's got something to do with feeling as though I don't know how to grow older out here doing what we're doing, without parents having done it all before us. It's got something to do with realising that this is probably my lot in life — pigs, chickens, self-sufficiency — and that I won't look back and laugh about it one day because chances are there'll never be a one day when I'm not doing it. It's got everything to do with wondering if someone of my age shouldn't be more tangibly successful."

She'd stopped shaking the saucepans. "I don't understand what tangibly successful means."

I took a sip. "Everything we own is botched together and homemade, which is fine when you're in your thirties, even early forties. But late forties? Fifties? *Sixties?* We're not exactly going to be growing older elegantly."

"You don't think we're elegant enough?"

I thought about it. "I don't know. My parents were elegant, and so were yours — your mum's one of the most elegant ladies I've ever known. I'm just not sure that living the way we do we're going to be able to be the same; and I know that's copying your parents, but isn't that what growing older is all about? Looking at your mum and dad and following their lead in how to do it? Take a little of their style?"

"I think we have style."

"I did, though I was always aware it was a very individual style — not bad, just, you know, individual. In a lot of things. Stuff. And clothes. But then Ziggy said that homemade clothes were wrong."

"Since when have you ever listened to Ziggy? Simon, Ziggy lives in a different world from us. I *love* it that you make some of our clothes, and even if we had all the money in the world I'd still want you to make me things."

"Do you think we're eccentric?"

"Of course."

"Oh. I'm not sure I want to be."

"Bit late for that, darling, look around you."

"Yeah, well, that's what I mean! That's exactly it! Look around. When I took Ziggy down onto the land that morning and we did the rounds together and *he looked around*, I felt ashamed."

She winced.

"At the time I thought it was because he was next to me and suddenly I could see everything through his London eyes, and it all looked shabby, but now I think it was more than that. I think part of me felt that at my age I should have better things and I think that part of Ziggy felt that we should have better things too. Not be quite so surrounded by make-do and mend at our age." I rubbed the top of my head, the brain inside was beginning to overheat.

138

"But you said it yourself, you were looking at it through Ziggy's eyes. You were imagining what he was thinking. Did he say anything about it all? When I spoke to him he said he loved it."

"That's what he said to me, too."

"Yeah, so, let's be honest, I don't think you were looking at it through Ziggy's eyes at all, because if you were you'd see it for what it is, which is fantastic. I think you were looking at it through your own London eyes. I think you were looking at it from the perspective of Simon who lived and worked in London and what *you* would have thought had *you* come down here, and the fact that Ziggy was there just brought that on. True?"

I stopped rubbing my head.

She continued. "You were an estate agent, Simon. And whilst I loved you, you were not the same person you are now."

"I liked being an estate agent."

"I know, but you were very much a townie."

"Is that bad?"

"Only if you're still clinging to it."

She turned and dipped a wooden spoon into a sauce, tasted it and threw in some salt. Over to one side a clothes hanger hung from a cabinet. On it were strings of freshly made yellow pasta lusted in flour and hung up to dry.

"What have we got?" I asked.

She spoke without turning around. "Meatballs stuffed with cheese in a tomato sauce with pasta."

"Nice."

"I hope so. Does it make sense to you that you were looking at it through your own eyes rather than Ziggy's?"

"I don't know. Maybe."

"So when you said you were ashamed, how does that make you feel now you know it was yourself you were ashamed about?"

"Easy, I feel like I've walked into therapy."

"Sorry. I just really want to get to the bottom of this."

"I know. Um, how do I feel? A bit freaked, I think, that I'd be ashamed to show my younger self what I'm up to now. But even as I say that I'm not sure that it's right. I'm not sure it was my own eyes I was seeing it through. I still think it makes more sense that it was Ziggy's."

She nodded. "Okay. We can come back to that."

Suddenly I felt insecure sitting while Debbie was standing. I grabbed my wine and walked over to her and leant against the side of the kitchen. At least we were now at equal height — or would have been if she wasn't half a foot taller than me. I thought about getting a couple of books to stand on but decided that might be overkill.

"Dinner in ten minutes," she said, touching my arm.

"Great, I'm starving."

"Good. Taste the sauce, would you? See what you think. I'm also confused why you said you should have better things at your age when most people I know are up to their necks in debt and stuck in jobs they hate, and we have all this," she waved her arm at the messy kitchen.

I tasted the sauce. "It needs a bit more salt," I said, though in truth it didn't.

"Put some in then."

I pretended to. "You grow up with expectations, right?" I said. "At least I did. Buy your first Ferrari by age twenty-six, live in a pent-house by thirty and declare yourself a millionaire by thirty-five."

"But you didn't do any of those things."

"No, I know, but that's what I aimed for. They were my expectations. I had similar ones for growing older: watch a ballet from the Royal Box, have a face lift, get gout, have sex with a woman exactly half my age. You know, the usual."

She turned so I could watch her raise her eyebrows.

Continuing, I said, "I had expectations of what I'd have around me too. Big house. Perfect garden. Original art hanging on the walls. Antiques. Lots of first editions. Staff; a cook, a gardener, a cleaner, a chauffeur."

"You had all those expectations?"

"I've always been an optimist."

"You certainly were."

"I know. But that's what expectations are, they're the goals you set for yourself when you're young. In a lot of ways it doesn't even matter if you never get close to achieving them, what matters is that's the trajectory you put yourself on. When I was in my teens I decided on my list of expectations and set off in that direction.

141

It was only when I met you that I got blown off course."

"Oh, don't say it like that."

Laughing, I said, "Sorry, that was supposed to be funny. I love my life, *love it*! Okay, it hasn't ended up quite as I thought it would, but then I don't think you expected to live as we are now either, did you?"

"I suppose not, though I always hoped I'd be involved with animals somehow." She scooped the pasta from the clothes hanger and tipped it into a pan of boiling water.

"But I wouldn't change what we have for anything," I said. "And I can now see that my teenage expectations were fluff and rubbish, and if it had worked out as my younger self hoped, I'd have hated and would have joined the ranks of the in-debtors and stuck-in-a-rutters, and I'm so *so SO* grateful that I'm not in that gang. But that said, I seem to have reached a point in my life when those old expectations my teenage self set are coming back to taunt me."

She began plating up and said, "Ah."

We moved about in silence, not an uncomfortable silence, just a quiet one until dinner was ready. Then we sat at the table.

"I loved the card you gave me," I said. It was up on the dresser next to us and I glanced at it.

"You're disappointed," she said.

"Not at all, I love it."

"Not with the card. With us. What we've done. What we've got."

"No, you're putting it the wrong way around. I'm not disappointed with what we've done or what we've got, I'm disappointed with what we haven't done and haven't got. There's a big difference."

"I'm not sure you can separate the two."

"Of course you can."

"But you said that when you were with Ziggy down on the land you felt ashamed of what we have."

"Yes. Because it looks scruffy, and it looks scruffy because I built with bits and bobs that were lying around. But I still love it. It still makes me happy. And the animals love it. That's important. The animals are my mates. My best mates. Everything I do — everything we do — is for them. Of course I'd prefer them all to have lovely new houses, but that's only my ideal."

We both ate for a while, twizzling pasta and sauce around a fork and stabbing meatballs that oozed melted cheese. Scrummy. Utterly scrummy.

"So, if I've got this right," Debbie said, "you're disappointed that you haven't achieved the things you set as goals when you were a teenager, even though you never expected to achieve them anyway and it was only ever a path to follow?"

"Kind of. Even though it was only a path to follow, I expected to make it part of the way and by doing so pick up some nice things en route." I shrugged.

"You don't feel like you have nice things?"

"Anything with any value is long sold."

"Nice things aren't just things with a value, you know."

"I know."

"Then, what we have doesn't make you feel successful?"

"Not in the eyes of the teenager who set the expectations and began walking that path, no."

"And in your eyes? Your eyes right now? Do you look at our life and see success?"

I thought about it. "On Saturday I'm going to start my new job shovelling shit for seventeen horses," I said.

"That one," she laughed, holding her glass and pointing at me, "I'm going to give you."

Oh, so that's what it means!

It was only later in bed that something struck me about the conversation. That my *thing*, my unease, was all . . . was all about the things I had around me. I supposed it made sense, but it wasn't what I expected. I felt quite shallow. I wasn't stressing over the fact that I'd reached the grand old age of 47 and didn't feel as though I'd read enough books, or seen enough plays or films, or listened to enough music. No, I was stressing that I hadn't acquired enough stuff that my younger self would be impressed with. Why was I worried about my younger self anyway? He became an estate agent!

You know what I realised? I was such a fool! Of course all my angst was about the things I had around me and that I was suddenly judging my life by the bits and pieces I'd collected on the way, *because that's the first thing that ends.*

144

Clearly there has been an ending. In my head. A switch has been flicked. A chequered flag waved. A black ball sunk. A whistle blown. A tape broken. It didn't matter what I added to my stack of belongings from this point on because the race to reach my teen self's list of expectations had come to an end. Something inside my brain had chosen now to make a finish line. It wasn't my choice. It was nothing I'd consciously considered. It just happened. Suddenly it all made sense. Jeez, that's why I wasn't panicking over the other stuff like body shape and how I looked, or whether I'd improved my mind sufficiently, because that was yet to come.

I thought hitting middle age was a one-shot deal, but of course it's not. This was just the beginning. First there would be the "*what have I got to show for my life?*" Which is where I was now. Then I guess would come the "*my body hates me and has started to go all wonky and refuses to work as it should*". Closely followed by blurred reality where conversations would begin with "So you're saying I shouldn't wear pants on my head? Who are you anyway? You call yourself a doctor but anyone can put on a white coat and smell of formaldehyde."

Oh bugger. No wonder I felt so deflated.

So that was it. *That was my thing.* I felt oddly elated that at least I'd figured it out, and for the most part avoided my usual method of addressing any problem by layering so many questions over the top of it that I could no longer see or remember what it was that troubled me in the first place.

My thing, my unease, was because something in my head had reached an end point in the race to acquire as many of the items my teenage self set as expectations, and was now forcing me to tally up.

So what the hell, let's do the tally:

Did I get a Ferrari?

No.

Penthouse apartment?

No.

Become a millionaire?

Clearly not.

Watch a ballet from the Royal Box, have a face lift, get gout, have sex with a woman half my age, own a big house with a perfect garden and original art hanging on the walls, and antiques, lots of first editions, with staff?

No. But then my younger self thought it would be a good idea to sell houses for a living, so he couldn't have been that bright in the first place.

Do I feel troubled that I haven't attained any of the things my younger self thought important?

Not at all, because my life changed part-way through and none of those expectations mean anything anymore. What would I do with a bleedin' Ferrari anyway? You can't fit a Great Dane in one, or a heston of straw. As for the rest of it, well, they're just things. Shame my teen self didn't have the wherewithal to include: make best friends with a pig, milk a goat or watch a chick hatch from an egg between your wife's boobs (yes, that really did happen).

However, although I did feel a sense of relief that I'd figured that out, it made me realise that I had reached

146

an age where midlife anxieties were starting to happen. For instance, I still felt as though I was on the brow of this hill and that this was the highest point in my life before I started the scoot down the other side towards pensionhood, and I acknowledge that I did want to hang around up here for as long as I could before plummeting over the edge yelling that my hips and knees hurt and I can't run very fast in slippers, even if I could remember where I had put my slippers, which I couldn't. Maybe I left them on the cruise . . .

More than ever I was convinced that the answer, of course, was Ziggy's nine commandments: clothes, music, TV, internet, social media, attitude and outlook, hair, food and language.

"Simon, why are you sitting up in bed?"

I looked down. Debbie and Solly were cuddled up beside me, both with one eye open and both Cyclopes staring up at me. Solly gave his tail a single wag. "And why do you look so pleased with yourself?" she added.

"I've figured it out," I said. "My *thing*. My unease. I've figured it out. I know what it is. You were right that by talking it through we could get to the bottom of it. I know what's at the bottom. It's me, when I was young. But that doesn't matter because I've figured something else out too. I've figured out the future. Not all of it, obviously, just the getting older bits. The midlife bits."

She groaned. "Go to sleep. It's the middle of the night."

"Ziggy's list," I continued, ignoring her. "I need to do Ziggy's list."

Closing her eyes she said, "Oh God. Not that again. You've been doing Ziggy's list since you went out for that drink with him and you've done nothing about it yet. It's been over a week. I hoped you'd moved on from that."

"That's not what you wrote in the card."

"That was then. I was worried about you then. Then wasn't the middle of the night."

Solly yawned and closed his eyes. So did Debbie. The last thing she said before she drifted back to sleep was, "You haven't forgotten about tomorrow, have you?"

I assured her I hadn't.

With her eyes still closed she slapped the mattress. "I knew you had."

"I haven't," I said, and with that I got up so I could go and check the calendar, because I had.

Padding into the kitchen I turned on the light. Most of the clearing up had been done from last night but there were still a couple of saucepans soaking on the side. I waggled the kettle to see if it had any water in it and set it down on the hob, switching on the hotplate before snagging the calendar off the wall and sitting down at the table.

Actually I hadn't forgotten what we were doing tomorrow (today), and I hadn't forgotten because I had never been told. I swear she had not uttered one word about the day's plans. I swear it. Solemnly. That or I hadn't listened, which I find very hard to believe.

I ran my hand through my hair, which was more a force of habit than any real objective to feel tufts between my fingers, and read the day again.

Take pig to abattoir. Simon — results of Well Man test midday at health centre.

Not able to process either of those events, I walked into the lounge and turned on the television, remembering Ziggy's words: "Make a point of watching at least one reality show a week that does not include cooking or antiques." No time like the present!

I flicked through the channels until I came to a programme about a group of people taken out to a deserted island and left there to fend for themselves. "It's my life with sunshine."

I didn't question how watching something like this could possibly keep me up on the brow of the hill feeling young, but just went with it, and watched to the end credits — which were arguably more entertaining than the programme itself, though perhaps I'm just out of practice watching shows like this. Then, at last, I fell asleep and did not wake for hours. When I did I felt tired and heavy at the thought of taking a pig to the abattoir, which is just a shitty way to start the day, especially for the pig. So I decided not to do it.

I'd tell Debbie I overslept. It'd be fine.

We'd tell the abattoir we couldn't load the pig. It'd be fine.

I closed my eyes. It'd be fine.

Right now, the thought of taking a pig to the abbatoir was the worst thought in the world. I couldn't do it. I just couldn't. It had become worse than ever lately, this . . . I don't even know how to describe it. Hatred isn't anywhere near strong enough. Abhorrence? No, that's not right either. It was more a sense of fear and sadness and an overpowering gut-wrenching feeling of treachery all mixed into one, and then ramped up to eleven. That's what it feels like taking a pig to the abattoir.

Not brilliant when you make your living as a pig farmer.

I'm aware it would be easier if I thought of them as animals, as commodity, and not friends. If I didn't anthropomorphise them. Didn't talk to them. Didn't fuss them. Didn't laugh with them. I know that by treating them as animals it would be easier to take them off. But I don't know if it should be easier, should it? Is that what I should be striving for, to load a pig while laughing and smiling, with a light heart, and take it to be killed? *Surely* that's not right either, is it?

After ten years of this lifestyle and taking animals to slaughter you'd think I'd have it sussed by now, but I don't. If anything I'm more confused over it than ever.

Vegetarians, vegans, sometimes I think they've got it right. Sometimes I feel as though I never want to touch meat again. But then there's the other side of it, the processing. That's just beautiful, and feels totally right to butcher a carcass and use every part of the animal, making all the fun bits, such as bacon and ham and sausages and chorizo and Palmer-style hams and faggots and brawn and pork pies. Trouble is, you can't separate the two; the killing and the processing. Try curing a back leg into ham while the pig is still running around and they tend to get a bit upset.

It was now borderline if there was enough time to load and take a pig anyway, as the abattoir only kill in the morning. Debbie hates taking the pigs almost as much as I do, but it's just, she's a better business person than I am. And it is a business — selling the meat is how we earn enough money to scrape by. It's what we do. How we survive.

There were no sounds of movement coming from upstairs. It was sleepy silent. Good. I crept into the kitchen to make a drink.

"Why didn't you wake me? I nearly overslept," Debbie said, coming in and placing a mug next to mine.

She was alone, which meant the dog was having a lie-in.

I mumbled something about having only just woken up myself.

She put her arms around me. She knows how much I hate abattoir days because I tell her every time the subject comes up. Anticipating it she said, "I'm sorry, but we do have to take a pig. We've got a butchery course booked in for next week, and butchery courses never work well when you haven't got anything to butcher."

"I'm not geared up to take a pig today," I said, trying to keep my voice level and professional and emotionless, which was the opposite of everything I'm feeling.

"Don't whinge. You sound like a child."

"I do not!" I was that close to stamping my foot.

She half smiled. "I know you hate taking the pigs, but Simon it's killing me having to talk you into it each time. You think you're the only one who suffers? Well, you're not. It's as though you're making me force you

151

into it, and that way it doesn't make you feel so bad, and I understand that, but it's annihilating me."

"I didn't realise that's what I was doing," I said.

"We do everything together except this bit. I can't shoulder it on my own anymore. It's too heavy for me to carry. We need to share the responsibility."

Some of it's probably down to a low piggy sperm count

It was quiet on the smallholding, and still early. Most sensible people were still tucked up in bed. I hitched the trailer to the quad and backed it to a pig pen containing some of the older yobs.

Steeling myself, I called, "Good morning you guys," in as close an approximation of a light and friendly voice as I could muster. I fussed them and pulled their ears and called them stupid names, and even sung an out-of-tune made-up song to them until one wandered down and into the trailer.

Did I feel like Judas?

Yes.

Did I feel sick to my stomach and hate myself for what I was doing?

Yes.

Did they know I felt like this?

No, and that's the important thing.

By the time I had secured everything and made it down to the gate, Debbie was waiting for me with a borrowed neighbour's truck. I took the trailer with the pig inside off the quad and hitched it to the back. Neither of us spoke.

Later, when the abattoir thing was done and we were back on the land, Debbie said, "Tell me something, if you've got this midlife thing, worry, crisis — whatever you want to call it — sussed, why do you need Ziggy's list?"

We were sharing morning rounds, which is to say Debbie was letting out the cute, fluffy chickens while I was running away from the killer geese. As a couple we like to pull to our strengths.

I jogged back to her side. "Glad you asked," I said. "Turns out hitting middle age doesn't happen in one go — go figure! There are stages to it. Levels, going down — middle age is a descent, you see, that bit's important. It starts when the race to achieve all the things your younger self set out to achieve finishes, and you're forced to tally up — don't ask me why it finishes, it just does —"

"The Well Man test," Debbie cut in.

"Sorry?"

"The Well Man test. That's when all this started, when you got a call from the health centre asking you to come in for the Well Man test and you decided it was because of your age. Go on . . ."

"Um. Yeah. Anyway — was it? — that's also when you realise you're on the brow of the hill, the highest point in your life, and from there in front of you is the descent into middle age. See? I told you that bit was important."

She raised her eyes and shook her head.

I pressed on. "My answer to avoid gravity yanking me down the other side is, of course, Ziggy's list."

Her shoulders crumpled forwards. "Why do I feel like this is never going to end?"

Together we watched Senorita, still utterly infatuated with my collie dog, Dex, who was planning something special. Sauntering across the field towards his house, stopping every few steps to give her hefty backside the type of slow, sensual wiggle perfected by ladies who earn their money on street corners, she made her way down to his house.

He was in, lazing on a straw bed just inside the doorway.

Without bothering to announce her intention, she walked right up to him and before he had a chance to do anything about it skipped her feet up underneath her and flopped the full mass of her sexy body on top of him. One minute here was a puppy snoozing happily, the next he was splattered under adoring female porky flesh.

He yelped, and while she desperately tried to keep him under her by rolling out another layer of fat to block his escape, he was too quick, slithered free and legged it.

"Ah, she loves him," Debbie said.

"She nearly killed him," I complained, watching him bolt across the field and hide on the other side of some long grass.

Back in his house Senorita shuffled over a bit so she could look down at the spot where he had been, and sighed.

154

"Come on, let me show you Pru's babies," I said to Debbie.

She must have heard us coming because when we reached the stable Pru was already up and greeting us. "You're so beautiful," I told her, "And just look at those babies! Debbie, are those the best babies you've ever seen in your life?"

"Oooowww! Look at them!" Debbie said, making grabbing motions with her hands.

We both went over and sat down in the straw cuddling a piglet each, proud mum going between us and *oooof, oooof, ooofing* manically.

"It's such a shame she only had two, but they are to die for. And," I held mine up and sniffed the top of her head, "They still have that newly born smell, like melted chocolate."

"She's our oldest sow, she must be eight. I think she's done brilliantly to have babies at all. You're gorgeous my darling, aren't you?" Debbie said, going nose to nose with Pru and snorting happily at one another.

"I should get the General a cigar, his sperm has ignited life once more."

"Ignited life?" Debbie laughed. "Anyway, it's his sperm, or lack of it, that's the problem. He's an old man now, and older men aren't as virile as younger men. His sperm count must be way down which is why we're only getting tiny litters. Couple that with the act that the sows are all getting older too," she held up the piglet and spoke in baby talk directly to it, "And that's why we're only getting little piggy groups, isn't it? Yes it is . . . oh, yes it is."

His sperm count might be low, but I can vouch for his keenness around the ladies. It's hard to miss. Sex between pigs lasts about an hour, can be performed up to six times a day with each ejaculation producing approximately a pint of semen. The General is all man and fully up to the challenge. Bless him. Reminds me of myself.

"H-ha!" Debbie spluttered.

"Did I say that out loud? Sorry," I said, knowing I had and grinning.

We put the piglets down. I wanted to go and see the General, make sure he was okay. After all, we had snatched Pru from him rather abruptly, and she is his favourite.

He wasn't in his house and I had to go searching for him in the woods. Eventually I found him fast asleep in a hollowed-out snug beneath a tall tree, his pink tongue lolling so far out of his mouth it touched the ground where a pool of drool had gathered. Beside him a new wife, freshly delivered, was snuggled, clearly enjoying his closeness and his manliness and his sexiness, and was prepared to overlook the sticking-out tongue and the lake of dribble in the name of *lurve*.

"Is he okay?" Debbie asked as I made my way back and climbed out of the enclosure.

"Fine. Looking good. She can't get enough of him, and who can blame her, he's a catch, that's for sure."

"You know we need to think about getting someone younger for the sows, don't you?"

I nodded. "Yeah. I know."

"How old is the sow he's in with now?"

156

"Barely out of her teens in pig terms — eighteen months? Something like that?"

"Let's see how he does," she caught hold of my arm and pulled me close. "But if she has a tiny litter, and let's face it, she is in her piglet-bearing prime, then we'll know it's him and we'll have to put him into retirement. Agreed?"

If it came to that I already had an area set aside as an OAP nursing home where he could live out his life drooling and sticking out his tongue as much as he liked. I might even be able to sneak the odd lady in from time to time, just for old time's sake. But it wouldn't come to that. I had plans: if I could adopt Ziggy's list and avoid the onslaught of middle age, who's to say the General couldn't do the same? Low sperm count? Pah! All I needed to do was play a little Kwabs and put a baseball cap on his head while he's on the job and ta-dah! Instant killer stud again.

"Come on, you need to be showered and shaved and at the medical centre in an hour for your Well Man results," Debbie said.

I'm sorry, but doctors' surgeries
stress me out

I arrived at the health centre with no time to spare and dashed in to reception. The lady behind the desk was a different lady from last time — maybe it was her day in the café. In her place was someone else. Again, a familiar someone else. A very familiar someone else. This time, it was my neighbour.

There should be a rule that doctor's surgeries have to swap staff with other villages so you've always got an out-of-towner on the desk rather than someone you see every day. Someone you just know is desperate to greet you with, "Oh, hi Simon, what are you here for? Something intimate? Something embarrassing? I've got your file right here. It's not John Grisham, but it is entertaining . . ."

Instead she looked up, smiled, and actually said, all clipped and professional, "Hi, Simon. Take a seat, the nurse will be right with you."

I thanked her and sat. I picked up the book I'd brought, but I didn't open it. The room was bright and cheery with a panel of glass windows that took over one complete wall. There were magazines on every surface, a radio playing softly in the background and a distinct smell of bleach. Apart from my neighbour the receptionist, I was the only one there.

I glanced across. Receptionist/neighbour was busy looking something up on the computer.

I stared at the wall.

Had all the anxiety and my *thing* really begun, as Debbie claimed, with the phone call from the health centre asking me to go in for the Well Man test? If that was true, and I suppose it is likely that that was the catalyst, then is middle age brought on by trauma? *Something* happens that jolts awake the over-the-hill bit of your brain and a programme of midlife angst starts? If so, could the results of the Well Man test either speed up or slow down the descent? Get a good result and I'll be clubbing by the weekend, get a bad one and I'll be shuffling around in my slippers reading SAGA magazines and dreaming of cruises.

The wall was yellow with scuff marks where chairs had scraped against it. There were posters. I didn't read them.

I was healthy, wasn't I? I had a good diet, all clean, additive-free, homemade fresh food. Lots of fruit and vegetables. Low sugar. Low salt. I exercised daily (running away from the geese). I didn't smoke. Okay, I drank dodgy homebrew wine, but it was all fruit- and vegetable-based so it was practically one of my five-a-day.

I hadn't got man boobs.

I hadn't got a thunder belly — well, not one that I couldn't hold when the occasion required it.

I hadn't even had erectile dysfunction.

Those three have always been my main getting-older worries; tits, a tummy that wobbles like Senorita's and the dreaded moment when you look down to find that not all of you is paying full attention to the task at hand. But that's body image stuff. Luckily I'm not at that stage yet, I'm still on the, *"what have I got to show for my life?"* part of my *thing*.

Lucky me.

I wondered if all men get erectile dysfunction? I wondered if it's an unavoidable part of getting older that everyone experiences at some point?

I wondered if I should have eaten differently the day before I gave blood, had a salad or something vegan rather than a regular meal?

159

I wondered if there was a note on my file from the lady who took my blood saying I had a chronic inability to judge a person's age with any accuracy? I hoped I hadn't offended her.

I thought, I bet I'm stressed. I felt stressed.

I knew I'd get erectile dysfunction now, and not just because I was sitting in a waiting room next to a window with my neighbour sitting over to one side, either.

If they were going to check my blood pressure I knew I'd be done for. They'd call the ambulance and whisk me away.

God, I hated doctor's surgeries.

A lady in a starched blue uniform walked into the waiting room and said, "Simon Dawson?"

I got up and, smiling as I passed neighbour/ receptionist, my eyes switched to a table full of leaflets beside her, obviously arranged for patients to peruse and pick up. I find it very hard to pass a written word without at least scanning it, so I scanned the headlines. They were the usual help and advice leaflets: Smoking, Caring, Children, Pregnancy and so on, and then tucked over to one side was one that made me stumble to a stop. The leaflet was blue with white writing, and said: *Erectile dysfunction — what you need to know*. Without thinking I reached out, grabbed one and stuffed it into my pocket before hurrying after Starched Blue Uniform lady.

"Are you okay? You look very warm, would you like me to get you a glass of water?" she said as we walked into her room.

"Oh, no, I'm fine," I assured her, my face flushed.

She nodded. "Have a seat. Now, do you smoke?"

160

Okay, no small talk, straight into it. "No," I said, shuffling in the chair to get comfortable.

"Do you drink alcohol?"

"Well, yes. A little wine."

She made a note. "How many units would you say you drank a week? On average?"

"I don't know. How many am I allowed?"

She looked up and gave me a nurse's version of "The Look". All women have it. Hers was practised and professional and implied, "Let's get on with this, okay?"

"The thing is, it's homemade and therefore difficult to judge in terms of units." I told her that we're not very good at homebrew and the batches were hit and miss at the best of times. The thing is I gabble when I'm nervous, but eventually we came to an agreement on my vino intake.

"Is that high?"

She looked down even though she'd just written the number. "A bit, but I'm not worried."

Somewhere inside me a little boy did a happy cartwheel.

Blood pressure next.

"It might be up a touch," I said, "because I'm in here."

"Really? I find it quite relaxing in here."

"That's probably because you're not being tested."

"No. What do you do for a living?"

"Is that part of the test?"

"Why would you think that's part of the test?"

"Memory."

"Memory?"

"Yes, see if I can remember what I do."

"Can you?"

"Yes," I said. "I have a smallholding."

"That's nice. The good life."

"Yes. Would you like me to tell you the date and the name of the current prime minister?"

"If you like."

"Only if it helps?"

"No, then."

"Oh."

She stopped doing the blood pressure test. "Normal," she said.

Phew.

"How tall are you?"

"Five-eight. People were born shorter in the sixties. Probably something to do with all the tight jeans."

"Mmm. Now I'd like to weigh you."

"Would you like me to take my clothes off?"

"I'd really prefer you didn't. Just your shoes."

I slipped them off and stood on the scales.

"Okay."

I got off.

She looked puzzled.

"Can you step back on them again, please?"

I did.

"Odd. I think they might be broken — that or you're obese. How much do you think you weigh?"

"Um, about ninety-four kilos," I said.

"In that case they're not broken and you are obese, though I must say you don't look it."

"Should I go on a diet?"

"Do you have much exercise?"

"About five hours a day."

"Every day?"

I nodded.

"Then I wouldn't worry. You look fine to me."

She started scribbling in her pad.

"Do you need to know about my food?"

"What about it?"

"We're self-sufficient and everything is homemade and fresh. We don't have any additives or processed food."

"That's nice."

"That helps, doesn't it?"

"Of course."

"Are the results of my blood test back?"

"All fine."

On a leaflet she drew a cross on the green section of a graph, pointed to it and said, "Everything looks good. I've got nothing to nag about. You only have an eight per cent chance of developing a heart condition over the next ten years. Well done. Keep doing what you're doing."

"Really?"

"What did you expect?"

"I don't know. That sounds good though."

"It is."

Back home I told Debbie the good news. She hugged me with tears in her eyes.

"I was really worried," she said.

I hugged her back. "I wasn't. I knew it was going to be fine," I lied as only a man can.

My mobile rang and I broke away from the hug, digging in my back pocket for the phone, pulling it and the leaflet from the health centre out at the same time. The leaflet fell on the floor and Debbie reached down to pick it up.

"It's not what you think," I said, and looked at the phone. It was Ziggy. I pressed green. "Hi Ziggy"

"Oh mate. Oh mate, oh mate," he said. "Oh mate, she's dumped me. We've split up."

Bit of an insight into what it's like to be a snail

How do you character-judge a person you have never met before? The way they look? The way they act? The words they use? Tone of voice, body language, clothes, even the shape of their mouth, or ears? (I read somewhere that the larger the earlobe, the kinder the person.) Or should you let an animal judge for you?

I'd hate to think I'm the only one that does this, but when someone new comes into my home I watch how my dog reacts to them. If Solly likes them, automatically I like them. If he feels the need to sit on the opposite sofa and boggle at them, then I feel weary too.

Quite when this notion to seek my dog's approval started, I have no idea. In fact, I wasn't even aware it had until Stafford, a friend from the village, came around one day to give me a hand with some farm

164

work, and as soon as he finished and left Debbie looked up and said, "Solly liked him."

"Mmm," I agreed. "He even fell asleep next to him. To do that he must have trusted him, which is brilliant." The conversation progressed to cover every nuance of the dog's behaviour around stafford — for half an hour! Not, what did you think of him? Not, I thought he was nice because . . . No, all we did was discuss what the dog thought of him.

My dog, who spends half his time asleep and the other half passionately cleaning his genitals, is now picking my friends.

But it gets worse. Having passed the "does Solly like him?" test, we moved on. We moved on to talk about how the chickens felt about him. At one point one of us even turned the television down so we could concentrate better on our conversation. Two nearly-fifty-something adults sipping an evening glass of wine whilst engaged in the deadly serious topic of how the chickens felt when we introduced someone new to them. Then the ducks. Then the horses. And finally, the pigs.

"The General loved him," Debbie said.

"Didn't he! Did you see him showing off?" I was really warming to the subject now. "The General was actually talking to him, Oo, Oo, Ooing." I took a sip of wine. "Then he went and plonked himself down in his wallow — he never does that unless he's really comfortable."

Debbie pointed to the dog, "Same as Solly," she said. "They were all totally at ease around him."

165

I nodded in agreement. So Stafford had been proposed to the gang and, by democratic consent, been accepted. That's fine. Even now I feel less bemused than perhaps I should about using the farm animals to help pick out my friends, and even less so over the dog.

On the phone to Ziggy I didn't get much more than the fact that they'd split up because she felt he was too immature. She must have known what he was like before they started trying for a baby, surely? Anyway, he said he would call later and fill me in on the details.

I'd gone down onto the land and was sitting on the General's bum telling him about the results of the Well Man test when I heard Stafford shout my name.

"I've got to go, General," I said. "I'll tell you the rest later," and with that I got up and walked out of the enclosure.

Stafford, known to everyone locally as Tell-Me-A-Story-Stafford, is an ex-publican with so many tales to tell you'd think his whole life had been one continuous string of crazy adventures, but he could only talk while walking in tiny little circles — a throw-back to his publican days. If you wanted to shut him up, you just made him stand still.

We gripped hands and he said, "Debbie said you'd be down here. She also told me to ask about the leaflet?" When he let go of my hand he started walking about in front of me, first two steps one way, then two steps the other way.

I laughed. How do you even begin to explain about the leaflet? "I went for this Well Man test at the health centre today."

166

Two steps back the other way. Small circle. I wonder if he misses being behind the bar?

"How'd it go?" he said.

"It went well, all okay. Only I was sitting in the waiting room thinking about getting older and the things that happen to you when you do, you know, like losing your teeth and hair, going grey and all of that, and on the way out there was a table of leaflets."

"Let me guess, you took a leaflet on dementia?"

"Erectile dysfunction."

He snorted with laughter, because that's what men do when confronted with issues like this. It's like a nervous reaction. Debbie had laughed too, though for a whole other reason.

"You suffering in that department?" he said, poking his little finger out and then curling it so it pointed down. "The little fella downing tools?"

"No! I was just trying to work out if it was an avoidable part of getting older?"

"They didn't give you any little blue tablets and tell you to take one half an hour before bedtime, did they?"

You can't help liking Stafford. Everybody does.

"How old are you, Staff?"

"Sixty-seven, and no, it's not happened to me either. Mind you, at my age having a much younger and shinier wife than me helps. Which reminds me, did I tell you about the time . . .?"

He had. Several times, but that didn't matter — it was a funny story. While he spoke I edged him over towards the pig ark in the woods that needed renovating. Numbers one and two on the "list of things on my mind":

1. Must move Winnie (mum) and newborn piglets out of field shelter into a pig house in the woods.
2. *BEFORE* doing above, renovate pig house in the woods.

With a flourish he concluded the story with, ". . . the police were called and this guy's eighty-year-old mother was arrested!" Suddenly aware we were heading into the woods he said, "Where are we going?"

I pointed at the dilapidated pig house. "Can you give me a hand to move it? It's a two-man job and I just can't shift it on my own."

Where the house had been so wet that the structure had sunk into the mud and when I tried to lift one end the other sank deeper in and refused to budge. It needed two of us to lift it equally. "It just needs to go ten foot that way," I said.

The house was a squat metal and wood structure, and once I'd moved it onto firmer ground I could replace the broken panels so it would be watertight once again, put a straw bed down and move Winnie and her babies into it.

There was no floor to it, so the idea was that once it was roughly out of the mud, I'd climb inside and as it was such a short house, much shorter than me, I'd put my shoulders to the roof, stand up so the whole thing was raised off the ground and balanced on my back, and walk it over to the new spot.

With two of us the first part of the plan was easy. Together Stafford and I lifted it out of the mud. Next, I climbed inside.

It wasn't heavy, it was just awkward. "I'll lift from in here and walk," I shouted, "if you could steer because I can't see anything other than the ground."

"Right-oh," he replied from outside.

I lifted, and walked, staring down as I moved over the grass, the pig house balanced on my back. "If I see a snail I'm going to high-five it and call it brother," I shouted, and he laughed.

Two minutes later I dropped the dilapidated pig house on a new, clean and not muddy spot, and flopped down on the ground beneath it. Actually, it wasn't too bad inside. Snug. I'd sleep in there. Before I got any ideas of camping for a night I crawled out. Stafford was leaning against the outside of it, stationary, which meant he was quiet for once.

I started counting how many panels on the house had holes and needed replacing.

"Debbie said you're having a hard time at the moment," Stafford said.

Debbie was saying a lot.

"Did she ask you to come and chat with me?"

Without pausing he said she had.

I carried on counting the panels.

"Don't take that the wrong way, I was going to come down and see you anyway. Would have preferred it if you'd have asked me yourself, of course, but I'm happy to come down. She said you were struggling with hitting middle-age."

From what I could see most of the panels were salvageable, just three needed changing.

"Okay," he said, taking the hint when I didn't say anything, "but if you want to talk about it . . ."

I tipped my head back. I don't know if it was the moving of the house or the conversation but I felt my neck click.

"I don't know that I'm having a hard time," I said. "I think Debbie thinks I am, but I'm just a bit confused. It's no big deal."

"Why are you confused?"

The thing is, it's different talking to a guy from how it is talking to your wife. You can say anything to the one you love and loves you back equally, but to another man? I'm not afraid of opening up, especially to Stafford who I know isn't going to dump on me for it, and I'm also aware that having a best friend as a pig and pouring my heart out to him daily probably isn't the most healthy thing I could do, and I also accept that having a fellow human being to talk to would probably . . . arguably . . . maybe even almost certainly, be better. It's just that I'm not entirely sure that my standing on the brow of my hill and peering over the other side into middle-age theory would make any sense if I tried to articulate it here in the woods.

Mind you, would that matter? Is my new theory *that* important to me?

In a way, yes, because if Stafford gave me a "you're off your head" look, it would really throw me backwards just when I felt as if I was making headway.

Look, I'm sensitive on it. Over sensitive. I'm trying to figure it out the best way I know how and the last thing I need right now is a setback.

170

So I said, "Just the whole growing older thing, you know?" And then I did tell him my standing on the brow of my hill and peering over the other side into middle-age theory anyway. What the hell, sometimes you've just got to take a leap — though metaphorically, obviously, not literally hurl myself out in the OAP void, slippers and SAGA magazine flapping in the draft. I might be desperate, but I'm not suicidal.

"How old are you, Simon?"

I told him I was forty-seven.

"That's young to be looking at life that way."

I don't know why I felt the need to support my case, but I did. So I told him my other theory, or maybe that should be one of the other theories because I seem to be collecting them. I told him the one about hitting the *"What have I got to show for my life?"* wall, and the tally up I'd done between the list of expectations my younger self set and what I'd actually achieved. I told him I hadn't needed a pen to put any ticks down the side of the list.

"So I'm guessing you came from that kind of world, where success and happiness was sought through the wallet?"

"Yeah, you could say that."

"And now you feel like you've disappointed your younger self?"

"Yeah!" I was worried it wouldn't make any sense to him and he wouldn't get it, but clearly he did.

Looking me straight in the eyes he said, "Your younger self was a fool."

I nodded. "True."

He looked a question at me. "Then all you've done is grown into an even bigger fool if you haven't moved on from what *he* thought were good ideas!" Even though there wasn't a question mark at the end of the sentence it was still clearly a question.

I nodded in answer. Again, true.

"If I brought a fifteen-year-old kid fresh out of the smoke down here and asked him to judge you, would you take any notice of him?"

"Probably not," I said.

"Then why are you taking notice of the fifteen-year-old kid inside you, *'cos it's exactly the same thing*! Now you're getting me angry and I've got to look after my heart at my age."

"Don't die on me, I've got enough on at the moment without having to worry about getting my suit dry-cleaned for a funeral," I said. It would have been nice to sit down but it was nearly winter and soggy on the ground, so we leant against the pig house.

"You can get old at any age you like," Stafford said, quieter now. It has little to do with the years you've spent on this planet, and much to do with your state of mind. I'll be honest, sometimes when I look in the mirror I get a shock at the old man looking back at me 'cos that's not how I see myself — in my mind I'm still kid playing at being grown up. I don't even think I'm thirty yet."

I told him my mum says much the same thing.

"You reckon it was the Well Man test that brought all this on?"

I'd simplified that bit, though in all reality probably not by much.

"It's what Debbie thinks."

"And you? What do you think?"

"I kind of agree with her."

"But the results of the test were all good, so now you're just linging onto the strings after your mother has taken off the apron and gone for a lie down."

I smiled, more at the thought of my mother in an apron than is Stafford-ism. A couple of chickens out on an expedition found the spot from which we'd moved the pig house and started scraping away at the soft ground in search of tasty morsels.

Much as I didn't want to see his apron strings point, it was difficult not to as it did seem to be blinking in neon in front of me. Of the catalyst to my unease, my *thing*, was the Well Man test, and I'd passed that test with flying colours, then does it not stand to reason that the unease should relax?

Did I feel easier? Was my *thing* less of a *thing?* No, for the same reason a bush fire won't go out if you drench the discarded cigarette butt in water once the fire has taken hold. All things have momentum, even thoughts.

I looked up at Stafford, his tight curly hair now silver where once it was jet black. "I think the Well Man test started something inside me, a realisation maybe, I don't know. I can't help feeling that without realising it I was slipping into middle age, and now that I can see that, I can't help wanting to halt the progress. Ziggy gave me a list to help keep me young —"

"That boy's as big a fool as you are!"

"Bigger. Much, much bigger," I said, grinning. Having met when they were both helping me out on the land a few years ago, I knew Ziggy and Stafford spoke regularly, so I asked, "Did he tell you his latest?"

He nodded. "I got a Facebook message. No details, just that they've split up."

"That's all I know, too. You know what a drama queen he is, she probably only snogged him for five minutes rather than the usual ten before he went off to work and he interpreted that as a split up. Mind you, if it is true and she has pulled the plug on their relationship, it's going to devastate him."

Stafford twirled a double pirouette at the end of a two-pace straight. It was like talking to someone doing moves on *Strictly Come Dancing*. "That boy's too in touch with his feelings even for me, but yeah, I agree, it's going to take a lot of work to pick him up if she has called it a day. Tell me about this list he gave you."

I told him. Clothes, music, TV, internet, social media, attitude and outlook, hair, food and language.

"Hair?" he said. "I don't mean to disillusion you, but . . ."

"Yes, I know. Appreciated."

"You're very welcome," he said, grinning, knowing he was doing the routine that Ziggy and I shared. "So how's it going for you? Has the list made you feel young again?"

"I think about it a lot, but I haven't really done very much on it yet," I admitted. "I did watch some reality TV show the other night about a group left to fend for themselves on a deserted island. It's been years since

174

I've watched anything like that. It's funny, at the time I thought it was rubbish only because that's what I wanted to think, does that make sense?"

Staff nodded.

"But afterwards I've found myself wondering what happened next and looking forward to another episode. Oh, and Ziggy left me some music. Kwabs, you heard of him?"

"Can't say I have."

"Neither had I. He's pretty good actually — not sure I'd want to muck out a stable to him, but he's pretty good."

"And . . .?"

I shrugged. "I don't feel any older?" I said, my voice rising at the end, switching it from a statement of fact into a feeble question. I found I was doing that a lot lately? And yes, it was intentional?

He boomed with laughter. So did I; it was impossible not to find it funny.

"Oh, before I forget . . ." He pulled out a square of cloth and handed it to me. It was about the size of a dinner placemat and bright red with the words "Keep Calm" in white letters emblazoned across the centre. "My grandson's favourite top. Could *not* keep him out of it when he was young, to the point that we had to ban him from wearing it in the end and stashed it in a cupboard until he forgot about it. Whenever I see it, it reminds me of a happy time. Here," he handed it to me. "It's for Debbie's quilt."

I took it and hugged him. How did I ever get this lucky to have such wonderful friends around me?

When he'd gone I spent some time walking around the place trying to find somewhere I could scavenge three sheets of corrugated iron to repair the pig house in the woods. Unfortunately the pieces I had put aside for it I'd been forced to use on the stable roof. With no luck I found myself by the General's enclosure again, and climbed in. General was dozing on his bed. When he saw me he sat up and shook, his big ears slapping against the side of his head so it sounded like he was clapping, and for a moment a fog of dust hovering around him like a halo.

I went in. He was alone, and I guessed his wife-of-right-now must have nipped out for a bit.

"Sorry about earlier," I said, patting his back and watching the dust spring back up again. Dusty is a good look for a pig, trust me, the girls *love* it. "Stafford came down."

General flopped back down and I sat on his bum.

My phone trilled. I pulled it out. Ziggy.

"I'd better take this," I said.

Oh Ziggy . . .

"Have you got a minute?" Ziggy asked. That was unusual, normally he launched himself right in. I'd been worried about him and tried to judge how things were by the tone of his voice. It didn't sound good.

"Of course." I said. "Come on, what's happened?"

Deep sigh. "I messed up. Went out after work for a drink; it was only supposed to be a swift one, but you know what it's like, you start talking and before you know it it's one in the morning and you're pissed with your tongue in the wrong girl's mouth."

"*You got off with someone else?*"

"No, it's just a saying."

"Blimey, for a minute there I thought you'd completely lost your mind."

"In the old days I would have, wouldn't have thought twice about it. But things are different now. No, I wasn't unfaithful, but I was drunk and it was one in the morning when I thought to phone her. I went outside because it was so noisy where we were and found I had eight missed calls from her. I dialled her number and she answered on the first ring, like she'd been sitting with the phone in her hand and her finger over the answer button. I told her what had happened and she just screamed at me. Said she never wants to see me again. Never. Said this is what she'd been worried about all along. Said I was too immature and couldn't be trusted. Said I was a kid. A child. Said she hated me — *hated me!* She told me to go back to my mum. Then she cut me off, can you believe that?"

"Well, I can see she was somewhat upset."

"I know. I feel awful. And hungover."

General shuffled about underneath me, stretched out, and fell asleep. I was still sitting on his bum — you'd be surprised just how comfortable a pig's backside is to sit on.

"Have you tried to phone her since?"

"Of course. Just goes onto voicemail. I must have left ten messages. Do you think I should go round there?"

I thought about it. "I don't know, I think I'd be tempted to leave it for a day or so. She sounds pretty mad, but I don't think it's terminal."

"You don't? I do." His voice was as flat as I'd ever heard it. "You don't know her like I do."

"No, we've never met, remember?"

He didn't comment, just continued, "I need," he said, "to think of demonstration of my maturity. Do something to show her how wrong she is about me. Something that shows I'm an adult."

"You mean the opposite of going out and getting tanked when you'd told her you were going to spend a quiet evening with her?"

"Exactly!"

"Anything in mind?"

"Not a thing, that's why I phoned you."

"Thanks."

"Oh come on, Simon. I'm in trouble here, big trouble. Please, if there's a chance of getting her back, I've got to try it. Please. I really need your help."

No pressure. "Of course, but just for the record, I think you're dickhead."

"For the record, I agree, now are you going to help me or not?"

"I'm thinking, I'm thinking, give me a minute." I thought about it. Hard.

After a handful of seconds he said, "Tell me your thoughts. Tell me what you're thinking . . ."

I said, "I was trying to think of something with a long-term commitment involved. Something that says you're there for the long haul and you're not afraid of

178

committing — commitment's big on a woman's checklist for a partner, and it does demonstrate a more mature outlook. It also shows you love her and you're sorry for messing up."

"Something with a long-term commitment . . ." he repeated thoughtfully. "I could try and book us into Heston Blumenthal's Fat Duck at Bray for an evening meal, it's insanely hard to get into that place and you really have to put the effort in! Or . . . or . . . tickets to a show that's not on until next year! Or a holiday! Maybe not a holiday. But the rest of it is spot on! Oh, man, I've got to go, this is magic. You're a lifesaver, I'll call you later," and he was gone before I could tell him that's not quite what I had in mind.

I put the phone away and turned to the General. "Busy old day, eh boy? Now, where were we? Oh yeah, Stafford . . ." But before I could tell him about the conversation over the dilapidated pig house, the General's wife-of-right-now walked in.

He got up to greet her, which meant I lost my seat, so I got up too. It made us both look very polite.

"I'll leave you to it," I said. "I've got to go and start the rounds anyway."

The rounds took a solid couple of hours and it was dusk and cold and rainy by the time I started chopping wood. When two bags were full of split logs and stacked on the quad bike, I made my way back up to the house.

"Some more parcels for you," Debbie said as I stacked the wood next to the fire.

"Okay, thanks. Stafford came down to see me today."

"Did he?"

I smiled. "You know he did. You sent him."

"I know. But he was really keen to come down and see you. He thinks such a lot of you."

"He's a good friend," I said.

I grabbed the parcels and walked upstairs where I put the radio on so she couldn't identify what I was doing by the sounds, and dragged the suitcase from the top of the wardrobe. Then I opened the parcels. A blouse in every shade of blue from my step-mum, a Chanel t-shirt with a note pinned to it saying, "Don't worry, it's a fake" from an incredibly successful London friend, a Morgan top from my mother, a hand-embroidered square from Debbie's cousin and, of course, Stafford's "Keep Calm" piece.

Stashing them in the case and replacing it on top of the wardrobe I thought how individual everybody's square was, and how, when the quilt was complete, we'd be able to read something really interesting into it about the relationships Debbie had formed with friends and relatives throughout her life, and I wondered what a similar quilt for me would look like. Then I went back downstairs for a glass of wine and to light the fire.

The following morning I did the rounds and went to see the General, who was spooning in bed with his wife-of-right-now.

I hadn't heard anything from Ziggy, which I took to be a good sign — I'd half expected him to turn up on the doorstep again. It made me smile that his interpretation of commitment was to book a show or a meal at a posh restaurant, but that was Ziggy all over. If she loved him at all, she had to love that part of him because that bit would never change; it was in Ziggy's DNA.

I sat in a corner of the pig house trying not to disturb the happy couple. General looked up, saw me, and flopped back down again. Wife-of-right-now didn't even wake up.

I'd wanted to talk to the General, but it felt weird opening up in front of his wife-of-right-now. So I waited for a while in case she was planning on popping out for a bit, but when she showed no signs of it I got up and left them to it, figuring I'd come back later when they were up.

Keen to use the time wisely, I rummaged around in my collection of precision tools for a hammer and a pair of fencing pliers, found them, realised the pliers were damp-welded into one immoveable position, drenched them in oil, hit them with the hammer, swore, hit them with the hammer again, wiggled, ajoled, begged, swore again, hit them again, and eventually got them to work as they should. Then I took them to the dilapidated pig house in the woods, planning to remove the three broken panels so at least I'd made a start on the house.

When I reached it, I found three sheets of corrugated iron leaning up against the house that I hadn't put there and, judging by the fact that they were only partially worn and almost new, I didn't own.

What the hell?

It took a while for my brain to do the calculation. It could only be one person as nobody else knew about it: Stafford.

I wanted to phone him or text him or do something to say thank you, but I had no money on my phone.

There was a noise behind me and I thought it might be him, but it was only Curry the goat come to see what I was doing. I stroked her head and said, "I hope you helped him bring these down, Curry."

With the incentive that I actually had some materials to work with, I whipped off the damaged sheets and replaced them with the new ones. By lunchtime, the pig house was finished, better than new and ready to be inhabited.

It was Friday, which meant that tomorrow was my first day at my new job shovelling shit for Steph's seventeen horses. You know you usually get that anxious feeling the day before starting a new job? Well, funnily enough I didn't have that. However, the prospect of the wages did excite me. I needed straw to lay as a bed in the redeveloped pig house.

Could I ask for an advance, I wondered? Perhaps I could have some of my wages a day earlier so I could make a nice bed and move Winnie and her babies out of the field shelter and in today? Not really. That's a bit much, considering I haven't even started working up there yet. It's only tomorrow. I'll do it then.

Feeling pretty good I wandered back to the General and tried not to show how pleased I was to find his wife-of-right-now out.

"Oh man," I said, flopping down next to him. "When did Stafford come back with the sheets? Did you see him go past?" The General's house was right next to the path; from his bedroom he could see everyone coming and going.

He didn't answer. Maybe he'd missed him.

"Look," I said, "I've been trying to get to talk to you for a while. There's something I need to tell you. There's no easy way to say this but I think your sperm count might be slipping. The litters you're throwing are getting smaller and smaller. It doesn't mean you're any less of a boar, it's just your age, you know? Don't feel bad, it happens to us all. My count's probably useless too, mind you I have got the added complication of having electrocuted my nuts on more than one occasion." Electric wire running around the perimeter of the pig enclosures, I'd long ago decided, was a far bigger hazard to me stepping over it than ever it was to the pigs.

"Anyway, if your wife-of-right-now who, let's face it, is young and in her child-bearing prime doesn't have a good-sized litter, you're probably going to have to retire from stud duties."

There, I'd said it. I watched his face for a reaction, but he's more your strong silent type and doesn't give much away.

I shrugged a shoulder and looked up at the tin roof.

"In many ways, General, we're going through the same thing, you and me. Okay, I'm not trying to get the girls pregnant, but I am facing the prospect of getting older and my body not working as it once did." I looked back at him. "When you were young did you have any expectations of where your life might lead you? Did you dream of one day owning your own mud wallow?"

183

I had this crazy notion that I could help him to develop a younger outlook in much the same way I was hoping to develop one in me, and by doing so give him a bit of a spark that might boost his performance in bed. I'd pored over Ziggy's list, trying to work out the things we could do together. I'd thought of getting a radio and tuning it to Radio 1 and propping it up over to the side of his house, but we didn't have the money for that. I'd also mulled over the idea of giving him a trendy haircut — his hair was long enough for it! Maybe I could set up a Twitter account for him, @TheGeneral, or get him to grunt with a question mark? At the end of each sequence? Of grunts?

My phone rang. It was Debbie asking if I was going up for lunch.

"I'm glad we had this talk," I said, getting up. "I feel good. Do you feel good?" and I left him, jumped on the quad and zoomed up to the house.

It's a poultry savings plan for Christmas

Lunch was lentil and tomato soup served with freshly baked hunks of warm bread. While we ate I told Debbie about the three sheets of corrugated iron from Stafford.

"Oh, that's so kind of him," she said.

"Makes me feel bad. I need to phone him," I said, grabbing the house phone, but he wasn't in. I didn't leave a message; it wasn't a message-leaving kind of thing.

184

"You could always make him something as a little thank you," she said. "Why don't you carve him a wooden spoon? He'd like that."

Not a bad shout.

Dragging the kettle over to the hotplate I switched it on. Behind me Debbie snaked her arms around my waist. "You seem less pre-occupied today," she said. "More like your old self? Do you feel better after the Well Man results, knowing you're not in imminent danger of keeling over?"

I leant in against her. "Yes," I admitted, and I did — who wouldn't?

"Good, because we need to discuss turkeys and chicks. I've been in touch with a friend who'll let us have twenty turkeys at cost, but only as long as we collect them this week as she doesn't want to get a whole delivery of feed for them if she doesn't have to, and she's got meat chickens that are just about old enough to live without a heat lamp. We can have thirty or forty of those. What do you think?"

"There's no money, Debbie," I said. This is part of the problem, there are ways of making money on a smallholding, but you have to have something to invest in the first place. And we didn't.

"If we don't do it now it'll be too late, Christmas is only three months away. We're going to have to ad-lib them with food as it is. I've thought about it, and to raise the money the choices, as far as I can make out, are: We could not pay the rent for a month. Or we could not pay the electric. I've just invoiced for the butchery course next week and we could use that —

185

mind you, that was earmarked to pay some urgent bills. Which reminds me, I must phone the abattoir and see how much the pig weighed and make arrangements to pick it up."

"I'm not sure about using the house money to buy livestock," I said.

"Neither am I, but I'm not sure we can afford not to either. Turkeys and meat chickens are our Christmas savings plan. If we don't do it, we'll have nothing."

This is what brings you down. This is what kills you. What do we do? Go for broke for Christmas and risk the stroppy letters and angry phone calls, or pay the bills and suck a polo mint on Christmas Day?

"Can we cope with the fallout?"

"Don't we always?"

"Okay."

"Okay? As in yes for the chickens and the turkeys?"

It made sense, speculate to accumulate and all that. I knew it would make things difficult for the short term, but long term we'd be miles better off. So I said, "I've got a shed and run already set side for the turkeys, and we can put the chickens in a stable for a while until I've got somewhere outside sorted for them. I'm pretty much geared up for it."

I hadn't even finished speaking and she was reaching for the phone. I made coffee for us both while she sorted out the collection details. When she got off the phone she said, "Done. We collect them on Monday."

I gave Debbie the update on Ziggy, about his desire to demonstrate his maturity and my commitment advice.

186

"For Christ's sake! Booking a restaurant is not a demonstration of maturity and has absolutely nothing to do with commitment! Why did you tell him to do that?"

"I didn't, that bit was his idea."

"Commitment is moving in together, especially as she's pregant. Not picking out a bloody menu! Where's the phone?"

I listened as she dialled his number. "Ziggy?" she said.

Quiet.

"I see."

Quiet.

"Mmm."

Quiet.

"Yes."

Quiet.

"I'm not surprised." A look at me.

Quiet.

"I think that's a good idea. Okay. Bye."

"That didn't sound as though it went so well," I said.

"Apparently it's not so easy to get on the waiting list for the restaurant he wanted, so he couldn't do that. Instead," she shook her head in a way that articulated how she felt better than words ever could, "he booked tickets for Disneyland two weeks after her due date and went round to give them to her."

I made an "Ouch" face.

"Mmm. His words were, 'She thought the timing was inappropriate, but sweet.' She's forgiven him and it's all now tickety-boo and back on — his words again."

With the bread dough kneaded I put it in a bowl and moved it to one side to rise.

"I should be an agony uncle," I said, washing my hands. "This relationship malarkey's a doddle."

"Trust me, stick to pigs."

"Oh."

The phone rang. Seriously, if you had this image of self-sufficiency being a quiet, solitary life, think again. Debbie snagged it and looked at the caller display and said, "Chris C," before handing it to me to answer.

Chris C was my oldest, oldest friend. I'd known him since we'd gone to the same school and hung out doing what kids do, which was getting into mischief. These days we stayed in touch through the power of Facebook with a few phone calls in between.

"Chris C," I said, grinning from ear to ear. He'd always been Chris C ever since I'd known him, on account that our school had an influx of Chrises, so the first letter of everyone's surname was added to tell them apart. And it had stuck.

We spoke for a while catching up, and then he admitted why he was really calling — his son had got in with a bad crowd. "We've been told the group are into drugs and some nasty stuff. Garth says he's got nothing to do with that side of the group, but I'm worried. Fi [Fi is Chris C's wife] and I wondered if he might be able to come down to you for the half-term week? We absolutely insist he pays his way for bed and board, and maybe you could show him what life is really all about? What do you think?"

My first thought was, no, sod that, a teenager in the house? You must be joking! My second thought was, mind you, the money would be handy, might even pay for the chickens and turkeys. Plus, it stood to reason that a teenager would necessarily have a young outlook, which could shed light on the Attitude and Outlook part of Ziggy's list.

I said, "Let me speak to Debbie and I'll call you back."

"What?" Debbie said, the instant I got off the phone.

"I think I might have found a way to pay for the chickens and the turkeys without using the rent."

My world is full of poo

Shit. The world is full of shit, or, more precisely, the ground is full of shit. Seventeen big, hairy, horse-bums' worth of it. Did they have a party last night? Invite some friends over? Order a spicy runny-burn-inducing curry for all their horsey friends to enjoy?

I was up at Steph's for the first day in my new job.

The horses are split into two covered yards: girls in one, boys in another, with a gate in between. Each yard has a field running off it, but why go out there to poo when it's so much nicer doing it on the dry, on the nice concrete floor where it explodes on impact giving it that lovely poo-carpet spread?

If there is such a thing as reincarnation, I want to come back as a horse. If you add up all the time that I've spent nipping to the bathroom I bet it's a month out of my life. A whole month just making my way to the lavatory. What a waste! A horse just does it where it stands, "Ooooh . . . Ahh, there you go — someone clean that up for me, would you?" Oh, the freedom!

It was Saturday morning. The animal rounds were done, with no injuries to report from either side. Now I was up at Steph's for my hotly anticipated new career as a shit-shoveller.

I'd been given my instructions, which basically consisted of pointing me towards a shovel and a wheelbarrow, being told to watch out for Aliana on the girls' side as she likes to tip the wheel-barrow over, and Fang on the boys' as he can be a bully, and then directed towards the muck heap, which was way, way, way over there.

Great.

I decided to go in with the girls first, hoping they might be a little gentler with me on my first day. Buzzing with the anticipation of a newbie the girls crowded the gateway, eager to see if I was either edible, squashable, kickable, stampable or generally bullyable, and were delighted to find out I was all of them.

Unlatching the gate and pushing the wheelbarrow through the mass of equine muscle, I called, "Coming through, mind your backs, girls. Man coming in. I'm here to clean up after your runny bums and I'd appreciate it if you could all stop any bottom action from now until I leave so you're not adding to the job. The management thanks you for your cooperation in this matter. Complaints can only be received by email."

190

The trick — oh who am I kidding? There is no trick — you start at one end, fill the wheelbarrow, empty it on the muck heap, fill it again, empty it, fill it again and keep doing that until you reach the wall at the other side of the yard. That, at least, is my side of the operation. The horses also have a role to play; their job is to mill about in front of me, kick any big piles of poo about a bit, argue and bicker between themselves so I'm distracted from Aliana who waits for me to fill the wheelbarrow before hooking a foot into it and pulling it over.

"Aliana, you *bitch!*" I shout as she does it for the third time.

A pleasant hour shot by which hardly felt longer than six. Then it was the turn of the boys.

If the girls were devious, the boys were scaredy-cats. *Everything* was frightening to them and needed to be leapt away from, including, but by no means restricted to: other horses, the wheelbarrow, a shovel, me, the floor, a pile of poo, a tuft of grass, the gate, a wall, a hay net containing their own lunch, their own foot, somebody else's foot, my baseball cap, my voice, a cough from one of the other horses, a fart from one of the other horses, and, I have no doubt, themselves.

At one point I swear one of them went to do a Scooby-Doo jump up into my arms and I only just put him off by ducking behind the barrow, because, as scary as I am, I'm far less scary than a shovel leaning against a wall, and in *that* scenario, I was their obvious go-to protector.

"Oh, no, no, no, no!" I shouted, ducking down behind the wheel-barrow as Harry, part cart horse and part something else that's equally heavy, leapt up in the spot where I had been standing.

By the time I started thinking, "Actually, the smell of all this crap isn't too bad", which was about two and a half hours in, I'd finished. I'd love to say that behind me I left a sparkling surface for the horses to walk about on, but unfortunately they'd all taken in turns to creep up and shit on whatever spot I'd just cleared, though it did look considerably better than when I'd started. Collecting my wages by filling the trailer with straw, I drove down into my land.

It was good to be back. It was less stinky, and what smell there was came from the pigs, and that's just sweet perfume. It's funny how your own animals never smell bad.

"New bed tonight," I called, humping enormous slices of sweet-smelling straw into each pig enclosure and chucking it into their house. Years ago I used to put the beds down nicely for the pigs, but I could never be trusted to do it properly and the sows would always come in after me and rearrange it. Pigs love to do their own housework, so these days I leave them to it.

The last thing I did was lay a deep bed in the now non-dilapidated refurbished pig house in the woods. Then I went off to get Winnie and her babies from the field shelter.

Hooking the trailer to the back of the quad I drove it to the field shelter, where I backed it up to the gate. Inside, Winnie was lying down feeding her little ones.

When she saw me she jumped up with far more grace and elegance that you might give credit to a 300 kg pig. The only thing that let it down slightly was the line of babies refusing to let go and still chomping on her nipples.

"Easy, girl. I know, I'm pleased to see you too," I said, getting down to her level and snorting with her nose-to-nose. "I saw the General earlier. He told me to tell you, 'Yo babe.' '

Loading Winnie is always a breeze. We have an understanding: I open up the trailer and she waltzes in. Job done. Unfortunately, the understanding does not extend to her babies, who dashed around the field shelter like mini racehorses.

At the start it wasn't too bad. There were so many of them I just positioned myself near a corner and grabbed a leg as they went flying by, pulling them up into cuddling position number one and putting them over the side of the trailer in with Mum. It was the last two that were the most difficult to catch. Natural selection means it is the quickest, the most nimble and the most agile that escape the big bad predator — me — for the longest time, and are therefore the most difficult to catch.

"Oh, come on, chill. It's me. We're buddies, remember? I've changed your nappy . . . so to speak. I certainly sprayed your navel when you were born so it wouldn't get infected, that's got to count for something, hasn't it?" Clearly it didn't as they weren't letting me anywhere near them.

Suddenly one hesitated in a corner. It was the break I'd been waiting for. With the reflexes of a slightly older, slightly decrepit overweight cat — but a cat nonetheless — I dived for the piglet, and when I say dived, I mean full-on, body in the air, sportsman dive. It looked great, *it felt great*! Until I landed. In the corner. Hard. Alone. The piglet long gone. Probably into poo — I mean, why wouldn't I think I'd landed in poo as so much of my life seems to have become dominated by excreta? I'm forty-seven years old, I'm supposed to be dignified.

I sat up. The piglets were on the other side watching me. I brushed myself off. Normally it's only people in films who brush themselves off, but then normal people don't usually dive around in pig pens.

I hate the fact that I'm not the norm. It kind of bothers me.

I brushed myself off and slapped the dust from my top and consoled myself that actually I'd missed the poo. I was a poo-free man. I got up, thinking sex, drugs and rock and roll, man, sex, drugs and rock and roll.

Pitching my look somewhere between the child catcher in *Chitty Chitty Bang Bang* and Mr Bean — which let's face it is quite a wide spectrum — I approached the piglets and amazingly caught them without further mishap, injury or anything that could be considered a poo near-miss. Happy days.

Back in the woods I let them out into their new home. Winnie inspected the bedroom and found I'd done the bed all wrong and set about making it properly, while the piglets found a stick with which they could play tug-of-war.

Top gun chickens

Having moved Winnie and her babies into the woods, I returned the trailer to its usual parking spot in the chicken field. Senorita screamed abuse at me for using it, and then raised the volume and abuse to a whole new level when she went inside and found some other female pig had been in it.

"Sorry," I said, hands up and backing away. There must be a way I can get Senorita to overcome her aversion to other pigs.

Everyone done, everyone in, everyone happy (except Senorita). The last job of the day was cutting wood for the fire.

Since the goats had eaten my chainsaw helmet I'd become nervous of this part of the day. But what choice did I have? There was no money to buy another helmet so it was either cut wood without one or have no wood, no fire, no heat in the house and spend the evening shivering under blankets. Sometimes in life you have no choice but to just get on with it.

The thought that if something goes wrong there's no safety equipment in place to protect you really helps to focus your concentration. I cut wood so carefully you'd think I was going to use the pieces to build a cabinet. I even cut a blank for a wooden spoon — I still hadn't managed to get hold of Stafford to thank him for the

195

corrugated iron, and was determined to make something nice for him to show how much I'd appreciated what he'd done.

With the quad bike stacked high with bags of wood and Dex balanced on the back, I drove up the hill to the house, unloaded the wood, lit the fire, showered, ironed a sharp fitted shirt and my best trousers and slipped them on. I know it's pathetic, and I know that clothes don't maketh the man, but they do maketh him feel a whole lot less like a shit-shoveller.

"Are you going out?" Debbie asked as I walked down the stairs. Then before I could answer she got it, and smiled at me. That's what twenty-four years of marriage does for you, it gives you a whole other language that doesn't involve words.

She came over and kissed me. "Thank you for doing Steph's."

Feeling a bit self-conscious and exposed I said, "What's the gossip here?"

She told me while I inserted a new blade into my Stanley knife, dragged the log basket over between my knees and sat in front of the fire whittling away at the wooden blank I'd cut with the chain-saw, hoping I'd find a nice spoon buried within.

Okay, Debbie hadn't been quite as involved in the bottom-produce removal today as I had, but she had been equally busy. There's something very comforting about moaning about your day with the one you love. When it's just one of you moaning about your day it's not the same, but when you can both get worked up into a really good rant there's nothing like it to make you feel close.

"Aliana!" I said, my eyes flicking up into my eyebrows.

"I phoned everyone we owe money to," she said, throwing her arms wide open.

"Had to fight her off the wheelbarrow!" I said.

"I think I placated them all, just about," she said.

"Aliana, OMG what a bitch!"

Silence. Then, "What did you say?"

Whittle, whittle, whittle. "What a bitch —"

"No, before then."

"Aliana and the wheelbarrow?"

"You said OMG."

Whittle, whittle, whittle. "Did I? Well . . . that's sick, and like, well bad. Innit."

She took a deep breath. "I know what you're trying to do, but you just come across like a creepy old bloke. If you ever talk like that again, I'm going to have to euthanise you with that Stanley knife."

"Are you sure you're not mixing up creepy old bloke with a dude who's down with the kids? It's easily done."

"Trust me, it's creepy old bloke."

"Shame, I thought it rather suited me."

"Did you get back to Chris C about his son coming to stay?" she said.

"Not yet."

There was a knock at the door and me, Solly and the Stanley knife answered it. It was someone after directions. We get that a lot. The best times are when

I'm butchering and answer the door wearing a bloody apron and waving a big butcher's knife smeared in blood. What I really want is a banjo and to learn the *Deliverance* Duelling Banjo lick and answer the door with that, but Debbie won't let me.

Back in the house I said, "Could you cope with a teenager in the house for a week?"

She thought about it. "What's he like? How long's it been since you saw him? Or Chris C for that matter?"

"A while," I admitted.

She was mixing chapatti flour and water into a dough that could later be flattened into several disks and dry-fried. Behind her was a huge pot of Jamaican curry with currants and sultanas and our own chicken bubbling away in the sauce, and beside that some rice simmering gently.

"Smells great. Did I get any post?"

"Not today. What's with all the parcels?"

She knows. I know she knows. Oh, come on, of course she bloody knows, she's a woman! "Nothing," I said.

"Would you mind if I called Chris C and spoke to Fi?" she said.

"Of course not!"

After dinner Debbie phoned Fi for the low-down on Garth — why do I get the urge to sing the theme tune to the *Fresh Prince of Bel-Air* every time I think of him? Here's what she found out: Garth. Seventeen years old but thinks he's older — what seventeen-year-old doesn't? There is a girlfriend, but they're not sure how serious it is as he gets touchy when his mum tries to speak to him about it. At college. Lots of friends. Lived in London all his life and has no idea about anything outside of it. Since he started lacking about with a new group of friends Fi has noticed a change in him. That worried her. She's not sure about this new group, not sure at all. He's a good lad and she was obviously super proud of him, but she admitted he was going though a stage.

While talking Debbie scribbled on the back of an envelope: *What do you think?*

I scribbled underneath it: *Is he trouble?*

She put: *I don't think so.*

I put: *WTH, okay then.*

She put: *WTH?*

I put: *What The Hell.*

She put: *Go get me the Stanley knife, you need putting down NOW!*

I went to tear up the envelope but found it was full of an un-opened bill and thought better of it.

Arrangements were made for Garth to come down on Tuesday — the day after we collected the turkeys and the chicks. I poured us both a glass of rosehip wine — I wouldn't recommend it.

Monday morning and once again we borrowed my poor neighbour's truck. Tootling along on our way to collect the turkeys and the chicks, Sally Traffic came on the radio and I turned her up. When she started talking about how horrendous the M25 was, I nudged Debbie and grinned. "Remember those days?" Then I sped up just because I could before a tractor came out of nowhere and slowed us down to half a mile an hour because the universe hates show-offs.

Chugging along behind the tractor, Debbie said, staring resolutely at the road ahead, "I need to ask you something. Are you having an affair?"

"*What?*"

She didn't look at me, but said again, "Are you having an affair?"

"No. What made you say that?"

"Hiding your emails from me. Presents through the post."

I laughed. I couldn't help it.

"*Don't laugh at me, don't you DARE laugh at me!*" She was angry and she wasn't crying but her eyes were leaking. I reached out for her but she pushed me away.

"No, I'm not having an affair, you lunatic. I'm doing something nice for your birthday."

Sniff. "So you say. How do I know that's true? You could be off shagging for all I know."

"I think you'd probably know if I was. Which I'm not. Besides everything else, when do you think I'd get the time?"

She sniffed and hummed.

"Speak to Paula, or your mum. They know all about it. They'll tell you," I said.

"It might be her you're having an affair with."

"*Your mum!!!!!!!!!!!!!*" Forgive the extra exclamation marks, but trust me, they're warranted.

She laughed and said, "I meant Paula." Lately we're having more and more of these crazy conversations that

200

make absolutely no sense whatsoever. I mean, her mum's lovely, but she's *her mum!*

The window on Debbie's side of the car was wide open. Even though it was freezing out she kept complaining she was hot.

"It's two below zero in here," I moaned.

She was fanning her face and pulling her collar away from her neck as though we were driving through a desert as opposed to winter on Exmoor. "Internal central heating," she said.

As fast as things went weird they returned to normal and for a while the conversation zipped about, dipping in and out of a gazillion different topics, sometimes referencing something we haven't talked about for months. That's kind of okay and I feel as though I'm just about keeping up, and then she goes to the next level and dropping the second half of sentences as well, so now not only am I guessing what we're talking about but I'm also guessing what we're saying. By the time we reach the friend's house, I'm exhausted and have no idea what the conversation is about.

While Debbie was talking to her friend I nipped to the loo. On top of the cistern, as arranged, was a bag. I opened it. Inside was a square of material placed there by the friend for Debbie's quilt. Feeling like George Smiley on a mission, I slipped the material down the back of my jeans and returned outside.

The three of us loaded the chickens and the turkeys into poultry crates for the journey home.

I slid the last crate of six-week-old chickens into the back of the truck, made a barrier because turkeys and chickens must not under any circumstances come into contact with each other, put the turkeys in, tied everything down to make it safe, kissed the friend on the cheek and whispered, "Got it, thank you," and trundled out of the yard. As I drove into the line of traffic I glanced in the rear-view mirror. The uppermost crate was snug up against the back window of the cab. In the mirror I could see inside the crate, see the boggle-eyed chicks as they looked out at the moving world. I accelerated, and when I did they collectively stood up, put their heads down and spread their wings.

Of course! To them a moving world meant they were flying.

"Quick, head down girls, wings out, Top Gun Chickens you are clear for take-off."

"Does anyone know where we're going? Flap faster, Doris, we're speeding up."

"I know where we're going," flap, flap, flap, *"I could tell you but then I'd have to kill you."*

As we went around a corner Debbie screeched with laughter bouncing up and down on her seat. "They're leaning into it. Go round and do it again, do it again!"

I've had chickens for years, but in all that time I can honestly say I've never once worried they all might at a moment's notice soar off into the night sky. In fact, only the other day I watched one chicken as she tried to flap over the gate that separates her field from the woods. Watched, open-mouthed, as she horribly misjudged how much effort it would take to raise her not-insubstantial bulk that far off the ground, and winced as she crashed beak first into the wood struts of

202

the gate. She landed on the grass, bounced a couple of times, ruffled her feathers, looked around to make sure nobody was laughing at her and skulked off.

Meat chickens, by the very nature of what they're intended for, are much chunkier than egg-laying hens, and whatever way you look at it they are not designed for flight, and certainly not long-haul. Maybe long ago . . . long, long ago, they might have been, but not anymore. There are no Homing Chicken Clubs full of chicken enthusiasts who drive their chickens hundreds of miles from home, slip a ring on their foot and race them back — unless it's a running race.

Yet here were chicks proving that chickens still have aeronautical hardwiring. Aviation is in their blood. As my speed edged towards 35mph, they stopped flapping and began gliding. Partly because of my slow speed, but mostly because of my flying passengers, other cars on the road crept close up behind me without bothering to pass. I could see the drivers laughing.

Maybe it's the fact that chickens have wings that gives them the impression they can fly. Inside the crates they were still in gliding formation, even though their feet were on the floor of the crate.

"*Doris, where are you? There you are. Good. Doris, never leave your wing man. Got it? Never leave your wing man.*"

It took twenty minutes of slow driving from me, and careful flying from them, before we made it home.

"*Landing lights ahead, Doris!*"

As I slowed right down they went back to flapping, presumably not trusting the slackened pace to keep them, in their eyes, air-borne. I headed straight down onto the land.

The turkey house was ready, a reinforced shed with loads of wire netting stapled to the outside and a door that firmly locked at night. Beyond that was a safe enclosure in which they could mooch about during the day. I pulled out the crate and took it over.

Young turkeys, known as poults, are ugly. Sorry, but they are. Imagine a Tyrannosaurus Rex in miniature, give it a huge pair of flappy feet to walk around in and a pointy face and they're *fat*! So *fat*! Then give diddy T-Rex all the stability of a ten-month-old baby walking its first few steps, and there you have an eight-week-old turkey. How they ever made it through evolution is a complete mystery. If challenged by a predator they'd be hard pushed to summon more than a flappy foot in defence, and they certainly couldn't outrun anything!

Ugly, ugly, ugly. Not cute at all.

The thing is, I didn't want to like them. I didn't want to dislike them, but I didn't want to, you know, "like them". I didn't want to be fond of them. They were only going to be there for a while. They were making no plans for Boxing Day. So I was going to have to look after them, but keep my distance. I mustn't form a relationship. It was a self-preservation thing.

So to me they were just flappy-footed mini dinosaurs who followed me around, bumping into things and falling on their backsides. Stupid things. Incredibly ugly. They looked moth-eaten, with their dark feathers poking out and silly little heads and sharp little faces.

I hated it when they followed me about. Why did they do that? Couldn't they tell I didn't like them?

You should have felt their little hearts beating when I picked them up. Their big breasts were all soft and squishy like jelly and their heart slammed away in their chest — bang, bang, bang, bang, bang. I told them, calm down, chill, you'll be sending more blood around your body than you can cope with. It was probably all going to their feet, no wonder they were so huge.

I picked them out of the crate and carefully put them in their new house. From there they could explore, but at least they'd know where home was.

They didn't explore, though. They followed me, cheeping and calling. When I walked fast they tried to rush to keep up and tripped over, then sat there looking at their own feet in disgust as though they'd done it on purpose. I only stopped and waited for them because I didn't want them injured. Not because I liked them.

I had to find a way to stop them following me about. I'd run away from them, and I wouldn't stop even if they did trip themselves up. And I wouldn't listen to their cheeping calls as they shouted after me.

Tomorrow. I'd do that tomorrow.

Debbie arranged feed and water for the turkeys while I got on with the Top Gun Chickens.

I could put them out in a house in the field, but I just felt they were a bit too young for that — they'd not been outside yet. It might have been too much for them all in one day. They had been used to a stable, so I thought I should really give them something they knew on their first day; some sense of comfort and safety.

Decision made, I prepared temporary quarters in the stable next to Pru and her two babies, who were growing all the time into little bruisers.

"The neighbours are a bit iffy," I told the chickens when they were all in and settled. "Watch out for the two youngsters, they've already had an ASBO slapped on them."

Even while I spoke the chickens were zonking out, shattered after a big day. I wondered if they'd dream of flying. I kind of hoped they would.

Garth is *nothing* like I thought

The following day, while Debbie went to collect Garth from the train station, I did morning rounds. First stop was the stable and the new chickens. I pulled open the door expecting to see them up and about, but they weren't.

They were all dead, every single last one. Dead.

I leant against the wall and looked at the ceiling, feeling more anger than I can possibly describe. I wanted to punch something, a wall, anything, just to release some of it. A few years ago I would probably have given in and done just that, but as you get older you learn to deal with it in other ways. I took a deep breath and swallowed half of the anger down in one go. That's exactly how it feels, like you're swallowing it. Then I looked down.

Strewn across the floor of the stable were the broken, bloody bodies of all twenty baby chickens. Some were alone, some in groups as though they were clinging to one another for comfort or the hope of protection.

Most had their heads missing.

For a while I didn't move. I just looked. What a waste, what a terrible, horrible waste of life. I thought about yesterday and collecting them, packing them in a crate and carrying them to the truck. Then the journey of the Top Gun Chickens, wings out as though they were flying. I thought of Debbie's shriek of laughter as we went around the corner. I'd laughed too. They looked so cute. They were just babies.

I thought I'd made the stable safe. I thought it was fox-proof. I thought, I thought, I thought.

I picked up one of the bodies. Rigor mortis had set in and it was cold and stiff. I placed it next to the largest group, then collected the others and did the same until I had them all in a single pile. I told them I was sorry. I told them I thought I'd done enough to keep them safe. Then I ran out of things to say, so I shut up.

I walked out of the stable and shut the door behind me. I'd deal with the disposal later. Tonight. Not now. I checked the rest of the poultry and tried to count numbers but couldn't concentrate, so I gave up. It looked like they were all there, which was the best I could do.

I guess I was lucky the fox didn't get into the rest. But I didn't feel lucky. I felt rotten. I tried to stop the "what ifs" and the "should haves" from crowding out my mind, but there were too many to keep out. What if I'd come down earlier? What if I hadn't put them in the stable? What if I'd checked more thoroughly that a fox couldn't get in?

I should have seen the danger and addressed it. That's my job. That's what I'm here for, to keep everything safe.

So what should I do now, shrug my shoulders? Learn a lesson? Move on? These things happen?

Sometimes . . . honestly, sometimes I could just walk away from the whole thing. I know I won't feel like that tomorrow; time, a bottle of awful wine tonight and a night's sleep will cure most of that. But right now, I could happily walk away and never come back.

I did the rest of the rounds slowly, dragging my feet the way you might if you were marooned on a desert island with zero prospects of rescue. I could hear the turkeys chattering inside their shed or I might not have been able to bring myself to open the door. They were fine.

I let out Senorita and she wobble-bellied it over to me and just leant against my leg. The animals know when something has gone down. They're very supportive towards me. Amazingly so.

Dex took up his position of daytime guardian of the poultry. Shame he couldn't stay down there at night too, but it didn't seem fair on the boy. Besides, night-time was my responsibility. It was my job to ensure they were made safe for the night. It was me that fucked up.

I drove up to the house.

From the brief bio Fi had given Debbie I had a fair image in my mind of what Garth would look like; you

208

know, bit of a homey loaner who'd found somewhere he felt he could fit in away from the nest and was now doing all he could to prove himself to his new group of friends. He would probably be somewhere in that transitional period, so he'd have downcast shifty eyes, pasty white pappy skin from all the years spent in his bedroom, a bit greasy, a bit spotty, half-hearted hair that can't quite work out if it wants to be radical or trendy, and clothes that make a statement just for the like of the statement.

I was way off. *Way off.*

What actually walked in was a surf dude. Long, shaggy, blond air under a black beanie hat. He was tall as a skyscraper, skinny, tanned, high cheekbones, wide smile, oozing confidence, firm eye contact with eyes that were so blue they just had to be contacts, expensive top, ripped jeans, trashed leather sandals.

Behind him Debbie was grinning ear to ear.

"Hey, man," he said, walking straight up to me and holding his hand out like he wanted to arm wrestle.

"Garth is going to be an actor," Debbie said, peeking round behind him.

Tentatively I placed my hand in his and he yanked me forwards, our hands chest height between us, and bumped me into a hug. "Thanks for having me here, man," he said, his other hand patting my back like he was burping me.

"That's fine. I know your dad," I said.

"Yeah, he told me." Pulling away he said, "Oh, he told me to give you this . . ." and dropped down onto one knee to search through a backpack. I wondered if he had a cagoule in there.

I looked at Debbie, who pulled the type of face normally only seen at a Take That concert. I sent her a frown. Upon receipt she pretended to struggle to rearrange her features into something less like a giddy schoolgirl, but they weren't having any of it.

"Here," he stood up, holding out an envelope. I opened it. Inside was a wad of money. I snapped it shut.

"Thank you," I said. "I'll phone him."

He nodded, smiling.

"Let me get you a drink, Garth, and something to eat. Are you hungry?" Debbie said, bustling past and snatching the envelope from my hand en route.

"I'm okay, thanks, Debs."

Debs? Debs? Nobody calls her Debs. She detests it.

"Okay. Well you let me know when you are," she said, not bothering to correct him.

"So, Debs has been telling me about your life and the animals. Sounds sick. Tell me about it."

I should have shaved my head this morning. I felt scruffy. I bet I looked scruffy. Blimey, standing next to Garth-Brad-Bloody-Pitt here even Ziggy would struggle not to look like a nerd, and not one of the new trendy breed of nerds either.

Look, I'm not competing with Garth, I'm really not. I couldn't, there'd be no point, I'm forty-seven and he's thirty years younger than me! So why am I holding my stomach in so much that it hurts? Why do I feel so short, fat and *old?* I don't want to feel this way. I don't want to stand next to him anymore.

I walked over to Debbie and put my hand on her while she made the tea, realised how possessive it must look, put my hand down, then thought sod it she is my wife and I have every right to be possessive over her, especially when confronted with someone so disgustingly good looking, and put my hand back. Then I put the other one on her too, just for good measure.

"I was telling Garth about the pigs and he's really keen to meet them," Debbie prompted, though I'm not sure which of us it was aimed at.

Garth took the hint first. "Yeah, the General sounds interesting. He's your best mate, isn't he, Simon?"

Was it just me or was he using our names more than felt comfortable?

"Is that weird?" I said, wondering how that statement must look to a seventeen-year-old, and making sure I laughed so I could backtrack about me and the General being best mates, if necessary.

"You should see some of my friends."

"Your dad said you were in with a bit of a gang."

It was his turn to laugh. "Not quite a gang as you might imagine. Most of them are actors like me. We're not exactly the ronx, man, but Mum and Dad heard that a couple of them were into drugs and panicked. Thing is, there have been drugs around me since Year 6 at school, but I suppose I never really said much about it because it's not my thing, you know?" As he spoke he dug out his mobile, a nice shiny new one, and started tapping. "No signal."

"No," Debbie said. "Although you might get one on the doorstep. If you want to use the phone you can always use the house phone. Did you want to let your mum know you arrived safely?"

"Yeah, and my girlfriend," he said, still looking at his phone.

"Your mum mentioned you had a girlfriend. What's her name?" Debbie asked.

"Sophie. Mum doesn't like her. She's a dancer."

Debbie handed him a tea. "She didn't say anything to me about not liking her. What type of dancer?"

She's a dancer and his mum doesn't approve. Which is it, lap or pole?

"Ballet. She used to be in the Royal School of Ballet. Here . . ." he swished his phone a few times, then twisted it so we could see. It was a picture of a ballerina en pointe and her arms making a circle around her head. Beautiful, I mean staggeringly beautiful. I felt bad about the lap or pole thought.

"I bet you thought I was going to say lap dancer," he said, grinning at me.

I gave him my best "*what are you talking about?*" look but didn't back it up with any words as I didn't trust them not to sound false.

He said, "I'm going to see if I can get a signal on the doorstep. Is it okay if I take this with me, Debs?" gesturing at the tea. "Debs" told him not to be stupid and to treat everything as if he was at home, and closed the kitchen door behind him so he had some privacy.

As soon as Garth was outside and we were alone I said, "All right, Debs?"

212

She sighed. "I just didn't want to sound picky as soon as he got here. I'll correct him next time he says it."

"Nothing to do with the fact that you fancy him?"

"*I do not fancy him*! I'm old enough to be his mother!"

"Grandmother, actually," I said, and started going through the maths. It was tight, but it worked; if Debbie had a daughter at fifteen, and then that daughter also had a child at fifteen —

"Thanks. Thanks a lot," she said.

"Sorry. I just didn't expect him to be . . . quite so . . ."

"Good looking?"

"Mmm, and I don't like it that you've noticed."

She burst out laughing. "Difficult to miss. He's not what I expected at all. No wonder his mum's so proud of him. Mind you, I do get the impression there's more going on here than we've been lead to believe."

"In what way?"

She thought for a moment. "I'm not sure. Some of the things Fi said about him don't quite add up now I've met him. Let's face it, if you're a mum to that," she pointed at the door, though I suspect she meant the boy who stood the other side of it, "you'd hardly describe him as anything less than perfect. But she sounded really worried about him."

"Well, I'm sure you'll wheedle it out of him. Just try to mother him as opposed to fawning all over him, okay?"

"*I do not fawn!*"

"Shush, he'll hear you."

Whispered shout, "*I don't fawn*! Okay, it was funny to see your face when he walked in and I admit I played on that a bit. There's no denying he is good looking, but I was only messing about. I'll try to be more mothering towards him in future. Tuck him in at night, read him a bedtime story, that sort of thing." She was grinning ear to ear.

Honestly, she was never like this when she was a solicitor.

I picked up my mug and took a sip, more to allow a beat to pass in the conversation than for any desire to drink. Then I said, "We've got a problem on the land."

Instantly her face switched to worry. "What?"

I closed my eyes and sighed. "The chickens. The new ones. The ones we got yesterday . . . A fox got in." I opened my eyes.

"No. *Please*, no." Tears fell in thick lines down her face. "Did any of them survive?"

I shook my head, feeling that sense of anger return, but rather than make me want to punch a wall, it revealed itself in tears.

She moved in and rested her head on my shoulder. "Oh Simon, they were so happy. Oh, no. Oh, no. That's not fair. How'd it get in?"

"I don't know. I didn't hang around. I couldn't. I'll work it out tonight."

She started sobbing and I held her. I felt utterly deflated.

214

Release the teenager (into our world)

I can handle dead bodies. Of course I get upset over losing a life, but the body that is left behind I don't fear. Sometimes I think should, bearing in mind the terror I used to feel as a child surrounding death. Maybe I've got used to it. God, that's a terrible thing to think, that I've got so used to handling dead bodies that it no longer affects me. Does that make me a monster? I hope not.

The Top Gun Chickens were where I'd left them, in a heap on the floor of the stable. One by one I placed them carefully into a bag.

Garth was up at the house. I could hardly expect his first trip down onto the land to include dealing with a pile of dead chickens. It didn't bother me that he'd walked in on Debbie and me hugging and crying. Crying's part of living. An essential part, especially living out here doing what we do. I don't think it makes me weak because I get upset when things die, and I hope Garth won't either. Doing all this with the animals is emotional, it really is, and sometimes — a lot of the time, actually — you've got to let it out or it will clot inside you. So you let it out, and if that means crying, so what? That's not a bad thing. Then I can deal with the bodies left behind.

Wherever you are, Top Gun Chickens, I hope you're flying way up high in the sky.

Finishing off the rounds I chopped wood, then drove the quad bike home.

"Garth is chief fire maker for the week," Debbie announced as I walked in.

Sitting in front of a blazing fire with an expression I couldn't quite read but seemed to be a mix of pride, happiness and something like embarrassment, was a much younger-looking Garth. Maybe it was the fact that he was sitting cross-legged and his hair was different. No hat, combed out, it made him look about twelve. Curled up next to him with his head in Garth's lap was Solly.

"Nice job!" I said, looking at the fire and hauling the sacks of freshly cut logs over and between us, stacking them in the recess.

"I've never lit a fire in a house before," he said.

I laughed. It sounded a funny way of putting it. "Long as you keep it in the grate."

"What's that?"

I pointed at the log burner. "That."

He nodded, picked up the poker and prodded a log. "I love it. I could just do this all day."

Gathering the empty sacks I said, "Good. Believe me, by the end of the winter it becomes a chore. Talking of which, tomorrow you can chop the wood if you like?"

"How do you do that?"

"Seriously? With an axe," I said.

"Yeah, I'll do that! I'll do that all day long!"

Oh don't tease me! Trying not to look too delighted at the prospect of a week without logging I stashed the bags by the back door then went up to shower and change.

Dinner was pizza. Anything based on fast food is affectionately known as slut food.

"I can't believe you don't get deliveries. I couldn't live without 'em," he said around a mouthful while at the same time reaching for yet another slice.

"We kind of do," I said. "I phone Debbie and say, 'sweetheart, can we have slut food tonight, please?' and it arrives on the table."

"This pizza is ridiculous. I can't believe you even made the base!" He was doing a lot of can't believing, so much so that I had the urge to give him a taste of homemade butter and see if I could get him to say, "I can't believe it's not butter."

"Wine?" I said. They both lifted their glasses and I poured.

"*Whoah-whahhhaa*," he said, tasting it, eyes streaming and mouth gasping like a fish out of water.

Debbie and I both tasted ours.

"Not bad," Debbie said.

I said, "I agree."

"Dandelion?"

"Hum-mm. Broke out the good stuff for tonight."

He tried to speak again, but something similar to before came out, "*Whahaah*."

"You're turning red, old boy. Everything okay?" I said. "Would you like me to hit you on the back?"

He looked panicked and shook his head vigorously.

"Well, if you change your mind, do let me know."

After a while he calmed down, even going as far as to brave another sip. "Takes a bit of getting used to, doesn't it?" he said.

At five o'clock the following morning I knocked on Garth's door and went in.

"What time is it? It feels as though I've only just come to bed," he said.

I plonked a coffee down beside him.

"That depends on what time you actually came to bed."

"Three. Or half past, I think."

"Then you're right, you have only just come to bed," I said brightly. "But now, it's time to get up! It's a beautiful day out there!" I pulled the curtains open to reveal a world so dark the only way I knew it was pouring with rain was because I could hear it.

"It's still dark."

"Best time of day."

"I can smell coffee."

I told him it was beside him.

"I drink tea."

Stroppy teenager.

Downstairs Debbie said, "You look pleased with yourself."

"I've just woken Garth up."

"Wicked. He won't see the funny side of it, you know — you will look after him today, won't you?"

"Unless Senorita takes a shine to him, he'll be fine."

Not long after that Garth emerged, stumbling past us into the kitchen, saying, "They get better treatment than this at Guantanamo Bay. Who's Senorita?"

"Eagle ears. She's a dusky maiden who's likely to have a crush on you, and do feel free to interpret that quite literally," I said as Debbie handed him breakfast.

"Thank you, but I think it might be a bit early for me to eat. Is it okay if I have something later?"

We both assured him it was fine.

218

"So, this is what five in the morning looks like," he said yawning and slouching down on the sofa next to Solly, who wagged his tail and kind of thought about playing before deciding it was too early even for him and flopped back down again, head in Garth's lap. "Hello boy," Garth said to the dog, then, "I haven't been up this early since Christmas Day when I was six. Can I light the fire?"

He did and tended it with one hand while the other flicked about on his phone. "Have you any idea how slow your broadband is?" he said. "I ran a test, point three upload and point eight download. That's dial-up speed. How'd you cope, man?"

"On the subject of which," I said, "Can I ask you a favour while you're here? How hot are you on social media?"

He looked at me as though I'd asked him if he'd ever worn trouers. "You know?" he said.

"Great. Can you show me how they work?"

It's fine for Ziggy to put social media on his list of How To avoid The Onset Of Middle Age commandments, but where do you begin? I do Twitter and a bit of Facebook, but that's about it. I've heard of Pinterest, and Vine, and YouTube obviously, and LinkedIn, but I've no idea how they work. At the point where the internet started getting interesting I booked myself out of the game by moving away from London and focusing all my energies on surviving in this alien world of pigs, chickens and self-sufficiency. Sure I could figure it out, but it would take hours, and I didn't have hours. The answer, I hoped, was Garth.

But Garth was a teenager, and therefore a git. Grinning, he said, "Sure, pops."

No snacking, Senorita, save yourself for breakfast — which is heading your way on two tender seventeen-year-old legs.

"Come on," I said. "It's nearly light. Time to get going."

Normally a chunk of Debbie's day would be set aside for placating anyone we owed money to, but today was different. Thanks to the envelope Garth handed over from his father, which was enough to pay for the chickens and the turkeys with a fair amount left over, the phone calls would be asking for bank details so she could send them money. It made a nice change. Then she could move onto the normal everyday matters of doing the books, the accounts, the farm records and promoting the business while Garth and I swanned about with the animals. It's called pulling to your strengths, and my particular strength is swanning. It's on my CV right next to socialising.

Approaching the quad bike defences Garth said, "Jeez, those cows are huge and they don't look friendly at all. I think I'll wait for you here, man."

"Coward." Gathering Dex onto the back of the quad I drove out, stopped for Garth on the other side of the cows and continued down onto the land.

Of course I expected to feel a sense of shame bumping along the farm track past the General's house; that higgledy-piggledy hodgepodge in the woods, but I didn't. I didn't even mind when we stopped and Garth just sat there, open mouthed as he took in the variety of accommodation and all the little expectant eyes peering out at us. Actually I felt pretty good about it all. I'm not sure if that's something to do with how far I've come or more to do with Garth's reaction, but I didn't harp on about it, after all this was the boy's first trip out of London, so I guess anything that wasn't grey and brick-built would be jaw dropping.

Dex jumped down and I said to Garth, "Come on, you need to meet Senorita."

Together we walked over to the trailer and I reached in and unlatched her bedroom door.

"*No way!*" Garth screamed, and I really mean screamed, all high-pitched and squeaky as Senorita stomped her way down the ramp, looked about from side to side for someone to duff-up, saw nobody worth taking on — and that included me and would have included Garth if he hadn't been hiding behind me — and made her way over for a morning drink.

"She's a micro pig," I said. "Aren't you, pretty girl?"

With her mouth full she snorted a response that sounded like a swear word. I really must teach her some manners.

Garth was still behind me, his hands on my shoulders aiming me so that I was always between them.

"Will you put me down?" I said.

"Do I have to?"

"Yes!"

"She looks dangerous."

"That's just because you don't know her. She's very sweet and misunderstood."

"She looks like she wants to kill something, or is that the bit that's misunderstood?"

"No, that bit's accurate," I admitted.

"I should have worn my trainers, I can run faster in them. Be honest with me, is she safe?"

Huff. "Probably."

Then Senorita's idea of Mr Perfect wandered past us in the shape of Dex, and she morphed into a sexpot and swished her mighty hips into a trot after him.

"She fancies him rotten," I said.

"*She's piff?* That's weird."

Huh? "Piff? I've never heard that before."

He shrugged. "It means fanciable."

Last on Ziggy's list: language. Piff. With the word logged and stored, I said, "Anyway, you okay to help with the rounds?"

"Long as I don't have to go near her."

I assured him he wouldn't.

"Poultry next."

"What's that?"

"You don't know what poultry are?"

He shook his head no. "Should I?"

"Um, no, not at all. Tell me, what do you know about geese?"

"Not much."

Come on, hand on heart, be honest, if you were in my position, tell me you wouldn't do the same thing?

"Okay, that's cool. That door over there," I pointed. "If you could go and open it for me."

He walked off and I leant against the trailer. Oh, the anticipation . . .

222

I watched him reach out his hand for the latch.

The geese were going berserk inside.

Hand touched latch.

Geese screeched ever louder.

Hand opened latch.

Geese were going *mental*.

Hand grasped the door, and pulled . . .

In a *blur* the geese were out, flapping and hissing and spitting, and in a beautifully choreographed twirl arced towards Garth. Who stood there, rooted to the spot. You'd think he'd have run. You'd think he could have worked that out for himself. But no, for some bizarre reason he put his hands up. Probably something to do with all the late-night cop shows he watches. In the old days anyone violent approached and you'd leg it; nowadays you raise your hands. It's a lot less effort, and I get that, but I can't help feeling it loses a certain something. Fitness, if nothing else.

To be fair, in most languages lifting your hands is the universal sign for, "I don't want to play." Unfortunately the geese didn't speak any of those languages, and lunged at him anyway.

I'm sorry, I know it's wicked to feed a young person to your animals, and I'm not proud of myself, I'm really not, but it was hilarious. Realising they weren't taking any notice of his raised hands, he switched to waving them about so he looked like a cartoon karate character who'd wandered into a swarm of bees.

Declaring it a draw before one of them got hurt, and by one of them I mean Garth, I wandered in and broke up the rumble. Incredibly pleased with themselves, the geese walked off, chests out, heads up and that waddling gait that made them look like they had wet knickers on. Presumably for them this was a great start to their day and they screeched their pleasure loud and proud.

Garth and I both watched them leave. He was panting. "They're dangerous," he said.

"Oh, I don't know."

"One of them bit my junk," he said, looking down and prodding his crotch. Seconds passed while he made a thorough inspection, then he looked up, called me a bastard, and started laughing. Instantly we were both in bits, laughing so hard we were choking and fighting for air.

In a brief lull I said, "I'm sorry, I didn't know they were going to bite your dick." Which was meant to sound heartfelt and apologetic, but just came across as funny, and we were off again.

"I've got goose dick," Garth yelled.

It took us ages to calm down, but when we did, any distance that a thirty-year age gap might have held between us was gone. Laughter does that.

Garth's story — or at least the important bits

"Amber, Bee and Curry, meet Garth," I said, opening the door to the goats' cupboard. The introduction made me think of Ziggy. I wondered how he was doing. I wondered if he was okay and resolved to call him

224

later, if nothing other than to tell him about Garth's goose dick.

As usual Curry was first out and fawned all over Garth while I made ready the milking platform and unwrapped a fresh bowl from the stack. Then I got Amber and jumped her up.

Leaning against the wall, his hands full of Curry, Garth said, "What did my dad tell you about me?"

"Not much," I said, squeezing her teats so that milk shot out. "Both your parents seem very proud of you."

"They don't like my girlfriend. That kind of makes things difficult. My mum won't even talk about her."

I thought, they didn't say anything about not liking her.

"She's a bit older than me," he said.

Okay, starting to make sense.

"How old is she?"

"Thirty-two."

I did the maths and smiled.

"She's divorced, but no children," he said.

"How long have you been together?"

"About a year."

Maybe it's something to do with milking that brings people out of themselves. Ziggy, now Garth. They should use it as a chatshow theme on TV, call it something like *Spill Your Secrets In the Milking Parlour*, and get the guests to talk about their love lives. I'd watch that.

"How'd you meet?"

"At a party. I spilt a drink on her and we went outside and talked and talked and talked until it was morning. I got in so much trouble for getting home late. Mum went ballistic. How long have you been with Debbie?"

"Twenty-four years. Nearly twenty-five."

"Do you talk a lot? Me and Sophie talk all the time, and for like, hours."

"That why you were up so late last night?" I guessed.

He nodded. "It's not just on your front doorstep that you can get a phone signal," he said. "You can also get one if you hang out the bedroom window."

"Do you worry about the age gap?"

"No. Sophie does sometimes. I know she wishes I was older, and there are some friends of hers that she doesn't want me to meet because she's worried what they'd think. But I can't magic myself older, I am what I am. I don't act seventeen. I'm pretty mature for my age. Sophie says I am anyway."

I wanted to ask him why his mum couldn't discuss his relationship with Sophie, but having had a turbulent relationship with my own mother I knew how tricky that connection could be. I was born in the late 1960s when very little was known and even less understood about postnatal depression, and my mother had a severe case and just couldn't bond with me when I came along. Recently I've been told she even went to see a bunch of psychiatrists, which was pretty much unheard of back then, and did everything she could to overcome it, but nothing worked. It's not her fault. It must have been a bitch having a baby she didn't want. I had never thought it affected me much until I had a sheep who rejected her lamb and refused to let it feed or come anywhere near her, and that really freaked me out. If you're wondering why I've never had children of my own, or why I am the way I am, there you go, that's probably got something to do with it.

"How well do you get on with your mum?" I asked, still milking.

"Until I told her about Sophie, we got on brilliantly. Recently, not so much."

"You don't feel like you can talk to her about your girlfriend?"

He shrugged. "It bothers her that she's older than me."

"Has she said that to you?"

"I know my mum, man."

With the bowl nearly full and Amber empty, I let her jump down.

Laughing so he wouldn't take it the wrong way, I said, "They are only looking out for you. That is a parent's job."

He didn't laugh back, but he didn't seem to take it the wrong way either. "Well if they're only looking out for me, can't they see that she makes me happy and we want to be together?"

If it was Ziggy or someone I knew better, I could delve a little deeper, but I didn't really know Garth from Adam so I changed the subject. "Tell me about acting."

"What do you want to know?"

I thought, I want to know what expectations you've set for yourself. I want to know what you expect from life. I want to know what path that puts you on. And in return, I want to tell you that although it may not seem like it, that path you've chosen isn't a stroll along, it's a race, and one day, on a day that you have no control over, that race will come to an end and you'll need to tally up and have a little look-see how far you've gone, and how well you've done, and then compare that to the expectations you set for yourself right at the start.

"I need to do breakfast for this lot," I said. "All the feed's in the caravan. You want to come and get it with me?"

"Sure."

I picked up the bowl and made to walk out, but he stopped me. "Is that edible?" he asked.

"It's milk. All the tea you've been drinking, the glass of milk you had last night, this is where it comes from."

"You don't buy it?" he said, stunned.

I shook my head. "No, we don't buy any."

"But that's fresh, right?"

It was still frothy and warm in my hands. "About as fresh as it gets."

"Can I taste it?"

We don't sell it — nobody drinks it but us — so I handed him the bowl and watched him take a slurp out of the side. When he put it down he had a milk moustache.

"It tastes like warm milk. That's wicked," he said, grinning from ear to ear.

I took the bowl back. "Come on, I've got to get these something to eat or there'll be a riot. Have you been on TV?"

228

He'd had screen tests, even been called back, but nothing more. Yet. We walked, all of us — *all of us* — to the caravan. "This is where it gets tricky," I said, holding onto the caravan door. Behind us Curry head-butted a lamb, who skipped backwards into Senorita, who jumped about in a tight circle scattering chickens. Garth looked terrified. "Don't look so worried, none of them are going to hurt you, they're just very keen on food. You up for a challenge?" I didn't wait for an answer in case he said no and continued, "You start walking slowly that way while I get the breakfasts ready and then I'll make a run for it and have a head start getting back to the barn before this mob. You good? Good."

I went inside while he shuffled in the direction I'd pointed. You just can't beat cannon fodder in the morning.

Scoops made up and ready to go, I opened the door. The second I had, I heard Garth scream, "There he is," and as I dashed out and bolted for the barn, the silly sod overtook me as we all rushed for the barn, closely followed by Curry, Amber and Bee, several sheep, a couple of lambs, Senorita and a flock of chickens. As each group passed they took a moment to look across at me, as if to say, "I've no idea who he is, but isn't he fun!" and charged on. I was last. By the time I reached the barn Garth was pinned up against a wall by the animals, hands above his head (why does he keep doing that?).

I nipped in and put the feed in each spot.

"Come on, come and get it while it's hot . . ."

They didn't need asking twice, each group diving into their own individual areas.

"This is insane," Garth said, hands on knees, panting. "Are we done now?"

"Oh no. Now it's time for your audience with the General."

There's probably a statistic somewhere of how many best friends the average person has throughout their life. I'm not talking about the lucky few who sit next to someone in kindergarten and they're still besties when they're in the pension queue at the Post Office seventy years later. I mean the average person. Joe Bloggs. I bet it's higher than you'd imagine.

My list of best friends runs as long as my arm and ends up somewhere around my wrist with the General.

I wonder what happened to some of the others? Friends from early jobs. From the pub I went to every night when I was in my early twenties and I knew everyone and everyone knew me, *Cheers* style. But most of all, school friends; Keith, Glen, Richard, Nicola, Zoe, Leslie, Little Mark, Ben and his brother Tango, Paul, Toby, Bret, Gareth, Duncan and of course Chris C. Names I hadn't thought about in thirty years — except Chris C, whom it would be very difficult not to think about considering his son was walking beside me. I wonder what happened to all of them?

"Do you keep in contact with the people you went to school with?" I asked Garth as we made our way along the muddy path towards the General.

"Some. Mostly through Facebook. You?"

230

"Not as many as I'd like to," but it suddenly felt really important that I did. "Come on, let's see if the old boy's in." We'd reached the bottom of the General's enclosure and I led Garth up to the gate. Inside I could see the General lazing with his wife-of-right-now.

Garth took one look and, backing away, said, "No way! U-huh, he's enormous! No way am I going in there with him. I expected a nice little pig, not . . . that!"

"Shut up, you'll hurt his feelings." Then to the General I called over the gate, "All right, General, how's it going? This is Garth, he's an idiot."

"How big is he?"

"About 350 kgs, but he's very big-boned."

"*Three-fifty kgs!*"

"Yeah, bless him. Come on, come and meet him," and I made towards the gate.

"Is it safe? I mean, be honest with me, is it safe?" Garth said, his face all concerned.

I thought about it. "Probably. Come on, you tart, come and say hello."

"Any, um, health and safety tips I should know about?"

"Yeah, try not to let him eat you."

"Thanks for that."

We went inside. Of course I stood between Garth and the General. Of course I never once took my eyes off the General. Read his body language. Sent chill-out messages to him that everything was fine. That Garth was a friend. Not a threat. Nothing to worry about, because, after all, the General might be my best friend but he was still a 350 kg boar.

Explaining how to approach him; side on, head tipped forwards, shoulders slumped, arms loose, passive, non-confrontational, Garth went over and stroked the General's shoulder.

"Talk to him," I said, crouching down beside them.

Giggling nervously he said, "I don't know what to say."

"Tell him . . . tell him about Sophie. Tell him about the first time you saw her dance. She's a ballerina, right?"

For a second he looked panicked, then he calmed down and started talking. It was probably the actor in him, that ability to deliver under the extreme pressure of cameras and crew yet come across as though he was totally relaxed and comfortable. Okay, this was a different type of pressure, but I figured the theory was sound. And it worked.

He told the General they'd been going out for a couple of months when Sophie invited him to a performance. It was the first time he'd ever been to a ballet. He'd had no idea what to expect, but he loved it, and Sophie was amazing. She wasn't the lead, so she didn't have any solo dances, but when she was on the stage the whole place lit up. She was so beautiful and delicate and beautiful and elegant and beautiful and beautiful, it made you want to rip your heart out and use it as a tissue to wipe your eyes — apparently.

"I can't believe I've just told that story to a pig," Garth said, still stroking the General and showing no signs of moving away.

232

"He's a good listener."

Not wanting to outstay our welcome, we left the General and his wife-of-right-now to contemplate the ballet — I do like my oinkers to be cultured — finished off the rounds and went back up to the house.

Walking into the kitchen Solly greeted us like we'd been gone forever. The radio was on in the background. Radio 2.

"I'm more a Kwabs man myself," I said, nodding. "Along with, you know, Woman's Hour. Early Drenge, that sort of thing."

"Who?" Debbie said, then turning to Garth, "Are you hungry?"

"Actually, I am, Debs," he said.

"So am I, *Debs*," I said. She caught my eye and made a brushing, dismissing motion with her hand.

"Sausage sandwich, Garth?" she said.

"Yes please."

"Tomato ketchup?"

"Yes please."

"Right, you boys make the bread, I'll get on with the butter and the ketchup then we'll all make the sausages together, okay?"

I opened the cupboard and fished out the bread flour and the yeast.

"You're kidding, right?" Garth said.

"Nope."

"Why don't you just buy all that stuff?"

What were we supposed to do, tell a seventeen-year-old that we couldn't afford it? No way. So Debbie sidestepped the question by going up on tiptoes and gently slapped the back of his head, told him not to question his elders and betters and to get on with it. Unfortunately he mistook "Get on with it" for, "Why don't you take our phone out and play with that while we do all the work?" It's easy to confuse the two.

As I kneaded the dough and Debbie whizzed cream into butter while heating ingredients together on the hob for the tomato ketchup, Garth entertained us beautifully with a teenager's take in our intermittent mobile phone signal and slow internet connection, which was nice.

"What if I miss a call from my agent for an audition?" he said, suddenly panicked, and went up to his room where he said he could get a signal if he hung out the window.

"What was he like down on the land?" Debbie whispered.

"You don't need to whisper," I said at normal volume. "Can't you ear the music?"

For a while we both listened. It sounded tinny and speeded up and rubbish and the words were garbled, which probably meant that whoever they were they were almost certainly The Beatles of the current generation.

"He was fine," I said, carrying on. "I got him to let the geese out."

Debbie drew in a breath.

"One of them bit his crotch and nipped his willy. It was hilarious."

"Simon!"

234

"He's fine. Okay his future children may all have a healthy phobia of geese, but other than that it's unlikely to affect him. Much. Oh, and I need to tell you about Sophie, his girlfriend. She's way older than him by some fifteen years."

"Really?"

I filled her in on all the gory details, then she quizzed me for a further ten minutes until she was satisfied she'd extracted every nugget of information. Then she had the barefaced cheek to call me a man because I hadn't found out all the details she felt she needed.

Shaping the dough and transferring it to a baking sheet I left the bread to rise.

"How did you get on this morning?" I asked.

"Bathroom," she said, spinning around to face me. "Oh! My! God! How many towels does that boy need? The toilet seat was up and he clearly can't aim! But, that's not the worst of it. Toothpaste. It was everywhere! Spray on the mirror, the taps, all around the sink, the side of the bath, the floor! I mean, what does he do, brush his teeth while doing the pogo?"

"Aah, do you remember the pogo?" You have to be in a certain emotional place to get nostalgic over a jumping up and down punk dance.

"Yeah, but I never did it while brushing my teeth! In some ways he's really mature, but in other things he's still such a kid."

"He is only seventeen," I said.

"With a thirty-two-year-old girlfriend."

"True."

Grand Designs for Senorita

Between us we made sausages, not your standard banger either, but gorgeous continental sausages with garlic and nutmeg and white wine. They smelt scrummy.

"Are you getting on with him okay?" she asked when all the skins were stuffed and the sausages linking and twisted in threes.

"Yes. The geese attacking him really broke the ice. It's funny, everyone seems to open up to me when I milk the goats."

"Did you tell him about Ziggy's list?"

"No."

"Are you going to?"

"I don't know. No, I don't think so. Why, what made you think of that?"

She leant against the side. The sink was piled high with washing up, but we'd do that in a minute.

"I thought that was why you were keen on him coming down," he shrugged. "Someone young in the house you can learn from."

In my mind I'm not as transparent as clearly I am. In my mind I'm a mass of subtlety and stealth so complex there are chess masters who'd struggle to keep up with my thought processes. "That's part of it," I said, adding, "Along with the money."

She came over and said, "Just be careful. I worry about you. Garth, Ziggy, even me, when you talk to us we all bring our own baggage. That can be good, but it can also muddle things. I couldn't live with someone

236

like Garth, or Ziggy for that matter." I went to say something but she cut me off. "And I'm worried you're trying to be like them because you see them as young and trendy and a good thing, and the one thing you're not factoring in, the one thing you're ignoring that is more important than anything else, is you. You're not factoring in you. You're so intent on being someone else you're forgetting who you are, and I . . . love . . . you. It breaks my heart that you no longer like the music we used to love together, or I walk in and you're watching a TV programme that you would have run a mile from a month ago. I'm scared you're going to go too far with all of this and become a different person. That a gap will develop between us and I'm going to lose you. I'm scared I'm losing you already."

"You're not going to lose me," I said, opening my arms and wrapping them around her. "That's never going to happen. I love you. All I'm doing is trying to figure out how to get older without plunging into old-man phase. That's all. Maybe maintain a scrap of youth before it's all too late and I go shopping for a Zimmer frame."

"It doesn't help that you're blocking me from your emails. We share the same computer. I want you to reverse that. I want you to let me read them again. Now is not the time to be secretive, okay? And these bloody parcels you keep getting . . ."

She went over to the table, picked two up and threw them at me.

I bent to pick them up. They were so well inspected they looked like a child had been left alone and told not to touch, but curiosity had got the better of them. The corners were even torn a little.

"If you start laughing at me, I swear to God I will fucking kill you, okay?" she said, switching from concerned loving wife to murdering angry woman in a heartbeat.

"I'm not going to laugh."

Two hours later and lunch was ready.

Garth came down and brought his handheld game console thingy with him. I wanted to ask him to show me how to play it, but I looked across at Debbie first and she was staring really hard at me, so I didn't.

The sausage sandwiches were ace, and we all scoffed every scrap. Afterwards I took Garth back down onto the land for an afternoon of graft.

"What's the plan?" he said as we wandered into the chicken field.

Senorita, Curry and one of the lambs came bundling up.

"I'm desperate to sort out a permanent home for Senorita. Living in a trailer is really not good. She needs a place of her own."

"Okay. So what does that mean, we have to make her a house?"

I nodded, "Yep."

"How do we do that?"

"That's a good question. I don't know. We need to improvise. Be creative." I shrugged, "Botch something together."

Having realised that we weren't there to provide afternoon tea and scones, pig, goat and lamb all trundled off.

"Where do we start?" Garth said.

238

"We walk around looking for things to use."

We walked, and he said, "It's not exactly the way I'd envisioned working."

"No," I agreed.

We walked some more. "I was hoping you'd have a tractor. You know, one of those open-top ones."

"Sorry to disappoint."

"And fields we'd have to drive around all day. And make baystacks."

"Wrong time of year."

"Does that happen in the summer?"

"Not here, no. Not enough land. We're supposed to be looking for things to build a Senorita house with."

"There's nothing here other than trees and . . . bits of scrap."

"Yeah, well, it's the bits of scrap that we need. And possibly some trees."

Having made a complete circuit of the land, we went back to the chicken field and sat on a clean bit of grass.

"What have we got to work with?" I said.

He didn't answer, just raised his eyebrows. So I answered, "There's a double-glazed window that might be useful. A shower door. Couple of pallets. An old freezer. A broken trailer with a wheel missing. Some fence posts."

"It's like an episode of *Bargain Hunt*."

"You watch that?"

"I'm an out-of-work actor and a college student, which is another way of saying I'm addicted to daytime TV."

"I thought . . . Doesn't matter."

"How about . . . what if we got the freezer, tipped it on its side so the door opens up, then we could secure the door so it's like a roof, put the shower door one side, the window on the other, and kind of do something to the front to make a door . . ."

DIY programmes clearly weren't off the daytime viewing list either.

"For a useless teenager, Garth, you're something of a genius," I said.

Beaming, he said, "Would that work?"

"No, she'd smash it down in a day and probably eat the glass — anything glass can only be used as a roof, *but*, we could take the essence of your idea, the freezer, and work with that. I was using it as extra storage, but every time I opened it to get something out or put something in, the chickens would jump inside, so I gave up with it after a while. How about if we cut an opening into the door and then bolted the door onto the main frame of the freezer so it no longer opened? Then we could lay the freezer onto its side and put loads of straw inside. That would be snug, wouldn't it? She'd love that."

"I still prefer my idea. How are you going to cut a hole in the freezer door?"

"No idea. Never done it before. With a saw, I guess. I have some precision tools . . ."

Together we emptied the freezer and dragged it into the chicken field before doing battle to remove the door. Freezer doors are tough to take off. Those suckers are not meant to be tampered with.

When it was off I went for the precision tools. It took a while to rummage through but eventually I found a saw that had almost half its teeth intact. Back at the freezer I handed the saw to Garth who looked at it and declared, "That's a precision tool?" but started sawing anyway.

We had to take frequent breaks as assorted animals came over to check on progress. Except Senorita, who was eerily silent on the matter — maybe she understood the prospect of sleeping in a freezer, which now I come to think of it is a little like us sleeping in a coffin since a freezer is where most pigs end up. But she wouldn't know that, would she?

Start, stop, start, stop, brush chickens away, start, stop, start, stop, remove sheep, start, stop, start, stop, push Amber, Bee and Curry away, start, stop, start, stop . . .

"Hang on," I said for the umpteenth time, grabbing a curious goose who was checking things out underneath and about to be decapitated with Garth's energetic sawing.

"Oh for God's sake!" he said, throwing all his toys out of the freezer. "This is doing my bloody head in!" and he stormed off in a red-faced temper tantrum.

Shame, we were getting on so well.

It's no good, we'll all have to go Garth-hunting

Debbie isn't losing me.

Is she?

I don't feel any sense of a distance developing between us. She can still (annoyingly) read my mind and (even more annoyingly) plant the odd idea in there just by thinking it, which must mean there's a strong connection between us. Doesn't it?

Beside me Curry leaned against my leg and lovingly prodded a horn into my thigh. Taking the hint, I reached down and stroked her neck.

It had been nearly an hour since Garth's little storming-off sessson. So far I had avoided going to find him, but if he wasn't back soon, I would have to. "I'll use you as a sniffer goat to sniff him out," I told Curry. Not to be outdone, Dex muscled in on the act, leaning against my other leg and staring up at me. In the interest of balance I said to him, "And you, Dexy, you can help sniff him out too."

I wondered where Garth was. He wasn't at the house because I spoke to Debbie, telling her what had happened and asked her to phone me if he turned up. We talked briefly about emails and who she'd spoken to, but not about anything else. Nothing important. Couldn't help searching her voice for any hint of strain between us, but everything seemed fine. Relaxed. Easy. Normal. As if the conversation we'd had earlier about her being scared had never happened. So I hung up without telling her the things I should have said to her.

The freezer was finished, the opening cut and what's left of the door bolted back on. It made a neat house. I wanted to show Senorita, but she'd disappeared too. I was beginning to think it was me.

It had been almost twenty-four hours since Garth arrived. A full day of having a teenager in our home and in our lives. Did I feel different? Did I feel rejuvenated?

242

Not really. All I felt so far was the urge to look up old school friends on Facebook. I guess Garth wasn't as extreme as I thought he would be. Sure, there were loads of differences between us, he explodes toothpaste for one, but there was also a lot of common ground. Maybe he was more mature than I thought he'd be — he was certainly more mature than I was at his age.

Digging out my phone I went through the album list until I found the Clash and hit play. The sound of "White Riot" filled the air. It made me smile.

It's not impossible for me to access the teenager inside myself. Not impossible, but it is uncomfortable. I was just so angry when I was young. I should have done something with all that energy, turned it into something positive, but I didn't. Instead I went down the destructive route. Got involved in some things I shouldn't. There were fights. Some substances. Some shenanigans. Things that make me squirm to think about now. But very early on I realised I didn't want to become that guy, so I changed. Turned things around. That's when I formulated my list of expectations and set off in a new direction towards them. Soon after I also fell in love with Debbie. That helped.

The chicken inspection crew were checking out the freezer-house. Apart from the straw bed I put in that needed kicking and scratching about, it seemed to pass the test.

There was still no sign of Senorita.

Or Garth.

Still, I was pleased to tick off another item on my list of things to worry about:

7. Work out where to house Senorita Small, the rescued micro pig who isn't a micro pig.

There can't be many things left on the list to work through now.

"White Riot" finished and "London's Burning" started. Music's okay for a while, but I don't crave it the way I used to. If I'm honest, after a while it kind of drives me mad. Flicking through my phone I searched out a podcast and hit play on that, and "London's burning" faded out to make way for the podcast, fading up two middle-aged guys talking and laughing about life, love, sex, food, work, religion and politics — rock and roll for the over-forties.

It was no good, I'd have to go and find the idiot.

"Come on, guys, let's go Garth-hunting." Dex and Curry ran on ahead, but they didn't have far to go as Garth was in the first place we looked, the barn, and he wasn't alone. He was sitting in the straw cuddling Senorita, who was cuddling him back. Man and pig sharing a moment. They both looked up at me, and both grinned.

"Sorry, man, I was going to come back, but she came in and lay down next to me. What was the music you were listening to?"

"The Clash." I did a quick recap of the conversation I'd had with Debbie, the one where I hadn't realised he could hear me, and tried to remember if I'd said anything I shouldn't have. I didn't think I had.

"How's the freezer-house?"

"Finished."

"I don't know how you work like that. It was killing me."

I shrugged. "You get used to it."

"I suppose."

No apology? No, I'm sorry that I stormed off?

His phone rang and he answered it, "*Wassup?* Dude, I'm in bed with a Senorita. Na, I'm not fuckin' wid ya."

Maybe he's not that mature after all. I wonder if he speaks to his friends like that when he's with his girlfriend? I bet he doesn't. Leaving him to it I wandered off, and when I turned I saw Senorita had followed me. Great! Time for a viewing on her new home, I called her and together we went over to the freezer-house.

She was going to love it!

She was going to adore it!

A pad of her own, she was going to . . .

. . . Hate it.

She took one look, turned and ran away. She didn't even walk, she *ran*!

"Why'd she do that?" Garth said, coming up behind me.

"No idea. She just needs a bit of time. She'll come around — it's got to be better than sleeping in a trailer, surely? Actually, I've got an idea. I had put fresh straw in thinking it would be nice to have it all new and clean, but what I should have done is take her old bed that smells of her and use that. That way she'll recognise it as hers." And that's what we did, swapped the straw over so she had her old bed in there. But I needn't have bothered. She still hated it.

Evening rounds were interesting.

Whereas before Senorita was the first to be fed and put to bed because I could shut her in her trailer bedroom with her dinner, now that was no longer the case. The freezer-house was door-less.

As chaotic as the rounds seem, there is a system because it's vitally important that every group of animals gets their own dinner and does not share. You can't mix feed between different types of animals. That's a big no-no.

The problem was, although Senorita was a micro-pig, she was a hefty lump of about forty to fifty kgs, and bloodyminded with it. There was no way I could convince her to stand back while I fed the others on the promise that she'd get hers at the end. She was definitely a "I want it, and I want it *now!*" type of girl, and the thought of someone else getting in ahead of her was out of the piggin' question.

So I shut her in her old house first. Without dinner. She was not impressed, and demonstrated it by trashing the place and screeching her head off. It sounded as though I was decapitating her with my precision saw.

With all the others fed and put away, Garth and I returned to the trailer. Time had not mellowed her. Or turned the volume down.

"She's not impressed," I yelled over the noise.

"What?"

"I said, she's not impressed!"

"She's angry, man. Woo-hoo, reminds me of a girl I used to date."

Inside the bedroom she had utterly lost it; she was foaming at the mouth and her eyes were doing this mad spin-around thing, and all the while she was flinging herself against the walls and biting them.

"Have you read *Jane Eyre?*" I shouted, thinking of Mr Rocheser's wife.

He looked blank and shook his head. I thought he was an actor, aren't they supposed to do the classics?

"Doesn't matter. Okay, you open the door, I'll have the food ready and she'll follow me over to the freezer-house."

Holding up his hands and backing away he said, "No way, man! You want that action, you can do it yourself."

I couldn't blame him. Shame, though. I put my hand on the latch that held her bedroom door closed. The noise inside reached crescendo, as did the flinging and biting of the walls, though that was slightly less vocal. "Stand back! She's about to blow!"

In one swift motion I unlatched and opened the door . . . and legged it.

She came out like a cannonball, down the ramp and flying after me. The speed was breathtaking, especially from the point of view of the one pursued. Compared with a pissed off and hungry Senorita, geese were kitten play.

Not bothering with any niceties, I dumped the feed into the freezer-house and spun out of the way just in time to avoid her gnashers. She didn't even try to slow down until she was on top of the food, and you might think that by then it would have been too late, that the sheer momentum involved would render it impossible for a wobble-belly like her to go from flat-out top speed standstill without the residual energy going somewhere, which did. It went into her fat. She stopped, but her fat didn't. It all ruffled up her body in tidal waves. Then sank back into place.

"That was *ridiculous!*"

I was inclined to agree.

Finishing off the evening rounds I showed Garth how to chop wood and left him to it while I went back to check on Senorita. Dinner would be over and I expected to find her flopped out in the freezer-house, shattered after her hissy-fit and nestled in the straw, but it was empty. Where the heck was she? I walked the field, checked her old bedroom, searched all over, but she was nowhere to be seen.

What is it with the disappearing acts today?

In the end I found her asleep in Dex's house. Given the option it seemed she didn't want her own digs, she just wanted to sleep where her boyfriend stayed during the day. If I'd known that she could have done it ages ago. Senorita and Dex could hotbed, she having the night-time session, he the daytime. That works.

"So the freezer-house is no good?" Garth said when I told him what had happened. He was surrounded by chunks of wood and had an axe slung over one shoulder. "All that work we put in!"

"We? We?" I stuttered, launching into a Jim Carey-type impression of Garth storming off, all hips and hair and over-dramatic hand flourishes, complete with dialogue "This is doing my bloody head in!"

"That is not me!"

"'Tis."

"'Tisn't!"

"'Tis."

"Who's got the axe?"

"Good point." We bagged up the logs and went up to the house.

Garth showered first, and while he was in there I heard him playing some familiar music: The Clash. Charging down to Debbie I said, "My work on this planet is done!"

"What on earth are you talking about?"

"Listen."

She did. Then she said, "He's playing your music?"

I shook my head and held out my phone. "He's playing his own. I had it on earlier and he asked who it was. He must have down-loaded it. I'm so proud."

She didn't look as excited as I thought she would. I gave her a hug but Garth came in so we had to break away.

"I'll light the fire," he said, then turned and walked out. Debbie and I are very tactile. That's just how we are. I think it's nice. But it was beginning to feel as though there had been too many moments where he'd caught us and I didn't want him to feel like a gooseberry, so I didn't bring her back into my arms and went up to change.

When I came down the fire was alight and Garth was sitting in front of it playing on his game station thingy.

I pulled over the log basket and sat next to him, taking out the wooden spoon I'd started carving for Stafford, and began whittling.

"What are you doing?" he asked.

I told him. In response he laughed in my face, even putting his hand up a fraction too late so he accidentally-on-purpose didn't cover the explosive outburst.

Nice. Friendly.

"Sorry, I didn't mean to laugh."

Yeah you did.

"It's just, I can't imagine anyone being pleased to get a wooden spoon. Some things you do I admit are cool. But that ain't one of them."

Getting up I went into the kitchen. He was still laughing. I could hear him, and I got the impression I was supposed to hear him. Out of sight I gesticulated to Debbie in a way that said, "What the hell is up with him?"

"Why don't you two swap?" she said. "Garth, you carve the spoon while Simon beats your best score. What game are you playing?"

"*Call of Duty*. There isn't a best score, it's not that type of game."

"Well, have you got one that is like that?"

"I guess."

"Why don't you go and get it then?"

While he was upstairs she said, "He feels threatened. You make him nervous."

"*Me!*"

"Yes. Show him how to carve the spoon."

So when he came down, I did. He made it very clear he thought it was stupid and a waste of time, but once he got started he didn't stop. Meanwhile I played his game, a car chase through the streets that he seemed to delight in how realistic it was. Anyway, I was useless at it.

"Your game's rubbish," I said, crashing for the millionth time.

"Computer games have evolved over the last few years. Unless you're used to them, you probably wouldn't recognise them now. Anyway, you want to worry, I'm carving a wooden spoon!"

"I never got into computer games."

"I can tell. You must have a drawer full of homemade cutlery by now, though."

Side swiping my virtual car into a building, I said, "I heard you playing The Clash upstairs." It was a cheap point, but they all count.

He shrugged. "Whateva."

Him: Whittle, whittle, whittle.

Me: Crash, crash, crash.

The silence wasn't exactly companionable. It felt strained. In an effort to bring it back I made loads of inane comments about the game, but he didn't pick up on any of them. Just sat there, stony faced, working on the spoon. I was just about to put the game down and start the, "Look mate, what's up . . ." speech, when the sound of the front door hurling open startled us all.

Like a Formula One car off the grid, Solly was first to react, barking a single warning bark that was clearly meant to give the interloper fair notice that just as soon as he'd got the hang of where all his limbs were supposed to be he was going to be on their case, and they'd better beware.

251

Then the newcomer said, "Shit, shit, shit. I hate this front door." The words were slow and slurred and followed by the front door slamming shut behind him and the unmistakable thud of a heavy holdall being chucked on the floor.

Only one person makes an entrance like that.

Ziggy.

Implosion

"We've split up," Ziggy said, slumping down onto the sofa.

"Again?"

"Yes. Is there any wine? I would have brought some only the cab driver refused to stop."

I poured him a glass. It was murky and smelt of old socks steeped in lemon juice. It wasn't the good stuff, but neither was it any of the really ropey wine. That stuff you needed a tolerance for before taking anything more than three sips without needing a paramedic in attendance, and we tended not to inflict it on others.

"I'm Ziggy, by the way," Ziggy said, holding out a hand to Garth.

"Garth," Garth said, reaching out his own.

"He got you doing his menial tasks," Ziggy said, nodding towards the half-finished spoon and Stanley knife balanced on the side of the log basket in front of Garth. "Insist on more than a shekel an hour, 'cos that's all he'll want to pay you."

252

"Garth's the son of an old school friend," I said. "He's here for a week."

"Sorry, I, er . . . should have called first." Ziggy said.

"No you absolutely should not have!" Debbie said, stepping in. "You know you're always welcome."

"Even a text message would have been nice," I said, only half kidding. He had a 250-mile journey down from London, sitting on a train, and he couldn't have spent one minute to tap out a message that he was on his way?

"Sorry. I didn't think," Braving a sip he pulled a *whooah*! face and spluttered, "That . . . is . . . revolting! Mind you, give it a minute or two and it . . . kind of . . . kicks in, and . . . grows on you."

It's difficult not to love him, even if he is an annoying idiot.

"That's not even the good stuff," I said.

"I can tell."

On second thoughts it isn't *that* difficult.

"Nice Man U shirt, Garth," Ziggy said, pointing needlessly at his top.

"Ziggy's Arsenal," Debbie said proudly, "Like me."

"Gooners!" Garth said, making a cross with his fingers as though warding off vampires.

I get it that people bond over football. That it's a language anyone can use to strike up a conversation and find some common ground, even if that common ground is to search out a team they both dislike and hate for a while. I understand all that. It's just, the truth is I can't find it in me to be interested. Don't get me wrong, I like people, and I'm endlessly fascinated as to how they communicate and come together, it's just I can't stand football.

The topic skipped about for a while, lightly touching on some of the more outlandish decisions made by managers, players and umpires, and by no means were all of those outlandish decisions confined to the pitch.

At one point Garth asked, "Who do you support, Simon?"

"He doesn't," Ziggy said, speaking up for me. "He's a freak. Doesn't like the beautiful game. Prefers his pigs."

"You are a prat," I said.

"Tell me it's not true," Garth challenged.

"Yes it is, but you make it sound like I'm a weirdo when clearly I'm not."

Garth and Ziggy looked at one another and burst out laughing.

"Appreciated."

"Welcome. What's your story, Garth? What brings you out to the back of beyond — I'm guessing it was your old man's idea if he and Simon were chums at school."

"Actually it was more my mum's idea," he said. "She doesn't like my friends. She certainly doesn't like my girlfriend, and this week is half term at college and she didn't want me hanging about with either. So they came up with the idea of sending me down here."

"You cool with that?"

"Not really. I mean this place is awesome and I've loved every second of being here, but the circumstances of why I'm here piss me off. My girlfriend's a little older than me."

"Thirty-two," I offered, grinning.

"Bit of mature, I like it. I lost my virginity to a thirty-two-year-old. Very fond of them. Totally approve. Well done."

"She's a ballerina," he said, digging out his phone and searching through the pictures to show him.

"Captivating."

"And you," Garth said, sitting back. "You said something about splitting up? Is that why you've come down — sorry, if you'd rather not talk about it . . ."

Debbie choked from the kitchen. I choked in the lounge and even Ziggy had the decency to cough. Regaining his composure he said, "Oh, I don't mind talking about it. How old are you, Garth?"

Rolling his eyes he said, "Seventeen."

"Interesting. How do you find being with someone older? No, scrap that, how does she find being with someone younger?" he said, reaching for the wine again.

He shrugged. "Okay. We talk about it and she says she's fine with. it"

Ziggy and I shared a look over the use of the word fine, knowing we were both thinking the same thing, back to the last time Ziggy was down and he found out what fine really means when spoken by a woman.

Ziggy said, "Did she actually say she was *fine* with it?"

"*Ziggy!*" Debbie yelled from the kitchen.

"What?" Garth said, looking confused.

"Nothing. In-joke," Ziggy said. "So do you find yourself trying to act older when you're with . . .?"

"Sophie. No, not really. I'm just myself."

Ziggy sat forward, the expression on his face almost one of pain. "She doesn't want you to act older, and you don't feel the need to act grown up when you're with her?"

Shaking his head, he said, "No. We're just ourselves."

"So you're comfortable being seventeen?"

"What kind of a question is that? Of course I'm comfortable being seventeen. I *am* seventeen!"

Crashing back into the sofa so hard he disturbed the dog, Ziggy put his hands over his face and wailed, "I don't get it!"

Mouthing at me, "Is he all right?" I assured Garth it was perfectly normal behaviour, which for Ziggy it was.

Figuring it was time to bring Garth in, I said, "Ziggy, you okay for me to sketch in some details for Garth, otherwise this whole conversation isn't fair on him?"

"Many as you like."

Turning to Garth I said, "Ziggy's bang in love with a woman who's having his baby, but she thinks he's too immature for either her or fatherhood and desperately wants him to grow up, and he can't — or, at least, he's having a hard time trying. That about right?"

"Simplified to the point of beauty." Ziggy said, who dropped his hands from his face, sat up and reached for his wine.

"What happened this time?" I said.

He took a sip. "She wants me to get a new phone number. Scrap the SIM. Throw it away. I tried to explain that I couldn't do that, that everyone I've ever met contacts me on that mobile number. Work, friends,

256

family — everybody. Throw it away and I might as well go and live on a desert island. She thinks I keep getting text messages from girls, which okay, sometimes I do, but I always text back a friendly message to say I'm now with someone. I told her it sounded as though she didn't trust me, and you know what she said?"

Neither Garth nor I made a comment.

"She said no, she didn't trust me, didn't trust me as far as she could throw me. How's that for love? I haven't been unfaithful once since I met her. Not once. And that's how she treats me. We had this big blazing row and she said, it's me or the phone. She actually said that, actually asked me to choose between her and my mobile."

"You chose the mobile?" I said.

"Of course I bloody didn't. I'm not a moron. I chose her. I said I'd get a new phone and leave the old one at the office. Not use it. But no, that's not good enough, she *actually* wanted me to hand it over so she could destroy it there and then. I told her, no way! Half my life's on that phone. You know what she said?"

It was starting to feel like being on a relationship quiz show. I shook my head.

"She put a finger on my chest and told me I was a child, because now she knows that's my Achilles' heel. Any time she wants to get at me, she calls me a child. Or I'm immature. Or a baby. I'm beginning to wonder if I shouldn't buy myself a Moses basket to sleep in at night."

Garth poked the fire and Debbie brought in a huge pan of curry and a plate stacked high with freshly cooked chapattis. "Dig in. There's plenty for everyone," she said. If ever there was a TV cooking competition where the competitors had to stretch a meal to accommodate ever increasing numbers of people *without* the quality diminishing, Debbie would walk it.

"So, who died?" she said into the silence, slumping down next me.

"Nobody. Ziggy was just giving us an update on the turbulent relationship between him and his mobile phone."

"We had a row because she wants me to lose my mobile. Do you mind if I try some of this? I wasn't hungry until you brought it in. It smells amazing."

"Of course! Please, everyone . . ."

Everyone did.

"So she wants you to give up your phone. Can't say I blame her."

"What? Why not?" Ziggy said around a mouthful.

"Come on, Ziggy, for the longest time you were a player. You've had more women than The Rolling Stones, and each conquest has a notch in the shape of a phone number on your mobile. No woman would be comfortable with that. Of course she wants you to give it up."

"But that's not fair."

"Yes it is. If you truly want her, then it's time to give up the little black book."

"I do want her. Absolutely. It's just . . ."

"Do you want me to look after it for you?" Garth asked, laughing.

"No," I said. "It would be much safer down here with me."

258

Digging me in the ribs, Debbie said, "You want to watch yourself, buster."

"No, you don't understand, I was going to sell it on eBay."

"To the highest bidder. Be like winning the lottery," Garth spluttered.

The only person not joining in with the banter was Ziggy.

Debbie looked across. "Ziggy, darling, if you really want it to work with her there are things you must give up. That bit of your past is one of them. You just need to grow up."

Slamming his fist down onto the sofa he yelled, *"Don't keep fucking telling me to grow up!"*

The silence that followed was like an implosion, swallowing all light and sound in the room, leaving an awful, empty, cavernous, old silence.

I said, "Ziggy —"

He held up his hand and said, "Oh my God, I'm so sorry." He got up and shambled over to Debbie, hugging her and then hugging me and even hugging Garth. Over and over he kept repeating, "I'm so sorry."

Debbie got up and took away all the wine and all the glasses and went to put the kettle on for extra-strong coffees all round. While she was out of the room Ziggy looked imploringly at me. "Do you want me to leave?" he said.

"No. We're not your enemy, Ziggy. Don't take it out on us. And don't ever speak to her like that again. Do you understand?"

He nodded. "Of course. I'm just so sorry."

I've never seen that side of him before. Never even knew it existed. I can only guess how tormented he must feel inside to have reacted that way, which is why I didn't labour the point. Instead I got up and went out to Debbie.

"You okay?" I said, slipping my arms around her waist.

She leant her head back into me and wrapped her own arms over mine. "Sure. Look, can you finish off the coffees, I just want to go to bed?"

Within half an hour we were all lying in our beds wondering how the night could have unravelled so spectacularly, though I suspect the one who got the worst night's sleep was Ziggy.

Ziggy decides he should leave

"Talk to me," I said, early the next morning, plonking myself down on the end of the sofa where Ziggy had crashed — our cottage has two bedrooms and Garth was ensconced in the only spare room, which left Ziggy a choice of the sofa or the floor in the lounge. The way he looked he might just as well have chosen the floor.

"How are you getting on with the list?" he asked.

"Rubbish," I admitted. "I can't seem to get started on it even though I want to. You?"

He rubbed his chin, the bristles making a sanding noise. "Waste of time. Don't bother with it. It doesn't make any difference. Nothing does. Is Debbie okay?"

"You frightened her."

"I know. I'm so sorry." He sighed deeply. "I've never lost it like that before, not even when I was a child at school. It's not me, it's not the person I am. At least it's not the person I was. Christ. It's like this angry person has moved into my body and is slowly taking over. Maybe I'm a schizo. Maybe I should be on medication. What did Debbie say?"

"Not much. I think she was really shocked."

He nodded. "You cool if I take her to one side and try to apologise and talk it through with her?"

"Long as you promise to stay calm."

"Of course. Thanks. I think I'm going to pack in the drinking too. Can't be helping." He picked up his mobile phone from the folds of the blanket in front of him. "And get rid of this."

"Does she know you're down here?"

He made a face. "I'm not sure. I think so. After the row I called a cab from her place to take me to the train station, bypassing mine to grab some stuff on the way, and I'm sure she overheard. I'd text her but using my mobile to contact her isn't exactly the ticket right now."

"You want to use my phone?"

"Maybe. In a while. Thanks."

It's been a long while since there was any kind of awkward silence between us. A long time.

"So . . ."

"Yeah . . . Look, I know I messed up last night, and I just want to, you know, thank you for not flipping out, which you had every right to do. You should have chucked me out on my ear."

"Agreed."

"But you didn't."

"No."

He nodded. Gave a half smile. "Appreciated."

"Welcome."

It was our bit, but it was like some part of it was missing. I don't now how long we've been doing it, maybe eight, nine years. But this morning it didn't feel the same. It felt light, lacking all the mass that it usually carried. That sense of connection and understanding that normally came with it was gone. I looked down and picked at my jeans.

"I should leave," he said, hanging his head.

I didn't say anything.

"Maybe Debbie could run me to the station? That way I can talk to her on the way?"

"I'll ask her," I said, still picking at my jeans.

"I'm so sorry."

I nodded. "I know."

I spoke to Debbie and she agreed to drive Ziggy to the train station, then I nipped out before Garth got up, which wasn't difficult as it was not anywhere near midday yet. Outside the morning was freezing. Driving down the lane with Dex standing on the back of the quad bike sheltering behind me, I tried to duck my head down so the biting cold wind wouldn't hurt my face. At least the traffic was light: no need to bother Sally Traffic with, "*And the General's dad says that his hill is chocka this morning!*"

Standard morning antics followed: geese first, then all the poultry — including the turkeys, who were

262

loving their new life and flourishing, putting on stacks of weight and developing breasts like Dolly Parton. Senorita wobble-bellied it out of Dex's house when I called and he slipped in behind her, the hot-bed situation working quite well. Goats milked. Breakfasts done. Sheep and horses checked. Pigs fed and watered. Everyone happy.

General was on his own. "Do you ever wonder where your wife-of-right-now goes during the day?" I said, slipping in beside him. The bed beneath us was thick with straw and surprisingly warm, though lying on my back I could still see my own breath fogging up towards the tin roof.

He grunted and rolled over. Translating his porcine into English I replied, "No, I suppose not."

I shouldn't have let Ziggy leave like that. He's my best friend, "Present company excepted, General," I said out loud.

But he had erupted, he had frightened Debbie. I couldn't have that, I'm her husband, it's my job to protect her from crazed brain-not-functioning lunatics. Isn't it?

But in the cold light of day, and I mean that quite literally as another tiny cloud appeared in front of my face as I breathed out and hung about there for a handful of seconds, I think I could have been more supportive towards him.

Mind you, I hadn't exactly ended up besties with Garth last night either, even before Ziggy arrived. That situation hadn't worked out as I thought it would. Having a teenager in the house is harder work than you'd think. They seem normal and you're hugging along laughing and joking and connecting and being real, and all of the sudden they say something and you think, "Where did that come from?"

At the point when Ziggy crashed through the front door, I'm not even sure Garth and I were getting on.

I might have upset him with the Clash music comment. I think that was it. Or maybe it wasn't, maybe it was something earlier. Maybe his storming off was still under his skin. I don't know.

One thing's for sure, he changed when Ziggy came into the mix. People do, Ziggy's that type of person. Plonk him into a room and it's like everyone in there has suddenly been given a mouthful of chocolate ice cream. They love him and go all animated and gooey and laugh and light up. Lucky bugger.

Shame it all went wrong, I'd love to have seen the three of us spend some time together. The three different age groups: Garth, the youngster happy with his age but in a relationship with someone older; Ziggy next, trying to grow up because his partner wants him to and because they are about to have a child; then, me the oldest, desperately trying to halt the onslaught of middle age. It would have been a hoot comparing issues, even if Ziggy would have had a barrel load more worries than the rest of us put together. But let's face it, there's entertainment even in that.

Putting my hand out I rested it on the General's side.

I'm not sure where I am on *my thing*. It seems to have gone quiet after I figured out that the expectations my younger self set were pretty much made redundant at the point I nodded "Oh yes," to my beer and my life went . . . *bang!*, taking a sharp right turn into a world of self-sufficiency and wacky animals. I still feel as though I'm up on the brow of this hill, but I don't feel as though I've started slipping down the other side yet. I still haven't worked out how to grow old out here, I still feel as though I'm trailblazing the whole getting older on a smallholding thing, but that doesn't feel too huge at the moment. Probably because I don't feel that old. The up side of having a teenager in the house, I suppose.

"I guess having Garth around has helped more than I thought," I said to the General. "Even if, and here's irony for you, he ends up copying my music. All the way along I thought I'd get an education on today's music from him and I end up hearing him play The Clash."

Which made me think of Debbie saying, "It breaks my heart that you no longer like the music we used to love together."

I hoped she was okay taking Ziggy to the train station. I knew that he had blown up last night, and at the time it felt horrible, but now, the next day, it didn't feel as bad as it had. I knew I could trust him, and I knew he would never do anything to hurt Debbie. I didn't want them to be at loggerheads, they were my two favourite people in the whole world. I wanted them to get on.

I should call him.

Actually there was a whole host of things that I should do, not least of which was as soon as Garth had gone I should have a Barry Manilow-fest with Debbie. Make a night of it.

I knew I should be there when she got back, be there waiting to make sure she was safe and okay.

"General, I've got to go."

Up at the house I parked the quad bike and opened the door. As soon as I did I heard laughter. Many voices of laughter.

Debbie and Solly came out.

So did Ziggy, who looked at me, held out his arms and shrugged.

"I convinced him to stay and go home tomorrow," Debbie said.

Then Garth appeared, and behind him Stafford and his wife Serena. Now retired, Serena had been a stewardess on British Airways for years. Age hadn't dulled her elegance or beauty one iota.

"You smell of pigs," Debbie said.

"Great, house full of hangers-on and strays. Will you lot bugger off into the lounge and let a working man get washed up?" I said, smiling as wide as it's possible for my face to split.

All bar Ziggy laughed and turned back. Looking serious he said, "This okay?"

I held my hand out to him the way Garth had to me, which was up high as opposed to down low. Without missing a beat he took it and grasped.

"Just promise me you won't do that again?" I said.

"My word, as a gentleman," Ziggy said.

266

"You're such an idiot."

He laughed and said, "I know."

No bit. No "Welcome" or "Appreciated". While washing away the General's pong and changing into clean clothes I wondered if we'd ever do our bit again. Shame if we didn't, but I guess everything moves on.

Downstairs men were doing what they do, which was talking football (yawn), so I went into the kitchen with Debbie and Serena.

"Everything okay with the animals?" Debbie asked.

"Sure," I said, pecking Serena on the cheek.

Debbie said, "These came for you — more secret bloody parcels! Serena, how would you feel if Stafford suddenly went all MI5 on you, started hiding things, keeping things from you, getting things through the post — they could be girl's underwear for all I know!"

There were three parcels. That's a lot of knickers to be sent in one day.

She was mild-ranting. ". . . not letting you look at his email account? What would *you* think, Serena?"

"First thing I'd want to know is if the undies fit me — a girl can ever have too many pants. Then I'd think he's up to no good. A bit of fancy on the side. Unless, of course, it just happened to be a special birthday of mine coming up soon."

Debbie raised her eyebrows. Had she really not thought that everyone was in on it?

Back in the lounge the conversation had moved on, with Ziggy taking centre stage. Standing in the middle of the room he was working it for all he was worth, cracking one-liners like a stand-up. Garth and Stafford were in stitches, but I didn't think they knew him well enough to spot the edge of desperation in his act. Not that he would have cared if they had, after all, everyone knows there's comedy in sadness. Some of the finest comics ever who have stood in front of a crowd and destroyed were seriously troubled souls. Ziggy was just hitching a ride on that bulging bandwagon. They were all relationship gags, or, more precisely, the inner code of relationship gags. "What she really means when she says . . ." and "What she really means when she doesn't say . . ." type of things. It probably wouldn't get him a set at the Edinburgh fringe, but in my lounge it was hilarious.

At one point I cornered Stafford. "I, um, you know, thanks — for the sheets. The corrugated iron sheets. For the pig house. That was really nice of you and I'm so grateful." I felt bad that he'd done something so kind and it made the words come out stuttery and awkward. Had I known he was coming round today I would have made pains to finish the spoon, but as it was it was tucked away in the bottom of the log basket half-finished.

Shaking his head and looking slightly baffled he said, "You're welcome. They were spare and I thought you could use them. Have you finished it yet?"

"I have. I keep on at Winnie to buy you a thank you card but the lazy sow hasn't got around to it yet. I told her, get yourself down to Clinton Cards, girl, but she's not having any of it. Pigs!"

He nodded sagely.

268

A while later I said, "Okay, well, I hate to break up this happy party but I've got to start evening rounds and there's no way I'm going out to work and leaving you lot up here enjoying yourself, so you'll all just have to come with me," to a chorus of childish boos and nays.

"Mature, really mature."

The boos and nays increased in volume, and I was pleased to see the loudest of them all was Ziggy, whom I thought might have gone the other way. As it was, Stafford and Serena had to leave, which just left the famous five.

"I'll stay up with Solly and start dinner," Debbie said. "You boys go."

Piling on the quad and with half a mind on health and safety, I drove at a snail's pace with Garth and Ziggy down the hill. The welcome committee at the bottom comprised of, in no particular order: Senorita, Dex, Curry, chickens, geese and three sheep. It's good to be popular.

"Will you lot . . ." Garth started.

"Move, I can't move, they're all around my legs!" Ziggy said, trying to put his feet down off the bike but not managing it.

"Ouch! I just got bitten!"

"Sorry. They're hungry," I said, clambering off the bike into the mêlée.

"When was the last time you fed them?" Ziggy said.

"About four hours ago."

Garth said, "Damn, breakfast really goes down fast for them, huh?"

Walking away I was stalled when Ziggy said, "Is the General okay?"

Fear for someone you love is completely different in texture from fear over yourself. It's hotter. Brighter. More intense. "What? Why? What's wrong with him?" I said, all but hoofing the mob out of my way in my rush to get back.

"Don't panic. It's nothing bad — at least I don't think it is. It's just, he seems to have changed colour."

"What are you talking about, changed colour?" We both stood there and looked up at him. He looked fine to me . . .

. . . and then I saw it.

I'd been spending so much time with him lately that I hadn't noticed. He was grey. Really grey. Old-man grey. It was like my inner mental picture of him was suddenly overlaid with a fresh one, and the contrast between the two was so great that for a second it was almost as though he was a different pig — a much, much older pig. My heart melted and my hands twitched in their desire to hug him, which is kind of embarrassing. "Oh, my boy," I said.

"What's wrong with him?"

"He's getting old," I admitted. "He's going grey."

Ziggy breathed out. "Is that all it is? Thank Christ for that!"

"I'm not sure your body decaying into old age is really a thanking Christ matter."

He shrugged. "It's natural. It's what happens. It also makes the two of you look like brothers."

270

Behind us Garth roared with laughter. "I'm sorry, but it does," he said.

Do I look like the General? People look like their dogs all the time, so why not? I'd be happy to look like the dude. However, admitting that to those two idiots was not an option, so I pantomimed storming off, tossing two-fingered salutes at them over both shoulders.

Receiving no help whatsoever with the animals, I set Garth and Ziggy to chopping wood while I got on with evening rounds. As I fed, watered and bedded down, my thoughts sought out my internal photo album and the newly updated picture of the General. How had I not noticed him ageing? How had I not noticed him going so grey?

Inevitably as soon as one image updates, they all update. As I rushed around settling each set of animals down for the night, new pictures overlaid previous ones in my head. It was harsh. Pretty fluffy sheep became seven-year-old OAPs. The sows — Winnie, Pru and Pippa — were wrinklies. Georgie Girl, my stunning horse, looked all of her twenty-four years. Even Dex looked like an old man. Somewhere inside me I knew that I'd been avoiding this, clinging on to old pictures because I didn't want to face the fact that everyone was knocking on. None of them looked bad. They were all still utterly beautiful. Just older. Greyer. Wrinklier.

Of course, not everyone has a foot in the grave. There are youngsters too. Winnie's babies, for instance. The turkeys. This year's lambs. Curry. Senorita, who still hadn't placed a hoof inside the freezer-house since

271

her initial viewing and continued to hot-bunk with Dex. Funnily enough, all those internal pictures were spot on and needed no updates at all. It was just the older stock that needed rebooting.

By the time I made it back to the lumberjacks, who it seems had turned log chopping into a boy's competition by seeing who could split the biggest log with the fewest number of swipes with the axe, I felt like someone had put an ageing spell on half my farm. Oh God, what about my own internal image of myself? When was the last time I updated that?

"Your turn," Ziggy said, handing me the axe. Over to one side Garth was hiding a laugh behind his hand. I could see that on top of the log Ziggy had set down for me were several marks where they'd tried to split it but the wood was too dense and the axe had bounced off.

"Now," Ziggy elaborated, "The game is you have to whack the log as hard as you can and see how many hits it takes you to split it. Garth's record is three. Mine is two."

"I'm guessing you've got me the nastiest gnarled-up bit of old wood you could find, right?"

"Cynical and untrue. There was one that was worse, but Garth threw it in the pile and we couldn't find it. This is the second nastiest. You've got to beat two hits to become the champion of the world. Three hits for runner-up, or more for a completely forgetable also-ran. Do your worst, big boy."

There's a trick to splitting logs. Don't ask me how it works, but it does. It has little to do with strength or aggression, and everything to do with concentration.

272

Standing in position, the axe hovering a hands-width above the wood, knees flexed, back soft, I focused on the log, staring so hard my peripheral vision blurred and began to darken, making the log itself stand out like it was under a spot-light. Then my ears started fading out the sounds of Ziggy and Garth so all I could hear was my own breath. I listened and slowed down; in, out, in . . . out, in . . . out . . . in . . . out . . . and when my concentration felt at its peak, I lifted the axe high above my head, focused hard and slammed it down. The log smashed into two halves. Magnanimous in victory I was not. Punching the air I yelled, "Champion of the world!"

Not bad for an oldie, not too shabby at all.

Standing next to a teenager, in front of a mirror, both topless, is the most depressing thing anyone can do

The reference I have in my head when I think of myself is pretty accurate and doesn't need updating. I checked when I got in, staring at my reflection in the mirror above the sink, the face of a forty-seven-year-old man staring back.

"You look beautiful, now budge up," Garth said, shouldering me sideways. Clearly he'd got bored queuing outside for the bathroom and decided there was room for two. Now the topless image of myself was joined by the topless image of a seventeen-year-old boy.

273

Never do this. If you're in your forties, never, never, *never* stand next to a teenager in front of a mirror without at least one layer of clothing on, preferably two (the under layer as tight as you can get it in the wild hope that it might keep things from sagging too far away from their station). It was like we were two different beings distantly related. Very distantly related. One all tight and smooth and tanned, the other all loose and wobbly and milky-white — I'll leave you to guess which is which, but in case you need it, here's a clue: I was the one who looked at the comparison and groaned, "Oh, God," shut my eyes and, working blind, finished up washing as fast as I could before walking out, not opening my eyes until I was well out of there.

Luckily, downstairs Ziggy was in the mood to talk, which meant we could all sit back and feel better about ourselves as he outlined his current worries, starting with: his inability to grow up; his relationship with Miss Perfect that was more on/off than a kettle; the fact that he was going to be a dad; his decision to give up drinking, all while lamenting the looming loss of his mobile phone (without being able to let it out of his grasp). Then he dipped into his back catalogue of woes, which was wide and expansive and hugely entertaining.

Feeling happy that despite all that was confusing and uncertain about my life, at least I wasn't Ziggy, I followed Debbie into the kitchen and, looking down, asked, "Do you think I have man boobs?"

"What? No, not at all. What made you ask that?"

274

Still looking down. "I stood next to Garth in the bathroom. Neither of us had a top on. It was a very depressing sight."

"Oh, sweetheart. I think you look gorgeous. Miles better than a seventeen-year-old. Mind you, just to be on the safe side, what does he look like semi-naked?"

"Debbie!"

Laughing, she reached over and kissed me. "I'm kidding." She poured two glasses of wine, shouting out if anyone else wanted one, to which the answer was a sensible no.

"How were the animals?" she said.

"I hadn't noticed how old the General's looking. Or the sows. Or the sheep. In fact, half of them down there are ready for the nursing home. When did they all get so antique?"

"Is the General doing what he needs to do with his wife-of-right-now?"

There weren't any signs. Mind you, from what I could tell she was hardly there.

"I don't know. Possibly. Probably."

"I take it that's a no, then?"

Yeah, that's a no. When the General is up for it, trust me, you can't miss the telltale signs of six or seven shagathon sessions a day.

Nodding, she said, "I think the time's come to get a younger man in. Put the General on gardening leave. If we don't have any piglets, we don't have a business."

Over the years we've become very good at living on fresh air. We can survive on practically nothing by making just about everything we need. But the animals can't. They need proper food, shelter, bedding, and plenty of it. And that costs. I felt bad that the General would be shoved to one side while some whippersnapper came in and took the leading role in his shagathon sessions, but what alternative was there? Sink or swim, survive or close the farm gate forever, if he wasn't up to the job we needed someone who was.

"I suppose. What do we do, advertise in the Situations Vacant section of PorkyFriends.com?"

"We can't bring in a boar. They're too unpredictable. We need something we can trust and feel safe with. We need something home-produced. We need a General Junior."

"One of his sons?"

She nodded. "How would you feel about that?"

Actually, of all the scenarios, this one didn't feel too bad.

Changing the subject she said, "We'd better go back in. I think Ziggy's wrapping up."

He wasn't. He was still in full flow.

". . . doesn't understand. She really doesn't. Of course I don't want to act like a child for the rest of my life. Nobody wants that. But then I think, do I really act like a child? I mean, really? I can —"

"Bore everyone to tears?" I offered, taking a seat next to Solly. "Wake up, Garth!"

He wasn't asleep but looked at me and smiled.

Not missing a beat, Ziggy continued, "— drive a car. I own my own home *and* pay all the bills. A child doesn't do that! My phone has got my life's work on it."

276

"She just wants to feel safe with you, Ziggy" Debbie said from the doorway. "She sees that giving up your phone with all those girls' numbers on it is a commitment to her, and a sign that you're prepared to give up your old ways. She feels vulnerable. And scared. She's pregnant, for God's sake! She knows you want to be with her right now, but what she wants to know is if you are still going to want to be with her in a year's time when there's a screaming, puking, pooing baby to look after." She shrugged. "Just saying."

"I asked her to marry me," he said.

"What did she say?"

"She said no."

"Well, even so, she's definitely testing you."

"You think so?"

She gave a look as an answer.

He continued, "If she feels vulnerable and scared, why on earth does it feel like she keeps pushing me away?"

"To see if you'll come back."

"But I'll always come back. She knows that."

"Prove it to her."

"By giving up my phone?"

"Afraid so."

He looked down at the mobile in his hands, then tossed it onto the floor in front of him. "But what about all this 'you're acting like a child' business?"

"It's all part of the same thing," she said.

"You mean it's all just another test? I don't get it, so does she want me to grow up or not?"

Debbie shook her head. "I don't know. I don't know how she feels about that."

"Well, can't you guess?"

I think she knew how desperate he was, so she didn't get exasperated and quietly said, "No, Ziggy"

I went for another glass of wine but caught Debbie's frown. I looked a question at her.

"Nothing. It's just, you don't normally drink the night before you go on the radio."

The radio! "*Shit, it's Thursday tomorrow? Are you sure? Oh shit!* OhShitOhShit — don't swear! Nobody is to swear, okay? I need to get all swear words out of my head. How can I have forgotten something that important?"

"Arse," said Ziggy picking up on the "nobody is to swear" plea as only he would.

"Balls," said Garth, joining him.

"What am I going to talk about? *What am I going to talk about?*"

"You go on the radio?" Garth asked.

"He does a weekly spot on The Voice FM, local radio down were," Debbie said.

"Skeen."

We all looked at him.

Shaking his head he said, "How old are you lot? It means cool."

"Not going to be cool if I've got nothing to talk about. It's going to be very cold and very silent."

"You can talk about me if you like," Ziggy offered.

"It's got to be farm-related."

"Why don't you do the freezer house we built for Senorita?" Garth offered.

"You know what? That's perfect!"

That night I lay in the dark with Debbie and Solly next to me and worked over what I'd say on air in the morning. The funny bits I could include. When I was happy with it, I let my mind do an about face and returned to Ziggy's continuing plight. Poor sod, I did feel sorry for him. One thing I could relate to was that feeling of confusion over the immediate world around you. So it seems he'd ditched the How To Mature list I gave him. Shame. Not that I've done much on his How To Avoid The Onset Of Early Middle Age list myself, even though I knew I should. It's like going on a diet, it's hard to get motivated and the cheat-outs are just too enticing. Stretching out on the bed I ran through the list anyway and stopped at social media. Garth had promised to show me how to use some of the platforms that were less familiar, but I could still do some of the stuff I knew. Especially Facebook. I pulled out my phone and fell asleep searching for old school friends and sending out friend requests.

In the morning the house was freezing, the fire long out. Ziggy was curled up on the sofa. This time yesterday I'd wanted him to leave. Today, I was glad he hadn't.

"Good morning," I called, strolling past him on my way to the kitchen. He didn't answer. Just snored. I made coffee and went over the Senorita freezer-house story I'd use on the radio today once more,

279

crow-barring in a joke reference to Garth's tantrum. I thought he'd appreciate that.

A little voice from under the covers in the lounge said, "What time is it?"

I looked. "Nearly five," I said.

"Sadist."

Behind me the kettle boiled. I pulled out two mugs.

"What time is it?" Garth said, walking down the stairs.

"Stupid o'clock," Ziggy said. "Farmer DJ here's under the deluded impression that the day starts four hours before daylight."

I pulled out another mug. "You don't have to be up, you know," I said.

"Yes we do. We're coming with you," Ziggy said. "You're going on the radio, so are we."

Hopps is going to love me. I sent him a quick email asking if it would be okay to bring two idiots into the studio with me. Fast as Senorita chasing Dex, he came back. Sure, no problem, he said. More the merrier.

Skidding through morning rounds in record time I finished up, showered, changed into non-farm clothes and we all bundled into town.

As much as I love the farm, it's good to be out.

"What time have you got to be there?" Garth asked as we walked along Barnstaple high street.

"I'm on just after the ten o'clock news," I said.

"What time is it now?" Debbie asked.

"Can't be bothered to look," Garth replied. I get it that he was probably tired from getting up early, but the more time he spent with us, the more his mature shroud was slipping and the surly teenager began to peek out from underneath.

As it was we were half an hour early so we decided to go for a coffee. There are a lot of coffee shops in Barnstaple and we chose one that looked the warmest. I sat down with Debbie while Garth and Ziggy did the honours.

"Are you okay?" she said. "You know what you're going to say?"

"I think so."

When they came back I picked up my drink and, rather than raising it nicely to my lips as people wishing to sip should, I brought it halfway up and dumped the entire contents of boiling hot coffee into my lap.

"*Whooooooo!*" I wailed in only the way a man can when he feels boiling liquid caress his genitals.

"What are you doing?" Debbie said.

"Mate," Garth said.

I'm sure Ziggy would have been sympathetic if he wasn't sprawled across the table in hysterics. I looked down. The coffee was milky and sugary and the stain looked like I'd properly wet myself "Bloody hell that's hot," I said, my voice two octaves above normal, then stood up, trying to hold the molten jeans away from my skin.

"Don't swear," Debbie said. She was trying not to laugh.

"What am I going to do? I can't go into the studio like this! They know I get nervous as it is. They'll think I couldn't make it to the toilet."

"Just tell them the truth," Debbie said.

Ziggy howled.

So did Garth.

The gits.

"I can't tell them the bloody truth, they'll think I'm lying even more!"

"Don't swear," Debbie said again.

"Put a coat in front of it," Garth said.

"Aaaaahhhhhhhh please, I can't breathe . . . this is killing me," Ziggy stammered, his face so red he looked like he was going to explode.

"Right. I'll have to phone them and say I can't make it in, say something came up."

"If it does you'll be in trouble," Garth said. Spoken like a true teenager.

"You can't cancel," Garth continued. "I got up at stupid o'clock for this, I'm not going to miss it now. Go to the gents and dry them. They'll be fine."

Good call — worth a try, anyway. Edging out from behind the table I made my way towards the toilets.

"I'm not missing this," Ziggy said behind me, following.

"Me neither," said Garth.

Great, just what I need — an audience. Walking in I heard Garth say, "Quick, take your jeans off, I'll guard the door."

We all paused.

"Did that sound as bad as I think it did?" he said.

I didn't answer, but I did take off my jeans and held them in front of the hand dryer. Ten minutes later the jeans were dry, though you could still see the stain and it didn't look great.

"Just go and buy another pair," Garth said. "I'll come with you."

Knowing me well, when Garth had turned his back to leave Ziggy tried palming a couple of notes to me, but I smiled and stood back in a "I really appreciate it, but I wouldn't dream of it" gesture.

A curt nod back and he put the money away.

Pulling the jeans back on I looked down. It really did look like I'd wet myself.

"There's a Primark over the road," I said. "Let's go and have a look."

"It's always good to go for quality," Ziggy said. "I'll go and sit with Debbie."

I followed Garth out and across the road. The shop was heaving. There were people everywhere, and every single person was deep in concentration unfolding all the garments they could lay their hands on and dumping them back on top of piles that had once been neat, as though that was the sole reason for being in the place.

"Jeans are over here," Garth said, pushing his way past a lady who couldn't make the pile of neat tops in front of her look scruffy fast enough, so had enlisted the help of her child who was yanking them out from the middle of the stack and wheeling them through the air so they landed in a heap on the top.

We looked at the jeans, but it was a half-hearted look. There was no way I could justify spending the money. Then I had an idea.

Turning to Garth I said, "Can I ask you a favour?"

I had no intention of walking out with anything, but the opportunity to see what a seventeen-year-old would go for was too good to miss. Clothes were number one on Ziggy's list of How To avoid Middle Age.

"Sure, fire away," Garth said.

Neatly folding the pair of jeans I was holding, I put them back. "How good are you on fashion?"

"I try to keep up with what's in for work. Going for auditions they like you to have a reasonable grasp of what looks good. Why, you looking to update?"

"Not right now, but yes, at some point. What would you recommend?"

"Muted colours are in right now. Blues, greys, darks. As are suits and suit jackets with skinny trousers or jeans."

"How about casual?"

"Yeah, that is."

"Oh. Well, more casual. What would you buy in here?"

"Just slouch clothes for home. Nothing I'd wear out. There are better shops for that. It depends what you're after."

I thought about it. "Just an idea," I said.

"Okay" he started looking around. Pointing at a rack he said, "Hoodies are timeless, and if you get it right can look good."

"Less vague. I've never worn a hoodie in my life so I don't know what getting it right or wrong means."

He looked astonished. "That's something that should be put right immediately. Come on."

284

The rack of hoodies spanned almost the entire length of one wall. About a third of the way along was a section that looked more like cardigans. That's where we headed.

Garth picked out a grey one and handed it to me, then he went off and got a funky t-shirt for underneath. "Try them on."

Aware of the time I said, "Oh no, I won't try them on, I just wanted to, you know, look."

"Try them on," he insisted.

I looked up. "I can't see any changing rooms, and I haven't got time."

Coming close he said, "If you don't try them on, I will sing and dance the opening number to *Billy Elliot*, right here, right now, at the top of my voice."

"You wouldn't . . .?"

Standing back so he had some space, he put his arms out wide, chest out, head up and took a deep breath . . .

"Okay! Okay!" I said, whipping my jumper over my head and stuffing the t-shirt and hoodie on as fast as I could. I looked in the mirror. Pulled the hood up. Garth pushed it back.

"It looks better down," he said.

I looked again. So this was what I looked like in a hoodie. It looked okay, but I'm not sure I looked any younger.

"I don't mean to worry you," Garth said after a while, "but if you are on after the ten o'clock news, it's nearly ten now."

Changing back we collected Debbie and Ziggy and made it to the studio with no time to waste. Ushered in I sat in front of the mic and did my thing, Ziggy and Garth slouched on a sofa to one side like they belonged there and Debbie sitting quietly beside me. It should have been the worst talk ever; ill-prepared, nearly late after flash-boiling my junk and stripping in a public toilet. But it wasn't. It was one of the most confident and together performances I've ever given. There's probably a lesson there somewhere, but if you're a budding radio presenter looking for tips, I wouldn't read too much into it.

Outside we low-five'd because that's what you do when you've killed it on the radio.

"That was sick," Garth said, grinning.

Walking with my coat nonchalantly draped over an arm that just happened to be in front of my jeans, I felt pretty good. I didn't feel old and knackered, I felt rejuvenated. Going on the radio does that. It gives you a hit of youth. I walked slightly ahead of the others. In the lead. The leader of the gang. It was a good feeling, and I was milking it. If I'd known how bad things were about to get, I'd have milked it for all it was worth.

"Do you have such a thing as a mobile phone shop down here?" Ziggy asked. "I'm going to chop my phone in. Then, if it's all right with you guys, I'm going to head home after lunch."

"Actually" Garth cut in. "If you're getting a train back to London, I might as well join you."

Pippa. Oh baby girl . . .

Ziggy and Garth both left in the afternoon. It made sense. They could travel back together. Doing the evening rounds on my own was a breeze anyway. A breeze! I could do what I wanted; catch up on podcasts while I worked, chat with the animals. Anything I wanted. Shame, though, it did feel a bit lonely. It's amazing what you can miss.

If I'm honest I'm not sure Garth had a great time. I think he missed his girlfriend, judging by the amount of time he spent on the phone to her. But I think he missed city life too. I get it. This place isn't for everyone. And I guess I had hoped we'd end up better friends, even though there is a fair old age gap between us. He plays Sunday League football and has a match this weekend, and when he left I asked him to let me know the score, and he gave me the website where they post the match results. That kind of spoke volumes. I don't know, maybe I'm overreacting. But I don't think I am. Teenagers are hard work, even if they are mature for their age, and I'm not exactly down with the kids.

I got three texts in quick succession:

Home safe and sound. This is my new mobile number. The other one's in the bin and I didn't sync the two, so other than a few phone numbers, this new one's totally empty. How's that for a show of commitment????

Then a minute later, from the same number:

It's Ziggy, btw.

I kind of gathered that. It was quickly followed by:

Hi simon & debs — hd n awesome tme. Feel honoured to hv spent time wiv u, u both rock. Giv kisses to solly dex n senorita. & General!!!!!!!! Garth x

The phone rang two seconds later.

"It's me," Debbie said. "How long are you going to be?"

"I've only just started. Couple of hours at least. Why?"

"We've just had a call from an animal rescue centre. They're trying to place a duck and wanted to know if we could take it?"

"How old?"

"Young, they think. Can I say yes?"

"Sure, why not? We could do with youngsters around the place."

"Thank you!"

"I've heard from Garth and Ziggy. They both sent me texts," I said.

"What did they say?"

I was down by Pippa's pen. She was in with her teenage children. She looked tired — I knew how she felt. However, more worrying was the fact that she wasn't bothering to eat.

"Oh, you know, that they're both back okay, had a great time. You can read the texts when I come up. Look, I'm down with Pippa. She looks tired and she's not eating. I'm a bit worried about her."

"You want me to come down?"

"I think so, yes."

"I'll put dinner on hold and be on my way in thirty seconds."

I went in. Pippa was lying on her bed watching the others eat. I sat down next to her. "Not hungry tonight, pretty girl?" I said, forcing a smile into my words.

She looked up at me, her eyes full of something I couldn't read. I stroked her face softly, trying to work out how old she was. We didn't get her as a baby, but bought her with a litter at hoof. That was about seven years ago, and she must have been two then.

A few minutes later Debbie arrived, took one look and said, "That's not good. We need to get her out."

The last thing I wanted to do was start backing up trailers and trying to load her, so I simply opened the gate and walked her out. She was happy to leave and followed me without batting an eyelid. I walked her into an empty field and tried to encourage her to eat now she was on her own, but she really wasn't interested. All she wanted to do was lie down, her eyes returning to that look I couldn't read.

I suggested Debbie sit with Pippa while I finished off the rounds. When I came back, neither of them had moved. "How is she?"

"No change. I think she's dying," she said, almost in a whisper.

"What can we do? Shouldn't we phone a vet or something?"

She shook her head, not looking up at me but down at Pippa. "Can you get me a couple of horse rugs to put over her to keep her warm?"

Grabbing the rugs I also got an armful of straw that I slipped in under her head so she wasn't resting directly on the ground.

"Do you know what's wrong with her?" I said as I covered the rest of Pippa with the rugs.

Debbie nodded. "Old age. Vets can't cure old age. Nobody can. We've just got to make her comfortable."

"But she was fine this morning, and I swear I've been so vigilant since Winnie."

"It's not you. It's nothing you've done or missed," she said, looking a sad smile up at me. "Sit down, you're making her nervous."

Of course I knelt down next to them. Quietly. Slowly. It was nearly fully dark now. Above us the sky was clear and the millions and millions of stars shone ever brighter.

"It's her time," Debbie said, taking my hand in hers. "We've got to let her go."

Tears tickled as they spilled down my face and I cuffed them away. "I still feel like we should be doing something."

"What? Simon, she's nine years old. That's probably something like ninety in human terms. She's not in any pain. There are no symptoms other than old age. There's nothing to treat."

"How has it come on so fast?"

Debbie sighed, but I don't think it was exasperation. Just sadness. "It hasn't. It's how elderly animals go. If they're really lucky. They're fine, they're fine, they're fine, then one day they feel more tired than usual, lie down and slip away. It's a beautiful way to go. She's had a wonderful life and she's been so, so happy. She's had lots of friends and lots of babies and watched them all grow up. She's lived a full life. Now it's time for her to leave."

Dex came over and joined us, zonking out against me after a hard day's poultry protecting. Debbie and I both stroked Pippa and talked about some of her hooligan babies. Boy, some of them were spirited. If you were a mum and had her children, you'd be a twitching nervous wreck. Then there was the time Pippa herself wandered down to the local petrol station to see what was going on, and we got a frantic phone call to say she was helping some poor man put air into his tyres.

Just before she closed her eyes for the last time, we both told her we loved her and thanked her for being with us. And we cried. We told her we'd miss her. We told her the General would miss her. We all would. Everybody. We told her to wait for us at Rainbow Bridge. Go find the others and wait for us there.

Funny thing is as I cuddled her and stroked her I didn't think about myself, but just tried really hard to be present and in the moment with her, which felt oddly comforting.

The next time we checked, she was gone.

The body man collected Pippa early the next day. I wasn't there to see her go. I was at the abattoir collecting the body of the pig we'd had killed last week. *Here children, here's one I prepared earlier . . .*

Jesus.

I brought the pig back and slapped the carcass on the kitchen able. It was in two halves, and I covered them in ice packs — not that it was hot in there, the kitchen had all the warmth of a financial adviser's handshake — and threw a sheet over the lot of it.

It was still early and daylight had only just started pushing nighttime away. I hadn't even started the morning rounds yet. Debbie was already on the phone hustling. I moved the kettle onto the hob and listened to her conversation. It was to do with the foster duck we'd been offered from an animal rescue centre.

"Sure we can take him. We have the room, and the other ducks will love to have a new friend. Well, we're running a butchery course today, so the kitchen's going to be full of people, but if you want to bring him over Simon can take him straight down." Pause. "Midday?" she said, looking a question directly at me.

I nodded yes.

"That should be fine," she said.

Miming going off and doing the animals, she smiled and mouthed, "Okay"

Senorita met Dex and I at the gate. She wanted to be close and stuck by my side the whole way through the morning rounds, even as I did the geese, which is way above the call of duty. She didn't try to scoff the food when I put it out, other than her own. She just wanted to be with me.

"I can't work out if you're giving me support or if you're nervous and don't want to let me out of your sight," I said, bending down and rubbing the soft area of skin behind her ears. "But I love your company, girly."

Animals know. They do. Last night, when Pippa went, the farm was silent. I mean, imploding silence where every sound is sucked out of the air. This morning, everyone is subdued. There's an atmosphere. We're generally a happy family down here, even though there are squabbles and arguments and one-upmanships and a strict hierarchy in place amongst the animals that is constantly being challenged, but when one of our own goes, you can feel it. Sure, it's possible it's me transmitting how I feel to them and the animals purely reacting to that, but that's not how it feels. That's surface. This feels deeper.

After breakfast Senorita, Curry, Dex, a lamb and a handful of chickens all made their way with me into the field where Pippa had lain down for the last time. There were tyre marks and a big skid where her body had been winched into the back of a truck. All that was left were the horse rugs and a squashed pile of straw where her head had been. The rugs had been tossed to one side. In a heap — an empty heap.

Inevitably guilt cast itself in heavy metal and landed squarely in the centre of my mind. Guilt's horrible; it doesn't need to attach itself to anything, it can just hang around for the sake of hanging around. Pippa died of old age. I know that. She got old, and she died. It wasn't my fault.

So why did I feel so responsible?

I picked up the rugs and led my crew back out of the field. Job done, the animals dispersed. All except Senorita, who for some reason had decided I still wasn't out of the woods and so she continued to shadow me.

"Sweetheart, I'm going up to see the General," I told her. "You're welcome to come with me if you like."

Amazingly, she did. I let myself into the old boy's pad and she followed. The General was in bed, his wife-of-right-now off in the woods somewhere. Senorita sank down onto her tummy some distance away and watched me crawl in with him.

"General, how you doing?" I sat cross-legged in the straw, rubbing his shoulder, and told him about Pippa. It seemed the right thing to do. When I left Senorita didn't come with me. She stayed. She actually remained within the enclosure. Maybe she did want to be a pig after all? Okay, she didn't go up and make friends with the General, but then he didn't go over to her either. He's good with the ladies like that, not too pushy. Turning back I could see he two of them still watching each other from a distance.

My phone rang. It was Ziggy.

"We're back together," he said, launching straight into the nitty-gritty. "I showed her my new phone and we ceremonially trashed he old one, SIM card and all."

"That's great!" I said.

"Yeah, well, we'll see how long it lasts this time. You okay?"

I didn't want to answer so sidestepped by saying, "How was the trip back with Garth?"

He laughed. "The lad's surprisingly well adjusted for a seventeen-year-old. Amazing. You know he wants to be an actor? I'll think he'll make it too. That's kind of why I'm phoning. We're both coming down for Debbie's birthday."

"You are?"

"Of course. He thinks the world of you, mate, kept referring to you as his brother from another mother. You two do some sort of demonic blood-brother ritual or something?"

"I didn't even think he was talking to me!"

"You do make me laugh. Look, I've got to go, I'm nearly at the office. Laters." And he was gone.

By the way, the duck isn't waterproof . . .

Back up at the house, preparations for the course were in full swing and both Debbie and I dashed about like blue-arsed flies vacuuming, polishing and cleaning. When the people who'd signed up for the course arrived I unveiled the pig on the table by whipping off the sheet covering it. Two halves split nose to tail. Half facing up, half facing down, it was an impressive sight.

"Wow, that really is a pig!" they exclaimed.

"Oh yes."

"How old is it?" they asked.

"Nearly a year," I said.

"A year. And it's one of yours?"

I nodded, yes.

"How's it feel looking at it on the table?"

Everyone asks a version of the same question.

"Fine. You get used to it," I said.

Out of the corner of my eye I caught Debbie's frown.

"Everything dies," I added. I know it sounded cold and unfeeling, but I just couldn't cope with anything soft right now.

"What he means," Debbie said, butting in, "is that everything dies for a reason, and it's important we respect that animal by using every single scrap of it. Wasting nothing. It's only by doing that that we can do what we do."

Everyone was really nice and we had a great time, and when proceedings were interrupted by the arrival of the duck, they thought it was hilarious. The duck came in a cat carrier accompanied by the sweetest lady from the animal rescue centre, the type of person you want to kidnap and install as your grandmother. She chatted and smiled and thanked us for helping. Then as she left she stopped in a perfect Peter Falk *Colombo* moment, half in and half out the door, her hand still on the handle. She turned back to us and said, "Oh, by the way the duck isn't waterproof," stepped out and slammed the door shut behind her.

After a beat of silence, Debbie said, "Did she just say what I think she said?"

"How can a duck not be waterproof?"

Turns out, after some Googling, he was a show duck and had been bathed in washing-up liquid until all his natural oils had gone. Poor thing.

"You want me to kill him and we'll eat him?" I said.

"*No I don't!*" Debbie yelled. Then taking me to one side while the others tucked into lunch she said, "What's got into you?"

"What do you mean?"

"You can't kill the duck, we've just promised to give it a home! Are you okay?"

"I'm fine. I'll take it down, then."

Wedging the cat carrier on my lap between me and the handlebars of the quad, I drove nice and slow down the hill, the duck wack-wacking the entire journey.

"All right, fella," I said, shifting on the seat so I could turn onto our lane, which made him wack-wack even louder. It was only when we pulled up in the chicken field and all and sundry came out to greet us that he went quiet. All and sundry, including Senorita.

"How did you get out? You were in with the General. I don't understand how you got out?"

I have no idea how she did it, or how she got back into the chicken field. She must have sucked her belly in and sneaked under the fencing, though there were no obvious signs of a gap.

"I'm a good girl, I am. I don't mind spending a bit of time with the boys, but I'm not going to spend the whole day in there with him. Not with him in his bedroom 'n all! I'm a good girl I am."

Oh well. Maybe I'll try again in a few days' time.

Shaking out a scattering of fresh straw into a stable, I figured I'd gather my ducks and usher them inside, that way I could introduce the new duck to them in a contained area. Then I went to fill a bucket with water. But I stopped. Would a non-waterproof duck drown if he sat in a bucket of water? I had no idea, but just to be on the safe side I found an old bucket with the handle missing and cut the bottom off just a finger length up the side and filled that so that even if he did sit in it he could stand up if he started to sink.

He was still in the cat carrier. Perched on the front rack of the quad. Silent. Boggle-eyed at the new world he'd just been driven into.

I stood back and looked at him through the mesh front. He looked very majestic, no wonder he was a show duck. "You need a full-Monty name," I told him. "Something fitting." For a while I toyed with several ideas, but in the end settled on Bertie Wooster. Nice.

"Guys," I said, carrying the cat carrier into the stable and shutting the door behind me. "Best behaviour, we have a newbie. He's only young. Be nice to him, okay? The whole world, meet Bertie Wooster." I set the cat carrier down and opened the front. "Bertie Wooster, meet the whole world."

Confident little guy, he waddled out, stood as tall as he could and flapped his wings as though he were saying, "I say!" It's amazing how fast animals grow into their names.

I wasn't going to leave them in there for any longer than a couple of hours, just until evening rounds. I wanted them to get to know one another before I let them out into the wide world, and the stable seemed like a good place to get acquainted. Actually, it was the same stable that the Top Gun Chickens had been kept in, so I certainly wasn't going to leave them in there overnight.

Girls are really good at making friends. Girly ducks are even better than that. They took one look at Bertie Wooster's pecs as he flapped his wings and swooned. If you've never seen a duck swoon, it's kind of an open-beaked, boggle-eyed weak-kneed affair. In effect, a slow fowl faint.

I left Bertie, destined to be a hit, to it and went back up to the house.

"More parcels," Debbie said, pointing to two brown packets on the side as I walked in. I couldn't be far short of my fifty pieces of material target now. I'd also sent an email to Marco Pierre White's restaurant L'Escargot in Soho, London, which is where Debbie and I had got engaged twenty-four years ago explaining what I was doing for her birthday with the quilt and received a really kind reply saying they would send me a napkin to put towards it. How awesome is that!

I didn't bother hiding the parcels straight away, but left them on the side and got on with teaching the course with Debbie for the rest of the afternoon. When we'd butchered the carcass, boned, rolled and tied the joints, packed the chops and got the sausage pile ready, we turned our attention to bacon-making, curing and doing all the scrummy bits. Courses are great. So much fun.

Later than normal I went back down to start evening rounds. Despite the full day I had a lot of energy to burn and worked fast, feeding, watering and bedding down in a blur. It felt good to be busy, and the harder I pushed myself, the better it felt.

It doesn't take long for ducks to become tight, and they naturally flock together anyway so when I let them out of the stable they waddled and wack-wacked as a group in the direction of their house. Knowing dinner was waiting for them everyone except Bertie Wooster bolted inside, leaving the new guy alone and uncertain until one of the girls came out to get him. I told you they were friendly.

I left Pippa's babies until last.

They were four, nearly five, months old and well beyond weaning, so physically I knew they would be fine. It's just how much else they'd picked up about last night, about Mum and all that, but in fact when I threw their feed in they were as happy as a family with a Saturday night curry.

"You're sure they were okay?" Debbie asked as I described how they'd tucked into dinner with gusto. The course had finished and the people had left for the night, looking shattered but happy.

"Totally. They're amazingly resilient."

"So you're not worried about them?"

"No."

"Good, because we need to talk," she said.

In all matters that begin, "We need to talk," my strategy was simple, be charming, and wherever possible aim to settle the issue without the need for too much soul-searching, which can be catastrophic, especially when spoken aloud.

"Wine," Debbie said, handing me a glass. I sat next to Solly, who lolled his head into my lap and looked up at me. Debbie had put on some background music that I didn't recognise, and it was only when the track finished and the presenter announced we were listening to Radio 1 that I realised why. I haven't listened to

Radio 1 for more than a decade. Neither, to my knowledge, has Debbie. Until tonight, that is.

"You worried me today" she said, taking her spot on the other side of the dog.

"Why?"

"I've never heard you say that looking at one of our pigs on the kitchen table felt fine before. Did it really feel fine to you?"

"Everything dies," I said.

"Yes, that's what you said before. Simon," she held her hand out across the dog and took hold of mine. "The thing is, I'm a bit worried that your obsession with age and getting older might have moved on to death. That's . . . unhealthy. And frightening. I don't like how blasé you're becoming around it — normally you're the one who would do anything to avoid harming anyone, and yet you wanted to kill the duck this afternoon. I know Pippa affected you last night, and normally I'd be able to see the sadness in your eyes for days and weeks after, but I haven't been able to detect anything in you today and it only happened last night."

"I cleared her rugs away in the field," I said.

"I know."

"I don't think I'm obsessed."

She didn't say anything to that. Just waited for me to continue.

Sipping some wine, I said, "You don't need to be worried and certainly not frightened! I've been thinking about Pippa all day, it's just, we've had a course so I couldn't show it."

"Are you sure?"

"Absolutely"

"So why did you say that it felt fine with the pig on the kitchen table?"

What did I mean? So much for avoiding catastrophic soul-searching, here goes nothing: "This is not exactly cheerful evening conversation, but when I was a kid, and I mean really young, like amongst my earliest memories, I used to cry myself to sleep because I was so terrified of dying. It was a big thing and went on for years and years, well into my teens, until finally I learnt to shut the terror off by forcing myself not to think about it and building barricades to shut it out."

"I didn't know that. You never said that before."

"Well, as I said, it's not exactly cheerful conversation. Anyway, I haven't thought about it for a long while until we went to the vet's to collect the antibiotic spray for Bee's bad foot, and I started thinking about the day Brodie died. Since then, I've had a hard time shutting it out. It's like it's all connected with me hitting middle age. Do you remember ages ago the night I rolled the quad bike and you sat me down because you knew I had stuff on my mind — it was the night Ziggy arrived when you were trying to seduce me because you thought that might help me open up?! The night Ziggy told us he was pregnant. Remember? And I told you I felt unnerved about life, and that there was this dark presence in the corner of my mind that I couldn't identify but had something to do with my age?"

"You didn't tell me that. You told me you were unnerved because you couldn't figure out how to grow older out here doing what we're doing without parents and family around — oh, wait, there was something about a presence. Go on . . ."

"Well, I think I've worked out what the dark presence was. I think it was the barricades I'd built as a child coming down."

She got up and came around to me, putting her arms around my neck and tucking her face in. "So that's what all of this is about?"

"Stupid childhood fear."

"Did you tell your mum at the time? Did she know you were so upset and frightened?"

"Sometimes."

"What did she say?"

I couldn't remember. "I think she just used to tell me to go back to bed. She was a single mum and wasn't having the best time of it herself."

"So you found out how to shut the terror out on your own?"

I started laughing. I couldn't help it. I think it was embarrassment.

"What are you laughing at?" she said looking confused.

"Nothing. Can we change the subject, please?"

"No," she said. "So how did that affect you when you saw the pig on the kitchen table today, and why did it suddenly feel fine?"

I shrugged and stroked the dog, multitasking beautifully. "I don't know. I just think it's easier to get my head around taking a pig to the abattoir, rather than something like Pippa dying of old age. See, that's part of the problem, as soon as you get a nagging thought in your head it seems to be everywhere you look. Pippa. Top Gun Chickens. Taking a pig to the abattoir. There's been a lot of death lately, and the more you see it, the more it's around you, the more you think about it. The more you think about it, the more you try to work out what it means because, for me, these thoughts are all new since I'd blocked them as a kid, so it kind of feels doubly hard because not only am I suddenly having to confront that, but it's also connected with me hitting middle age. And so I'm trying to process the two. Does any of that make any sense at all?"

"Of course."

What we need is some youth around here

After dinner I said. "Ziggy and Garth have decided to come down for your birthday. How do you fancy having a party? Inviting a few close friends and family?"

She went and sat back on her side of the dog. "Could be fun. I was thinking of inviting some people anyway. I'd love to do a great big vat of mutton curry, and maybe a vegetable curry. Some rice. Poppadoms. Chapattis. Just on the table so everyone could help themselves. Can we?"

"As long as we made it all ourselves, it's not going to cost much. I think it would be great."

"You're not off the hook with these packages that keep turning up, you know that don't you?"

With the mood a little lighter, I took the opportunity to tease. "It's to do with your birthday. It's nice. So come on, what do you think I'm doing? If you had to guess?"

"If it turns out you're having an affair, rest assured, I will tie you up and cut your balls off."

"Spoken like an English rose. Come on, guess."

"I don't know."

"Yes you do," I said.

"No, honestly, I really don't."

"Yes you do."

"No, Simon, I really don't!"

"Spoilsport."

It was a nice full stop to a heavy conversation and we both felt it. After Pippa last night and running the course today neither of us had the energy to delve or tease any further. So while Debbie went off to fix dinner, I dragged over the log basket and resumed whittling Stafford's spoon in front of the fire.

The following day Debbie hit the phones early. In a lull between calls she said, "I've got an idea how to make life better for you down on the land. I'm going to try to get some young stock in so the age balance down there is a little more even, and make it feel less like a retirement home for aged animals."

I knew we had no money, so whatever her plan it didn't involve shekels but bartering, swapping and general ducking and diving, all of which she'd become ace at. Intrigued, but unable to wait any longer before going down to start morning rounds, I had no choice but to leave her to it.

"Let me know how it's going," I said, kissing her on the cheek. She nodded.

It was take-your-breath-away bitterly cold outside. My skin froze the instant I set foot outside the front door. Then it started raining. Perfect.

Geese care not a jot for the weather. Sunshine, rain, snow, ice, whatever the weather it's still their job to chase me, and they're very conscientious. There must be an easier way to let them out. Rope and pulley, like a drawbridge, maybe, so I could do it from a distance. That would work. In the meantime, they chased and I ran.

Bertie Wooster was the second duck out in the string, looking as though he'd been part of the gang all his life. It was good to see, although he was less than impressed when I scooped him up and marched him over to the stable with one of the other ducks to keep him company. "Sorry, Bertie Wooster, but it's raining and you're not waterproof." I said, feeling ridiculous that only I could end up with a duck that came with the same set of instructions as a Mogwai.

I let the chickens out and collected the eggs, checked on the turkeys, which were getting fat, and milked Amber. I never did show Garth how to milk a goat. Mind you, he in turn never showed me all the fancy social media sites he'd promised to do. I do kind of miss the boy. However, I was starting to get responses from the friend requests I'd put out on Facebook to old school mates. Nearly half of them had come back so far. It was good to catch up, see what everyone was doing and how differently all our lives had evolved, and it seemed that over the past few months a lot of us had the same idea and had been searching each other out. Maybe we'd all hit a similar phase in our lives and responded to that most primal of inner calls, the urge to Facebook old not-spoken-to-in-yonks schoolies.

Senorita was having a lie-in, which meant that until she got up Dex had nowhere to go. I think the ulterior motive behind it was the hope that he'd go and join her, but he didn't. Instead he came with me and helped put breakfast out for the rest of the pigs.

When everyone was up and ready for the day — except Senorita, the lazy sow — I paid a visit to the General.

"Dude," I said, shoving an armful of straw in ahead of me to top up his bed and crawling after it. "Mind if I come in?" He was finishing off breakfast and grunted as I moved up next to him. Wife-of-right-now must have left as soon as she'd finished eating because she was nowhere to be seen, as usual.

"Don't you get annoyed that she keeps going out without you?" I asked. With all the food gone, he went back for a lie down. While he settled I told him about last night and the conversation I'd had with Debbie.

"The thing is," I said, "I know we're all the product of our own set of experiences, but I really hate the fact that all this stuff from my past is coming back to haunt me. First the list of expectations my younger self set, and now this . . . stupid childhood fear over death. I hate the fact that my past is suddenly part of my life now when I was convinced I'd left all that behind. And why, because I'm about to hit middle age? What's that

307

got to do with it? I don't get it. It doesn't make any sense."

Not comfortable, the General rolled over so he was facing away from me. It didn't put me off. I was on a roll.

My phone rang. It was probably a good thing.

"It's Debbie. Do you mind if I answer this?" I asked the General.

"Is everything okay?" Debbie said.

"Yeah, fine. I was just topping up the General's bed." Well I was. To start with.

"Good news first, I've got some more geese."

"*That's the good news?*"

"Don't be like that. They're nice. They're *young*."

"Young terrorists are still terrorists," I said.

"We can collect them tomorrow. I thought it would give a better balance to the chicken field. Plus it might give Honey-Bunny something else to think about."

I failed to understand how things would improve if they went from a terrorist twosome into a homicidal gang. Still, youth is youth.

"Go on, what's the bad news?"

"I'm sorry, but you know what day it is today?"

"Er, no . . . go on . . ."

"Saturday. Steph's. The horses. Your job."

Oh my God! I'd completely forgotten about that!

Dashing up to Steph's I walked into the pen. The first horse to come over and say hello was Aliana. I called her a slut and pulled her ears and stroked her mane and she nuzzled me with her nose. To be fair, Steph had told me I could put all the horses out and work with an empty pen, empty, that is, if you didn't count all the poo, but the only thing that made the job interesting was interacting with the horses, so I left them in and worked amongst them, shovelling, sweeping and wheelbarrowing out all the muck.

While I worked I talked to Aliana and Harry and Fang and Spot and all the others, and listened to podcasts. When it was done I wanted to go around and put corks up all their bums so they couldn't make a mess.

"Spotless," I announced in the end, leaning the wheelbarrow and shovel up against the wall outside the pen. "And, well, you do know that in some of the better bathrooms there's a plate on the side for patrons to leave a tip for the poor sod who keeps the place clean. Might be worth a thought, what do you think? Anyway, that's me done for now. See you tomorrow, guys." Sometimes it's worthwhile dropping the odd subtle hint. You never know.

No time to collect my hay and straw wages, I zipped straight down to start evening rounds. All was going well until I checked the sheep and saw yet another mucky bum. My back ached and I wasn't sure I could face it, and memories of last time when I licked my lips and got a good taste of sheep faeces still gave me the willies. I even thought about pretending that I hadn't noticed and leaving it to sort out tomorrow, but the little darlings were my responsibility, and besides it would only be a worse job if I left it. So I huffed and swore and kicked a stick, which is the mature response to doing something you don't want to do, and went off to collect the bottom-shearing equipment.

The ewe was easy to catch. I stuck her head between my knees and bent over her bum ready to trim the wool and clean it up. But I couldn't focus. My eyes didn't seem to be working properly. I tried taking my glasses off, tried leaving them on. Tried tipping my head back, tried moving it forward. No matter what I did I couldn't get the image to sharpen. It was just fuzzy.

Weird.

It was at times like this that I wish I had money on my phone. If I did I'd phone Debbie. Tell her my eyes had broken. Ask her to come and help me.

My phone rang. I swear at that exact moment my bloody phone rang. Of course I was pleased. It was just a bit freaky.

"Tabitha, I was just thinking about you," I said.

"Tabitha?" Debbie said. "Oh, were you waiting for me to call?"

"Tell me what I'm thinking."

"No. It's rude."

I told you she could read my mind.

"What's up?" she said.

"My eyes. I've got a sheep with a mucky bum. It's between my knees and getting a bit upset." On cue it wriggled and barred. "But I can't see it. Not clearly. Not clear enough to shear. I don't get it. I think there's something wrong with my eyes. When I get close it just goes out of vision."

"Oh God."

"What?"

"Please don't go into a fiat spin."

"I won't. Why? What is it? You can tell me. It's bad, isn't it? Tell me. I can take it."

"Don't be such a drama queen. You probably need reading glasses, that's all. We probably need to get you some bifocals."

It's been a while, but I think it's time to take a good look at this body of mine

Old people have bifocals. I'll probably get one of those chains that go around my neck with a spare set attached for when I lose my first pair, which will probably happen while searching for my slippers. On a cruise. That I booked through SAGA. While learning bridge. And line dancing. When I get home I'll go wing walking. And become part of the swingers' "bus-pass-in-a-bowl" scene.

"Isn't it supposed to be 'keys-in-a-bowl'? Besides, swingers are not old people — are they?" Debbie said. We were at home trying to coax warmth out of the fire and into the rest of the lounge. Even Solly had a housecoat on.

"They are, everybody knows that," I said. "They all meet up in the post office. They can hardly keep their hands off one another in the queue. I've seen it."

"You've seen no such thing. How was Steph's? How was Aliana?"

"Don't change the subject, I haven't finished with my depression yet. I can't believe I need reading glasses at my age. Especially not reading glasses to shear the arse end of a sheep."

"You are forty-seven."

"So?"

"So, that's about the right age for your body to start changing."

I closed my eyes. "Stage two. I didn't think it would happen so soon. I thought you had a while to get used to stage one first. Maybe it does all happen at the same time."

"I have no idea what you're talking about," Debbie said.

Taking a deep breath and letting it out slowly, I said, "I kind of worked out that midlife hits in stages. Stage one is, 'What have done with my life?', stage two is, 'My body hates me', and the third stage is, 'Losing your marbles'. Needing bifocals is obviously part of stage two. I should have put more effort into Ziggy's list. Maybe I should join a gym."

"You do a physical job. You're not out of shape. You don't need to join a gym. Don't go over the top, please, I'm not sure I can deal with another crisis so close to the last one."

"Crisis? These are not crises! If anything they're observations surrounding the premature aging of the human body. More a study than a crisis. And for your information I have no desire to drive a soft-top sports car, so clearly it's not a midlife-induced thing, crisis, whatever."

"That's handy."

Deciding it was time for a toilet break, Solly got up, stretched, went over and pressed his button. Although we own twenty acres of land, the cottage in which we live is rented and does not have a garden. When you have a dog and no garden, it's a mega pain. Every time they want to go out, you have to escort them. Even the late-night toilet trips.

When Solly was a puppy we bought some pop-up button torches and dotted them around the place so if there was a puppy emergency and it was dark out, we could grab one and go. Over time Solly got used to the fact that each trip out was preluded by pressing the button torch. So he started helping us out and pressing it for us to quicken the process, and little by little it developed so that whenever he wanted to go out he announced it by pressing one of them with his nose.

"Solly wants to go out," I said, as he pressed it again just to make sure we knew the situation was becoming urgent.

"I'll do it," Debbie said.

While they were out I went up for a shower.

Although I fully accept that the male body can be a thing of beauty, it's probably fair to say that your average day-to-day example is a bit disappointing. As for bodies that have been knocking about for more than forty-seven years, the disappointment is likely to be greater still. Especially when the body in question is mine.

Washed, rinsed and dried, I stood in front of the mirror.

I looked. I mean really looked. Then I stood back so I could focus, and looked some more.

You know, in all the years I've been running this body this was the first time I'd paid it more than scant attention since I was twenty-something. Sure, I knew what it looked like. I knew the parts I liked and the parts I didn't, and like us all, I'd learned how to clothe it so that the good and bad are extenuated or hidden. But I'd done little in the past couple of decades to update or upgrade. I hadn't looked at myself naked in years. Doing it now, I could see why. Based on the evidence I would most likely have to change my backup life plan to something that didn't involve running away to join the Chippendales.

I touched some of the spots, twisting slowly this way and that. Thighs. Bum. Belly. Shoulders. They all wobbled. Not excessively but they all wobbled more than you would want. Arms up in He-Man pose. Muscles flexed. Not too bad, at least there was some definition there — that'd be the endless buckets of water I carried back and forth to the pigs. My biggest worry was the pecs. Fear of developing moobs was huge. I shimmied to see if they'd shake, and let me tell you shimmying is not easy unless you're well practised. But I gave it my best shot, arms outstretched and everything — if man-boobs slapped together I decided I'd kill myself there and then on the spot. Fortunately, they didn't.

The other upset was the amount of hair that seemed to have sprouted. My back was covered — when did that happen? And why? Why in evolutionary terms is it necessary for the ageing male *Homo sapiens* to grow hair on his back? Was it decided in some grand design meeting chaired by God that middle-aged man was going to need to be petted or something?

"Oh yes, we figure if man does ever reach the grand old age of Forty-seven, we'd better reward him by giving him some back hair. Then he can be stroked. Like a cat. That'd be nice."

Not all the hair was dark either. Some of it was grey. Quite a lot of it was grey. Braving a close-up I moved towards the mirror. The fact that the image lost sharpness was probably a blessing, but I could make out enough to search for wrinkles on my body. I looked for the best part of a second and a half, couldn't see any, and stepped back. Good.

Excellent.

Small mercies.

Then there was the waist. Or more precisely, the lack of it. The bit at the sides where it should nip in but didn't. What the hell happened to that?

Of course, what I couldn't see was inside my body. That I could only feel. I thought of shadow boxing because that's what men do in front of fogged-up mirrors in the bathroom — it's a primal thing written into our DNA — and occasionally dance, but less said about that the better. You thought it was only adolescents who did that sort of thing? Sadly not. We all do. It's a good way to give your body a shake-down and assess how it all feels. Get a sense of how the joints are working. The muscles. The lungs. Heart. Then there's balance, strength, agility, suppleness. Shadow boxing in the bathroom exposes weaknesses in all those. That and pulling your socks on without sitting down or doing the one leg crossed over the other trick, which has roughly the same effect.

But I didn't. I didn't shadow box or dance or anything. Frankly I wasn't sure my body could cope after a day of mucking out seventeen horses. Anyway, the readings would be false. Like doing a fitness test after running a marathon. If I needed an assessment of how things were going under the bonnet of my body, I'd do it in the morning. Tomorrow morning, in fact. Yeah, I'd do it tomorrow morning.

Amazingly, I did. Getting up and out of bed early the next day I made my way back into the bathroom. It was bitter and still dark out. The fire in the lounge would be long cold. Cold was good. Without turning on the light, I stood in front of the mirror shivering in the pre-dawn grey. Normally I'm the very last person ever to make good on a promise made to myself the night before, but this felt important. With my eyesight suddenly going all to wonk, I had to know how the rest of my body was faring.

Dancing was out as I'd need music for that, so shadow boxing it was. That was a better workout anyway. Jigging slowly from foot to foot, I raised my fists. Shoulders rolling, one at a time, backwards and forwards. Hips twisting. Knees loose. Bobbing, up, down. Warming up. A little weaving. Some twisting. Fists up higher. *Pow*, I threw an exploratory punch. Nice. No pain so far. No sign of trouble. So I went for it. I *went* for it.

For ten whole minutes I fought myself, and even I got that joke. When I'd had enough I reached up and turned on the light, swivelled and sat on the edge of the bath.

The good news was I had lasted ten minutes. The bad news was I might not last another ten.

My body was exhausted. My heart *pounded*.

I couldn't breathe. It hurt.

Everything hurt.

Why had I pushed myself so hard shadow boxing in the bathroom? What was I trying to prove? That I was still young? Well I wasn't. My body was forty-seven years old, and for the last fifteen of those years it had been bounced around on the backs of horses, made to charge after escaping piglets, been head butted by a succession of sheep and goats, walked a bazillion steps after chickens, run away from killer geese, tripped, slipped, banged and walloped itself all over the place with hardly a month between near-death experiences. I'd zapped my nuts on electric fencing, rolled the quad bike, stubbed toes, legs, head and fingers, chopped a tree down on my noggin and mucked out more horses than your average groom. As bodies go, it was, in short, abused. And how did I thank it for all the years of loyal service? I brought it into a cold dark bathroom first thing in the morning and tried to do it in.

Athletes warm down. Mortals sit on the edge of the bath and suffer.

So I sat on the edge of the bath and suffered. I wanted to know how my body was doing. Now I knew. When pushed it felt slow, and wobbly, and didn't work the way it used to. It had changed, and I don't just mean the hair or the disappearing waist, or even how things are starting to flop, and ache, and wobble, and feel tired. No, it had changed because it was ageing. It wasn't unfit, it was just getting older and slower.

It took half an hour before I could move, and then I put my socks on by sitting on the bed *and* crossing one leg over the other. Fully dressed, I drank coffee and ate toast and tried not to dwell on the fact that my body hated me. Then I went out.

After morning rounds I went straight up to Steph's to get an early start on the horse-poo situation. Catching the horses napping by arriving pre-lunch, they each made every effort to squeeze out all the remaining nuggets they could, so I had something to do. Not have a wasted trip. Bless 'em.

"I don't suppose there's any chance you could do that straight into the wheelbarrow and miss out the middle-man, is there?" I said, as a big bay cob stood in the middle of the yard and shat his own body weight while waving his bum about to give the produce splatting on the ground behind him some breadth.

Ear bud in one ear, podcast on, grabbing the wheelbarrow and shovel from where I'd left them yesterday, I started.

The podcast was *The Drunken Taoist* with Daniele Bolelli, a show I knew and loved, but wasn't in the mood for. After nearly losing a fist-fight with myself in the bathroom earlier I needed something sharper. Something with a bit more of a bite to it. Something like *The Bugle*, or maybe *WTF* with Marc Maron.

I swished down the list of dozens and dozens of different podcasts downloaded onto my phone.

See here's a thing, I listen to probably fifty different podcasts during the course of a week while I'm out working the land, on loads of different topics from science and scepticism, through Buddhism and religion, comedy, spirituality, news, current affairs, politics, satire, philosophy, deep conversations with Pete Holmes, self-improvement with Geoff Thompson, funny with Danny Baker, weird with Duncan Trussell, talks with Joe Rogan, and there's nothing within them that I don't agree with (except some of the really bonkers thoughts of Duncan Trussell, obviously), which doesn't make any sense at all as each one pretty much contradicts the others. For example, one minute I'll be listening to Professor Brian Cox talking about science saving humanity and everything else is mumbo-jumbo on *The Infinite Monkey Cage*, and I'll think, yes of course that's right! Then the next minute I'll be listening to Daniele Bolelli where he argues that extreme science without any room for spirituality is dogma, and I absolutely agree with that too. Only you can't agree with both. Can you?

Is this another manifestation of my age that I seem to have become a mass of contradictions, seeing and understanding every point of view no matter how opposed? It feels really strange, and most unlike me. I used to be such an opinionated git. But look at me now, rolling over for everyone.

External body, internal body and now my mind was changing. Living self-sufficiently with the animals

319

would alter a person, I accept that, but couple it with hitting middle age and it was all getting out of hand.

The podcast cut out and the phone rang. I dug it out of a pocket and answered.

"It's me," Debbie said. "You left before I could talk to you this morning. Is everything okay?"

Leaning on the shovel and keeping an eye out for Aliana and her wheelbarrow tipping-over trick, I told her it was.

"Good. You haven't forgotten about today have you? Collecting the geese?"

As if things couldn't get any worse. "Of course not. When do you need me?"

"About an hour."

"It might take a little longer than that for me to finish up here, but I'll come down as soon as I can."

I worked quicker, driving the wheelbarrow like a racing car and shovelling like a man who has somewhere else to be, as opposed normal when there's nowhere else on earth I'd rather be than here, surrounded by mounds of horse poo. I used to be a contender, you know. I used to be an estate agent. Cool suit, sharp tie, crisp white shirt:

"This is the home for you, Mrs Jones. It's been a long time since I've been inside anywhere that felt so comfortable. It just has a really nice vibe to it, don't you think? It's clean and smart and the kitchen is to die for!"

The geese were at the Station Inn, a local pub. Of course they were. "A pint of beer, large dry white wine, two packs of cheese and onion crisps . . . and . . . oh yeah! Six geese please." Only in North Devon.

It was a short drive to the pub and when we were halfway there Debbie said, "You were in the bathroom for a long time this morning."

"Was I? I thought you were asleep."

"Mmm, I was. For some of it. What were you doing? There were . . . noises."

There are some things you don't even want to share with your wife, so I said, "Not much," and hoped it would be enough. Of course it wasn't. It was nowhere near enough. I could feel her eyes drilling into me. Sighing heavily, I added, "I was working out. You know, trying to see what state my body was in."

"Why? Not because of your eyes, surely?"

"Actually it was."

"Okay. And?"

"And it was okay. I worked out for ten minutes and sat on the edge of the bath for half an hour to recover. Debbie, can I ask you a question?"

"U-huh."

"Do you feel like you're changing as you get older?"

Folding her arms she turned and looked out the window . . . ..and looked out the window . . .

. . . and looked out the window.

Just as we were about to pull into the pub car park, she said, "It's different for a woman."

"It's probably not as different as you think," I said.

"Yeah, it is."

We ordered two small drinks and found a free table while we waited for the owners, Lynn and Martin, to come and find us.

"Go easy" Debbie said as I gulped. "We haven't got any money for a second round."

Shame, you've no idea how good real beer tastes.

Six geese arrived, crated and ready for the journey. While Debbie was chatting, Lynn took me to one side and surreptitiously handed me an envelope. Inside was a square of material that she'd embroidered with a pig. "For the quilt," she said. Thanking her, I put the material back inside the envelope and stuffed the whole thing out of sight down the back of my jeans, downed the beer and carefully carried the geese out to the car. We'd parted with a chunk of rent money to buy the geese, which meant the rest of the month was going to be ultra tight, but we'd just have to get on with it. Sometimes you've got to adopt an attitude like that or you'd never get anywhere. Even if we were increasing the size of our resident goose kill squad. I wondered how Honey-Bunny would react? The female had made some sort of effort to sit on some eggs several months back, but nothing came of it. I just hoped they would accept the newbies. I knew what they were like.

In fact the worst they did was boggle at them, as if to say "Whose bright idea was that?"

"Come on, be nice," I said, scooting the newcomers into the goose house where they ran for a corner and huddled. Five of the six geese looked just like our hooligan mobsters — white, tall and proud with plenty of attitude. The sixth, however, was different. She had grey markings and the tips of her wings, the very ends, didn't sit close to her body as wings should, but stuck out so that when she walked she looked like a real

322

girly-girl tottering along in high heels, arms straight down by her sides with her hands pointing out level with the ground.

"That worked out better than I thought," Debbie said. "At least Honey-Bunny isn't attacking them."

The trick with introducing new poultry to existing stock is to do it just before dark. That way they have no choice but to settle down for the night and get used to one another over bedtime. Closing the door I said, "They'll be fine until the morning."

"Look at the turkeys, *look at the turkeys!* My God they're *huge!*" Debbie said as they came thundering over, their breasts arriving minutes before the rest of them.

"You want to see Winnie's two babies," I said, leading Debbie over to the stable. With unrestricted access to an all-you-can-eat buffet from Mum that was designed for ten or twelve babies, the two piglets had scoffed Mum's milk until they became bloated and podgy with faces nearly as enormous as their bellies.

Next to be fed and settled down was the General and his wife-of-right-now.

"No sign of her being pregnant at all?" Debbie said, peering in as I put their dinner down.

"No."

"Okay, so it's agreed we need a replacement?"

What could I say? "Yes, of course. I've been talking to one of the boys down the end and making a friend of him. His dad is the General and his mum was Pippa. He's a good, well-proportioned boy. I think he'd work well."

I fed the groups of pigs on the way down to him and once we were there pointed out the boy. He was indeed a big lad, about eighteen months old and not far short of his dad's size, which would have put him somewhere in the 200 to 250 kg zone.

"Nice. Have you given him a name?"

"I was thinking of Rigsby."

She nodded, smiling.

So that was it, Rigsby was our new boar. The General was put out on gardening leave. At some point I'd have to move him away from his wife-of-right-now and put Rigsby in with her. She'd be his first mission.

On the way back I popped in and gave the General an extra scoop of dinner. I didn't say a word about the decision to replace him, though I suspect he'd guessed. He's not stupid.

Out with the dad, in with the son

It was three weeks before I got a night in on my own.

I was in our bedroom. On the floor was the empty suitcase in which I'd been hiding all the packages people had sent or handed to me for Debbie's quilt.

A jumble-sale of clothes covered our bed; tops and skirts and shirts and blouses and jeans and t-shirts in a higgledy-piggledy spray of colour. Amongst the garments were off-cuts of material, some beautifully bejewelled and jazzed up, others plain and simple. Some were brand new while some looked as though they'd been shoved in a back pocket since Hadrian built his wall. Some were bright and vibrant, others understated and quiet. Each piece meant something to someone and they all had a name written carefully on a white sticker that was neatly attached in a corner so I could keep track of whose was whose. There were forty-six stickers.

Debbie was over at a friend's house and I was babysitting Solly.

From the centre of the heap on the bed, a little grey face looked up. Then a tail started wagging.

"You should not be in here," I said. I had tried to do it without his help, but when a Great Dane wants to join you in a room there's little you can do to stop him, and doors are certainly no match.

Forty-six pieces when cut to the right size equated to forty-six squares for Debbie's birthday quilt. I was four short of the magic fifty, but I'd already allowed for that with the animals. I'd pinch a piece from Solly's blanket for one. A section from George's rug for two. A snippet from Dex's bed for three. Which just left one square to find. For that, Debbie herself was going to unwittingly supply a square — from her wedding dress.

Of course it's necessary to have a piece of her wedding dress in the quilt! In fact, it's vital to make it really special. Besides, she hadn't worn the thing in twenty-four years — it was just folded up in a drawer. Obviously I wouldn't take it from the centre of the bust or anything stupid like that, but a bit taken out of the train wouldn't hurt. Would it? It would be a way of having a memento of the dress that she could look at every day and enjoy rather than have it tucked out of sight in a drawer. She would love that. Totally love it. The logic was sound, but that didn't make the prospect of attacking one's wife's wedding dress with a pair of scissors any less scary.

So that's it, I had all the raw uncut material to hand. Now all I had to do was figure out how to cut it and stitch it all together into a quilt, and there's only one place you go for that kind of information: YouTube.

Having upset the dog by putting everything back into the suitcase, we went downstairs, poured a glass of wine and switched on the computer.

One of the reasons I'm not brilliant on the internet is my laptop's a bit naff. The sound doesn't work so you can't hear anything, and the computer itself gives you intermittent electric shocks, which, admittedly, does make you type faster.

I went on to YouTube and wrote "quilt-making" in the search bar, found a video that looked as though it was more demonstration than talking, and watched it all the way through.

Then I watched another.

And another.

There is a possibility, and I'm hedging on this, but there is a possibility that I might have taken on more than I could handle with the whole quilt-making business. Mind you, what choice did I have now? I was committed. I didn't have an alternative idea to fall back on, and besides everyone had put so much time and thought into their piece it would be criminal if I gave up without at least trying.

That said, homemade sentimental presents only get you so far. If they look rubbish, no matter how thoughtful they are, they will find their way into the bin. And I didn't want that. I wanted this to be amazing.

Braving another bout of electric shock therapy from the computer (they're wrong about that you know, it doesn't cheer you up) I watched the videos twice more.

That night I dreamt of material and colours, patterns and wedding dresses and woke feeling more feminine than is entirely comfortable. So I picked my nose and cupped a hand down my pants while I made breakfast to help raise my masculinity. Then I went down to start morning rounds.

"Morning, Senorita," I called as I made my way over to the goose house. Introducing six adolescent geese had completely altered their dynamic. These days the focus when I let them out had shifted away from attacking me and much more towards ensuring the flock stayed together. Last out was always Angel Wings, the pretty grey girly goose with the wingtips that pointed outwards. I would open the door and the others would come out like a New York gang leaving the clubhouse, while she would totter and mince, and on occasion sashay after them. I was worried they might segregate her because she was so different, but there was no sign of it. They did get frustrated that she was always lagging behind, but they didn't ostracise her for it.

Chickens and ducks next, then goats. Quick scoot around the sheep and horses making sure everyone was where they should be and all legs were pointing down and not up, and then it was the pigs' turn.

In the last few weeks I'd spent some quality time with the new boar, Rigsby. Although he was the General's son, he was very different from his dad. Where the General was laidback and chilled with nothing to prove, Rigsby was a little edgy. I couldn't remember if the General was ever like that — I didn't think he was. Far as I could remember, the General was mellow from day one.

Which raised the problem of how to calm Rigsby down and mould him into the type of pig that would work for me down here. He was already tall and powerful and bulging with muscle, but I needed that muscle to be friendly and calm. In order to reach that chilled state, top of the agenda was to get him laid. He was still a virgin and needed a woman. He needed sex. Simple as that.

The problem was that the only available female was currently in with the General. Which meant I had to move the General out. Away from his wife-of-right-now. Shift the father away so the son could move in. Out with the old and in with the young.

I knew I had to do it, it's just — it felt sad.

I backed up the trailer. Slowly. Carefully. When it was in place I called the General down, kind of hoping he wouldn't come, but he did. He trusted me. What I asked him to do, he did. We were mates, why wouldn't he do as I asked?

His new home was gorgeous, a huge field shelter in a nice big field and, most important, a big double bed of fresh straw — he did like a nice bed. It was perfect. But he would be alone. When I could I'd bring him a woman, just for old time's sake, but right now there wasn't one available. The pattern was full. I'd come in and see him every day, but I was a buddy, not a wife.

Parking in the field I let down the ramp and pointed out the hotspots to the General. "Water is over there . . . Your new bedroom is there . . . You get two good meals delivered every day, no loud music and lights out by eleven-thirty. Any questions?"

What I didn't point out was the fact that he could also see his old pen, and in it his ex-wife-of-right-now. Okay, they hadn't seemed get on particularly well and there certainly was no sign of love in the air the way there had been whenever General was around Pippa, but even so, seeing your ex-missus shacking up with her new lover is going to affect you, especially when her new lover is your own son.

"You're better off without her," I told him as he sniffed his way over to a patch of sedge grass and started tucking in. "You're too good for her. Way too good for her. And as for him!" It's very difficult not to take sides in a split-up, you know.

When he was settled I drove the trailer out and trundled it down towards Rigsby.

What I had to watch was that I wasn't resentful towards Rigsby. It would be all too easy to slip down that road. In addition to being calm, I needed Rigsby to be a friend. It's unlikely I'd ever be as close to him as I was with the General, but it was vital we had a good relationship. After all, it wasn't his fault he was chosen to take over from his pops in the family business.

"Give me two minutes, Rigsby," I called, rushing to get everything in place so it would be easy for him to load. "Trust me, it'll be worth the wait. All your Christmases and birthdays are about to come true in the shape of a hot babe waiting for you just over there." I pointed so he got an idea of where he was going.

When the path to the waiting trailer was lined on either side with temporary fencing so he had a proper track to walk along, I called him down. He came, but maybe a touch too eagerly. It was my fault, I'd built up the anticipation too high with all the talk of hot babes and nookie. Faced with a steady trip in the trailer or making his own way, Rigsby chose the latter and bulldozed through the side of the path, flattening the temporary fencing like it wasn't even there.

Shit.

All I could do was accept the situation and adapt. Fast.

"You know, you're right," I called, grabbing the bucket full of food that I'd thought to keep handy in case something went wrong, and ran after him. "It's far quicker if we just leg it."

By the time I had caught up with him he was halfway there. Just up ahead the path snaked left to right. As it straightened out, I could see the entrance to his new home some fifty yards further on. "That's it, that's where we're heading!" I shouted, taking the lead and shaking the bucket in front of his face, hoping the prospect of an early dinner followed by an afternoon of

330

losing his virginity would be all the enticement he'd need to follow me.

We were almost there. "That's it. Good lad, nearly there now."

All I had to do was keep his focus on me. I rattled the bucket. It made a perfect follow-me sound.

Where it had been raining there were puddles all along the Farm track. I splashed through them. So did Rigsby. Neither of us cared about getting wet, but I was worried about tripping. The turning circle on a charging pig probably wasn't great, and the last thing I needed was him running over the top of me.

At the point where I needed him to come off the path and head up into the woods where the entrance to his enclosure stood, he stopped. Just stopped dead in the middle of the track.

I shook the bucket.

"Rigsby! Come on, Rigsby!"

But he wasn't interested in me. He wasn't interested in the bucket, or women, or anything else for that matter. Out the corner of his eye he'd spotted something far more interesting to a young full-of-himself male. As he turned, I followed the direction in which he now faced, and saw what it was. The General was standing by the gate opposite. He wasn't doing anything wrong. He was in the field in which I'd put him, he'd just heard the commotion and wandered over. Wandered over and found Rigsby running down the track on the other side of the gate.

"No, Rigsby, come to me!" I yelled, shaking the bucket for all I was worth. "General, go away! *Go away!*"

This was bad. Rigsby made his way to the gate until they were stood facing each other, nose to nose. Both boys chomping, white foam bubbling from their mouths. The prelude to fighting. The rumble in the jungle would have nothing on these two if they actually got in together.

"Rigsby! Rigsby!" I screamed. Nothing. Not even a glimmer that he was listening to me.

I rushed down. The gate separating them was metal, so at least stood more of a chance than one of the wooden gates. Mind you, 260 kgs one side against 350 kgs the other and even a metal gate won't hold up forever.

Both pigs were now pacing back and forth on either side of the gate, the foam from their mouths falling onto the floor in snowlike flurries. The noise they made as they chomped was loud and squelchy like a sink plunger rammed time and again up and down over a blocked drain.

I had to get Rigsby away. "Come on, boy," I said, pushing his bum and trying to spin him around, rattling the bucket full of food at the same time. For a second he looked at me, but the interest was only fleeting. He wasn't going to be moved that easily.

Tension was escalating. For the first time ever being around pigs, I was worried. The General had always been the boar on the farm since the beginning. We'd never needed another one, so I'd no reference point on what happened when two entire males clashed, but I guessed it would be ugly and bloody.

Suddenly I had an idea. The trailer! Leaving the bucket of feed on a nearby wall, I sprinted back to the quad bike. Behind it, still attached, was the trailer. Slamming the ramp shut I jumped on the bike and started the engine. It fired up first time. Slipping it into first gear I jammed my thumb on the accelerator and leant all my weight over the handlebars. The wheels spun on the gravel until they found traction, and we shot forward.

Following the path all the way back I pulled up beside the gate and the two warring pigs. Little between them had changed. They were both still pacing, foaming, angry and itching to fight.

Forcing myself to slow down so I didn't make any stupid mistakes, I let the ramp down at the back of the trailer. It landed with the dull *thwerump* of metal hitting soggy ground. The bucket of food was still on the wall. I lifted it off and went back to the trailer. Now all I had to do was get Rigsby inside.

It was pointless rattling the bucket. The whole thing was well beyond anyone stopping for dinner. So I picked up a stick, not to hit him with, but in an emergency there's a soft spot of skin just behind the ear that if you place the tip of the stick and push even the biggest pig will yield. I tried it. Put the tip in place and pushed. Not too hard, just enough. And he moved. Moved away from the gate. It was working. Then suddenly . . . suddenly, he switched back and just came at me. He was so fast I didn't stand a chance. He lunged at my leg, his teeth ripping through jeans and skin in a single bite. Blood gushed down my leg, turning the blue denim black. Then he turned and walked off.

Oh my God. FUCK! Okay, don't panic. There was no pain. Not yet. I tried putting weight on the leg and it took it. Good. I looked up. Rigsby had moved away from the gate and was wandering aimlessly, zigzagging the path almost as though he was drunk. I went over and picked up the bucket once more. Rattling it I called his name. "Rigsby Rigsby! Over here!"

He didn't come over. Didn't even acknowledge me. So I yelled harder, knowing that if he didn't approach me soon I'd have to go and get him, and at that moment that was the last thing I wanted to do.

My heart was thumping. I rattled the bucket. "*Rigsby!*"

Nothing. No response.

I looked down at my leg. The blood was now a tea-plate size around the rip in my jeans. It felt hot, and wet, but it still didn't hurt. Normally the sight of my own blood would have had me freaking out, but I didn't have time for that.

Christ, I wished I had money on my phone so I could have rung someone for help.

Grabbing the bucket and the stick, I went after Rigsby, figuring I had three options: one, to retrace our steps and get him back in his old pen; two, to get him in the new pen with love-of-right-now; or three, get him into the trailer.

He was further down the path. Not running, walking. The foam had gone. Cleared up. He didn't look demented; he just looked like the old Rigsby.

I got close and threw some food on the floor. That caught his interest. The closest of the three options was the trailer. When he'd eaten the handful of nuts I'd thrown, I went up to him and rattled the bucket.

He followed me. Right up to the trailer. When we reached the ramp, I threw the entire bucket and he followed it inside. I had him.

My heart *weerhumphed*

I rushed to hospital, but it was more precautionary than anything else. It looked a lot worse than it was.

"Doesn't matter," Debbie had said. "There's a risk of infection and all sorts. You need to get it looked at."

That's how we ended up at Barnstaple Accident & Emergency. Again. "They'll think I'm a regular," I said.

"This is only your third time in fourteen years."

First time was when a tree hit me on the head, and the second when one of the cats savaged my hand. "They're hardly going to invite you to the Christmas do on the strength of it," she said.

I sat quietly in one of the red plastic bucket seats with Debbie holding my hand.

"Are you okay?"

When I'd made it up to the house Debbie had washed and dressed the wound. It stung like crazy, but I wouldn't call it a bad pain.

"It's fine," I said.

"And you?" she pressed.

"I'm fine too."

She nodded and squeezed my hand. "Don't forget I'm a woman and I know what fine means."

When I was small and it became apparent that my mother was struggling with me over the bonding issue, my aunt kind of stepped in. "She's your second mum," my mother would tell me, adding, "I tried to get her to take you on full time but she wouldn't, though she does think the world of you." And regardless, she really did. On my seventh birthday my aunt bought me a tent and we pitched it in the back garden. The feeling of having somewhere of my very own was incredible. It was mine and nobody could come in without me saying they could, and I had this overwhelming sense of peace in there. It was amazing, and I loved it, loved it, loved it. I lived, ate and slept in there for an entire week — which when you're seven is a big deal. Anyway, soon after we all went out for the day, and when we got back I found a couple of the local kids had squatted in my tent while we'd been out. They'd used everything, touched everything and trashed the place. I tried to put everything back as it was, but the feeling it had given me was gone. I never slept in there again, and a couple of weeks later it was packed up and put away in the garage.

Forty years later, sitting in A&E after Rigsby had attacked me, I felt exactly the same. I felt betrayed, and I felt as though something special had been snatched away from me.

Look, I was overdramatic as a child and I'm overdramatic now. I know that. But I couldn't help the way I felt. Rigsby would have to go. I'd find him a new home. Which begged the question of whether the General could take back his position as Shag Master on the smallholding and be productive, or whether we'd have to look at yet another option. My money was on the General. I'd have put all my money on him.

"Simon Dawson?" a nurse called.

Getting up I made my way over. The nurse looked at my leg, then another nurse looked at it, then a doctor looked at it, and they all found it highly amusing that I'd been bitten by a pig. Of course they did. Taken out of context it was funny. They also told me I'd live, which was nice to hear.

We drove home, opened some awful wine and I sat on the sofa cuddling Solly while Debbie rustled up some dinner for the injured soldier.

It's funny how fear can be retro-fitted onto a scenario. I wasn't scared at the time — I was mindful of what could happen, but I wasn't scared. But replaying it in my mind I added fear, maybe not for what actually happened, but more for what could have happened. When Rigsby spun around and went for me, he was super fast. The only way I can describe it was like a snapping motion, the way you might imagine a shark suddenly turning on you in the water. It was that fast and that sudden. There was no way I could have avoided him. He was too quick. It was that instant turn of speed and the fact that I had no chance of getting away that was really playing on my mind.

I wondered how I'd be tomorrow. I wondered how I'd be around the General. I hoped I wouldn't be any different with him. After all, you can't tar all pigs because of one. But then again, tonight I'd seen a different side to pigs, one I'd heard about, but never thought I'd see. I'd always thought I was too careful. I'd thought I knew pigs too well. I'd thought we had an understanding. I'd thought, I'd thought, I'd thought . . .

No, I wouldn't be different with the General because I wouldn't let myself. We went back too far for that.

But it did make me think.

In time I could see myself at dinner parties telling the story of Rigsby's attack and getting a thousand laughs. I could add it to my repertoire of comic near-death experiences the way I had a tree falling on my head, rolling the quad bike or electrocuting my testicles. Play it up until I sound like an agricultural Evil Knievel; brave and fearless and constantly battered and bruised. Oh, the life of a self-sufficient smallholder!

Much to Solly's disgust, I got off the sofa and made up the fire, sipping wine while I loaded on the logs. Debbie was still in the kitchen and by the gorgeous aromas coming from there she was cooking Chinese.

One thing that was quite funny was my *thing*, my angst, my midlife crisis — there you go, I've said it. Of course it was a midlife crisis, *of course it was a midlife crisis*! It had only taken me most of the book to admit it. That feeling of being on the brow of a hill with nothing but a drop down into old age in front of me, didn't feel quite as looming as it had. Yeah, funny that. Go figure. Have a pig attack you and take a chunk out of your leg and suddenly life gets put into perspective. Hip, hip, hooray for irony.

But middle age suddenly didn't feel as looming. It really didn't. Tonight . . .

Who knows, tomorrow it might be back with all the weight of a dumpy-bag of cement landing on my foot.

But I didn't think so, and you want to know why? Because I didn't care as much. You've got to care to have a crisis.

"Come and get it," Debbie called from the kitchen. There on the table was a big bowl of noodles and vegetables and our own pork in a rich sauce, with homemade chopsticks at the ready because Chinese never tastes the same eaten with a knife and fork. Comforting and healthy. Beautiful.

The next morning I was up way earlier than normal. I checked the dressing on my leg, which looked fine, got ready and went out into the dark pre-dawn. That's the good thing about having land, when you can't sleep there's always somewhere to go.

Pulling my baseball cap low and my collar high, I drove the quad bike down with Dex balanced on the back.

I was worried about Rigsby.

Last night I'd slammed the ramp to the trailer shut when he'd gone in after the bucket of feed and gone off to hospital. There was no bed in there for him, and most importantly no water. He might have attacked me, but that didn't mean he should be neglected.

He was asleep. Sprawled out on his side, the metal walls of the trailer reverberating with his snores. He looked peaceful, like butter wouldn't melt.

Clutching an armful of straw I threw it in, figuring he could make up his own bed, then I filled a bucket with water from the stream and set it down just inside the door. He was awake, but still sprawled out on his side.

"Mess last night, wasn't it, boy?" I said. "Look, um . . . my leg's fine. Don't worry about it. Just a stupid situation that got out of hand. That's all. But I'm going to have to find you a new home. You can't stay here. Not anymore. You understand that, don't you? I'm sorry. But I'll find you somewhere nice to go, somewhere with some fit women, I promise."

He still didn't move, so I left him to it. There wasn't much else I could do.

The geese were happy to be let out early. Angel Wings was getting bigger, which only exaggerated her tottering gait, so wherever she went she looked like a lady with big boobs on four-inch stiletos getting a shove down a hill.

By the time I'd done the chickens and the ducks and let the turkeys out it was nearly light. I didn't disturb Senorita quite yet, or milk the goats, but instead made my way into the field where the General now lived — at least until I moved him back in with his was-ex-now-current-wife-of-right-now.

He was in the field shelter on his double bed. I leant against the wall, not quite in, but not quite out either. The sky was almost light now. On the ground was a shimmer of frost, the first of the year. In six weeks' it would be Christmas.

The General sat up and yawned. I couldn't dismiss the fact that he was part of the problem last night.

340

"Rigsby bit me," I said simply. "Did you know that?"

Of course he did, he was there. He yawned again, louder and longer this time.

"I'm fine. Thanks for your concern."

I don't know how to unpack how I felt standing there with a huge pig in front of me having been attacked by his son last night. A lot of the emotions are stuff I don't want to admit to, like fear because I'd now seen the other side of pigs and had a taste of what they're capable of, but also this sense that something deeper between us had been broken when Rigsby took a chunk out of me. I'm not even sure which of those two scared or hurt me the most. Then there were the questions. The inevitable questions. The ones about friendship between man and beast. Is it possible or had I been deluding myself all these years? Was Debbie right and all I was doing was anthropomorphising the animals so I felt like we had a bond? What if I'd made up the whole friendship thing in my head? God, what a thought, that this entire "my best friend is the General" could all be a figment of my imagination. That by putting human traits onto him I'd somehow built a relationship that simply did not exist.

Yawn over, he got up and came over. It was difficult for me to remain still. I wanted to move away, desperately wanted to move away, but a greater part of me needed to remain where I was. In the end I had to hold my breath to try to remain calm. Pathetic, really, but Rigsby had shaken me up. Just the speed and the fact that I couldn't get out of the way when he came at me. The fact that I didn't stand a chance against a pig of Rigsby's size, and the General was way bigger, faster and stronger than him.

Unlike dogs, who move about in the night constantly, pigs tend to zonk out in one position and stay there. The General was stiff after his sleep, and halfway to me stopped for a stretch. I'm not tall, I'm five-foot-eight. Stretched up on hoof-tip, the General's back rises up to my (firm, not at all wobbly) pecks. He's a tall lad.

"All right, big boy." I said, keeping my voice light.

Stretch over he continued plodding towards me. I, in turn, continued my battle against the urge to flee. We were both making progress.

Walking right up to me he went straight for my leg.

I jumped, I mean I *jumped*. Heart thumping, hands on head, girly screech — the works.

He went straight for my leg, my bad leg, and nudged it with his snout. Then he just rested against it. I was standing against the wall and he just rested his head against my bad leg. Gently, really gently. A minute or more passed, then he moved off to find somewhere suitable in the field for a poo.

Okay, he might have been tired. He might have smelt the cream the hospital slathered on the bite under the bandage and been interested in that. Then again he might not have noticed my bad leg at all and simply stopped for a rest as he passed by. There's any number of reasons why he could have done that. Was it the first time he'd ever rested his head against me? No. Was this usual behaviour? No, but then I had moved him into a new area, on his own, and perhaps I was the one constant he recognised as familiar and wanted to touch it. There are a hundred random reasons why he did what he did, and all of them are valid. But I know what I believe.

When he walked off my heart *weerhumphed* at the tenderness and I gulped back a cinema sob, feeling closer to him than I have ever felt in my life.

I went to milk a goat, which is obviously what you do when you crave physical contact because you're heart's just *weerhumphed*. I found Amber in her cupboard intertwined with Bee.

Untangling goats is harder than you'd think. They really cuddle in. Finally, having undone them, I escorted Amber to the milking platform, placed a new bowl under her and started drawing off the milk. We all have our ideal thinking spot. That one just happens to be mine. It's therapeutic.

Splash, splash, splash . . .

Is it really a necessary part of ageing that you have to constantly remodel your core beliefs? Things are so much easier when you're young and have life by the balls, and know, absolutely know, what it's all about. I don't resent the young — not exactly anyway. (Oh come on, who in their late forties doesn't resent them a little bit?) But I also envy them. Must be lovely to have it all figured out.

After Rigsby, things went weird for a while, but they had begun to settle again. The General had seen to that. Funny, just him resting his head on me and suddenly there was context in my life again. You look at what friendship is, and what it means, and it all comes down to a 350 kg pig resting his head against my bad leg. Distilled and simplified into that single sixty-second moment. That's kind of beautiful, don't you think?

Splash, splash, splash . . .

They should put hand milking on the NHS, you know. Suffer from stress? Milk a goat. Maybe that was one of the reasons why my *thing* hadn't returned; that this lifestyle actually helped rather than hindered a midlife crisis. There's a thought! Oh there was something still there, that sense of getting older, but it wasn't what it was. It had morphed into something else. Something less dramatic. That was good, that was very good. I was getting tired of feeling all the time like middle age was something you hurl yourself into off a high cliff.

"Good girl," I told Amber as the milk thinned the closer I got to emptying her. A couple of chickens had joined us. Curry is normally part of the first-thing-in-the-morning-gang while I milk, but she was nowhere to be seen, and Senorita wasn't up yet, so it was quite quiet and sedate, which made a nice change.

Change, it seems, was big on the agenda this morning. Weird how you get days like that. But it was also very much needed. Change brings with it an odd sense of clarity, not so much over the new position, but more over the old one. How annoying is that? It's not until you move on that you really feel you understand where you were.

Where was I? Well it was clear that everything from Ziggy's list to looking up old school friends on

344

Facebook was a way of stalling the sensation of heading over the hill. As a solution it worked, but it was a hard way of going about it. The other way, I now realised, the simple way, was to flatten the hill. In your mind, just flatten it. Bring it down. Level it. Make it as flat as the Cotswolds. That's what Rigsby's attack did, it helped to bring my thoughts together, which in itself was quite an unusual feeling, and allowed me to see what was in front of me all the time, that by putting so much emphasis on this feeling of being up high that the only direction I had to go was over the hill, and the more emphasis I placed on it, the more I concentrated and thought about it and tried to stay up there, the higher this hill became in my mind.

Then several things happened, including Rigsby attacking me. Okay it wasn't a bad attack — I wasn't savaged by any means — but it put the wind up me enough to make me realise that most of the stuff I worried about didn't actually matter. All that malarkey about being on a hill and afraid to go over it in case it made me old, was made up. My head invented it and presented it to me as truth — and I believed it.

There is no hill. You don't plummet into old age; you stroll at your own pace; on the flat. As Stafford said, you can get old at any age, the speed you move into it is largely up to you. Oh sure, my body is going to go through stages of hating me, but let's be honest, it's been going through stages of hating me since I was a teenager.

My phone rang. I let Amber jump down and wiped milky hands on my jeans. Then I answered it.

345

It was Stafford. "Staff! How's things?"

"Good. How are you? Good timing or bad timing?" he said.

"Fine. Just finished milking Amber."

"I hear there's going to be a party."

Stumped I said, "Is there?"

"By the looks of it. Just had an email from Debbie. She's decided to have a fiftieth birthday party and sent out a global invitation. How good is that?"

I might need some help finishing this quilt

Scissors.

Snip.

Snip.

Snip.

It took half a day to cut the fifty squares, accurately, neatly and precisely to the correct size — though not all the same size, as some pieces had to be bigger, which kind of made it a bit of a challenge to ensure I still ended up with a symmetrical oblong and not something that resembled a shape a child stuck together using Stickle Bricks.

It was kind of daunting, sitting there cutting into all these different sets of clothing that meant so much to people. There was Debbie's nephew's first baby grow. An embroided picture of Solly. Even her dad's towel that he used when he played indoor bowls for Scotland. And, of course, her wedding dress. My heart was hammering when I slashed into that one.

But I did it. Fifty pieces: all different colours, different textures, different fabrics. The quilt was going to look amazing! Absolutely amazing!

I cleared the bed and began laying out the squares.

It was going to look incredible.

Seven along the top row.

In-cred-ib-le.

Seven along the second row.

She was going to love it.

Five along the third row.

I hoped she'd cry when I gave it to her.

Five along the fourth row.

I bet she would.

Five along the fifth row.

I knew I would. I'd gone over how I'd present it to her so many times in my head, and I couldn't even think my way through it without choking up.

Seven along the sixth row.

Although I knew she knew exactly what it was. I knew she did.

Seven along the seventh row.

She hadn't mentioned it in ages.

Seven along the last row.

Of course she knew.

Done. That's fifty.

I stood back so I could get the full impact.

It looked . . . bloody awful.

Bloody awful.

An utter mess.

Worse than that, it looked ugly.

Oh God.

YouTube was no good. I could see what they were doing, but I couldn't hear the instructions.

I couldn't work out what I'd done so wrong, why it looked so bad.

Booked in to give a talk at a local WI group the following evening, I stood up and did my bit and then with all the ladies still sitting there, said, "Now I wonder if you might be able to help me with some advice?" and asked them how to put a patchwork quilt together, and especially how to lay out the squares so they didn't look ugly.

The trick, it turned out, was to arrange the colours as though it was a horizon, with all the blues at the top, then the reds, which presumably represented the sun, then the greens and the browns and blacks at the bottom.

Next time Debbie was out, I laid the fifty pieces out on the bed again, only this time in the new colour order.

Oh yes! Oh yes, yes, yes! *That's* how it should have looked!

Now all I had to do was stitch them together.

Whenever I could, whenever Debbie was out even for just an hour or two, I'd get the sewing machine and run a few more squares together. Bit by bit it took shape, each row complete before sewing the rows together. When it was done it looked great, but that was only half the process. Buying a new unfitted bed sheet as backing and some wadding in the middle with the patchwork on top so it was like a fabric sandwich, I pinned it all in place and then ran the machine up and down in wide

348

criss-cross lines. The result was a proper patchwork quilt. Fifty squares making a one-metre-ten wide by one-metre-thirty long quilt. I'd done it. I'd actually bloody done it!

"General, you are not going to believe this," I said, crawling up next to him. He was back in his house, the old routine reestablished, which of course meant his wife-of-right-now was nowhere to be seen.

Rigsby had gone. I couldn't help wondering if I'd overreacted. The thing is we have people down constantly. If we're not running a course we've got friends with us, and I need to be able to trust all the animals down here no matter what the situation. We stay in contact via Facebook with the farm where Rigsby now lives. Apparently he's very happy, and there hasn't been the slightest hint of a repeat performance. So yes, I do wonder if I made the right decision with him. But what's done is done.

For now General is back in charge of loving the ladies, or would be if his wife-of-right-now hung around long enough to let him.

"I've finished the quilt," I told the General. He was lying on his side in the straw so I sat on his bum. "Really, really, really, honestly finished it," I said. I expected him to whoop, but he's not exactly the whooping type of guy.

"I hope she loves it. I think she will. Do you think she will?" To be honest I could have done with running it by someone a little more verbose. Ziggy maybe. Or Stafford. "I think she'll love it."

The whole moving the General out and Rigsby in, then that going wrong and moving the General back, saga still left me with mixed feelings. There was something in there about the older generation and the younger generation that made me feel bad, and part of that was because I felt happy that it hadn't worked out. I kind of liked it that the General was back in his old role. Yet I also felt as though I'd let Rigsby down somehow. All the animals are my responsibility, and if something goes wrong, or kicks off, the buck stops with me. It's my bad, to use a phrase of Garth's. If this was a football team, I'd have had to resign.

But I also had to accept that it was more than simply the set-up with the pigs that changed the day Rigsby bit me.

"I've got something for you, General," I said, rooting around in my back pocket and pulling out a sheet of paper. I unfolded it. It was Ziggy's list. The one I'd written on the beer mat in the pub all those weeks ago. All nine commandments: *Clothes, music, TV, internet, social media, attitude and outlook, hair, food, language*. Ziggy's plan for avoiding the onset of middle age.

Ziggy was right, you know. Much as it now pained me to admit it, he was right. The lists we wrote for each other were a load of rubbish. I scrunched it up and gave it to the General to eat.

It felt good. It felt really good.

General did look old. He'd developed this habit of lolling his tongue out all the time — sleeping, walking and mooching about with it hanging in the breeze.

Sometimes he'd even let me grab hold of it and pull it like a cartoon tongue. Silly sod.

Forty-seven years old and I'm sitting in a make-do and mend pigsty that I cobbled together myself, in the woods, on the bum end of a pig — a pig who's got his tongue sticking out. Life doesn't get any odder than that. But it also doesn't get any better.

So many things now make sense. Not everything, not everything by any stretch, but a lot. I guess that's what happens when you work your way through a *thing*.

With Ziggy's list now passing through the digestive tract of the General, I thought it was time for a new list.

The things I now know and understand from the point of view of a man sitting on the bum of a pig, having recently experienced, and survived, a thing. By Simon Dawson. In no particular order:

1. My younger self was a dick with no imagination and should not be consulted on older-self matters.
2. Barry Manilow is cool.
3. So is watching *Come Dine with Me*.
4. Well Man/Woman tests should come with a health warning.
5. Over-forties should *never* strip to the waist and stand next to a teenager in front of a mirror.
6. Pigs make excellent best friends.
7. Parents do their best even when they themselves are dealt shitty cards.
8. "The Look" from a woman should be reclassified

as a dangerous weapon and placed in the same category as crimes with "Intent" in the title.

9. Micro pigs aren't.
10. Anthropomorphising animals is no bad thing if it helps you make sense of the world around you.

It's time to P . . . A . . . R . . . T . . . Y

Debbie stood next to her mother in the kitchen. On the table in front of them was a pile of presents all wrapped up in different-coloured papers and shiny jazzy papers, most of which were emblazed with "Happy 50th Birthday". Beside that mound was another of unopened cards. I made coffee and bucks fizz and we each had a glass and a mug and did "cheers" and "chin-chin" and "happy birthday" and clinked and clonked the drinks together.

"What do you think?" I said.

"I don't know where to start."

"You could start with my gift."

"No. Cards first," which was such a girly thing to say and frankly really annoying — *I want you to open mine, NOW!*

She opened the cards. All of them. Slowly. Looking at the pictures before moving inside and poring over every word printed and written. Oohing. Ahhing. Laughing. Smiling. Oohing some more.

Finally, when all the cards were separated from their envelopes and standing to attention in front of her, she turned to the presents.

"Mine first," I said, pulling the biggest one to the front.

"So do I get to read your emails after this?"

"If you want. *Just open it!*"

"Okay, okay."

The wrapping paper I'd chosen was blue, her favourite colour, and came in single sheets, not a roll, which had all been carefully taped together in a patchwork, which seemed appropriate given what lay beneath. She undid a corner. Then another corner. Then she turned the whole thing around so she could get at the other side and flipped open those corners too. All that was holding it together now was a long strip of sticky tape along the centre. Pausing, she stopped for a sip of bucks fizz — she actually stopped for a bloody drink! Then I saw her look out of the corner of her eye at me and grin.

"Second thoughts, I might save opening it for later," she said, and made to push it back into the pile.

The look on my face must have said everything because she crumpled and said, "I'm just teasing you, look," and swished her hand under the line of sticky tape.

The paper fell open.

I'd folded the quilt so only the outside would show when she opened it. She lifted it clear of the paper, turned it to face her, took one look at all the different squares of material, each with the name of a close friend or family member neatly written on a white sticker in the corner, shrieked and dropped the whole thing back on the table, her hands flying up to her face.

I'd thought of this moment a thousand times.

"Do you get it?" I said. "That's what all the parcels were. I asked fifty of your friends to send me a piece of material and made that with them. I even got one from L'Escargot, the restaurant where we got engaged."

Between Debbie and her mother they spread the quilt out over the table. They were both completely engrossed. I stood back and hugged Solly, battling a lump in my throat that was threatening tears. I felt exactly the way I'd hoped I'd feel, which was that if I could have bought her the diamond at the top of the crown jewels and given her that, I wouldn't have felt any happier with what I'd done.

Debbie came over, put her hands on either side of my face, kissed me and said all the things I'd hoped she'd say. "I love it. I love it *so* much. It's amazing. You've worked so hard. Thank you. I love you." It's been a long time since I'd seen her look so happy.

Success. Oh yeah baby,
That's What I Call Success
Number 1!

I'd quiz her later on whether she knew all along what it was.

"I need to go and do the animals," I said, and left Debbie and her mum hunched over the quilt, pointing out the different squares to one another and speed talking, which is, as far as I can gather, what women do when they want to cover a lot of verbal ground in the shortest amount of time and do it by shortening entire "do you remember" anecdotes into as few words as possible, sometimes only one or two.

The last thing I saw before closing the door was the two of them point at a square and both say at the same time, "Tow bar!" and howl with laughter.

So, my wife was fifty years old. How did that feel? It felt pretty good actually. Collecting Dex, I drove down the hill. I could have scooted through morning rounds and been back up in an hour, but it felt good to be down there. I even smiled at the geese as they lunged at me.

Bertie Wooster led out the ducks (it wasn't raining) and the chickens did their usual thing of the cockerels fighting between themselves for shagging rights over the ladies, all of whom hung around to see who the lucky victor would be.

"Senorita, your belly is enormous!" I said as she thumped her way past me, the bottom of her stomach dampening where it was brushing against the dew on the grass. "There are clubs you can join, you know. Support groups. I think I saw an advert with a smiley woman who gets all her dinners delivered through the post and she lost stacks of weight. Might be worth a thought."

Letting the goats out, Curry disappeared off to find her lamb friends while I milked Amber. The world was aligned.

"General," I said, looking in, "I can't hang around, but I just wanted to tell you the quilt was a hit. We did good, boy. We did good. Look, I'll fill you in tonight."

Back at the house I showered and changed just in time before guests started arriving for the party.

"I knew you'd be first," I told Stafford as he led Serena into the kitchen.

"When you get to my age it pays to be early and get things done. Besides, word is the birthday girl made curry and that's not something I want to turn up late for! And here she is, happy birthday, darling," he said as Debbie walked towards him, both he and Serena cuddling her and thrusting a present and card into her hands.

When they'd untwined, I said, "Staff, a minute?"

He excused himself and came over.

I felt a little silly and probably over compensated. "I never really thanked you properly for the sheets and stuff. For the pig house. The corrugated-iron sheets. You know? And, well, I kind of made you this." I handed him the spoon I'd made. Sanded, polished and oiled it looked okay.

Staff said nothing. So I gabbled, "To be honest it was just something to do of an evening, and it didn't take very long —"

"Shut up, you fool." He nodded, smiled and man-hugged me. "Thank you, that's way more than you should have done, but thank you."

The phone rang.

Debbie answered it. "Ziggy!" she said. "Thank you. Yes, first thing." She looked over at me. "I love it . . . I know he did." Silence. "Oh, oh okay. No, that's fine, I understand. Of course you can't come, it's two hundred and fifty miles, I wouldn't expect you to come all this way . . ."

There was a knock at the door. While on the phone Debbie vent to answer it, and opened the door to Ziggy himself standing on the doorstep with his mobile phone pressed to his ear and the biggest stupid grin on his face you've ever seen. Debbie was so flustered she actually said goodbye into the phone even though he was standing right there in front of her.

"I hope you don't mind, but I brought a friend," Ziggy said, stepping back to reveal Garth, both of his arms full of wrapped-up presents.

Over the next hour people arrived from as close as next door to as far as the other end of the country. Debbie's closest friend Paula came all the way from London just to spend a couple of hours with her, cousins came from Birmingham, Steph, my weekend boss from the stables up the hill . . .

"How's Aliana, the minx?" I said, greeting Steph. "Does she miss me?"

"Of course she does. In fact I was going to ask if would you like to work an extra day? Muck out three days a week rather than just the two?"

"Er, must go, need to circulate and all that . . ."

Aaahhhh-nnoooooooooo!

I did my bit with drinks and snacks and when I could I found the boys' corner in the lounge. Staff, Ziggy, Garth and most of the men had gathered there.

Turning to Ziggy I said, "Where's Miss Perfect? Thought you might bring her along."

"We've split up," he said.

Both feet . . . mouth . . . and commence plunging. "Oh no. Again? You're joking?"

He shook his head sadly.

"What happened?"

"I'll tell you another time. Meanwhile Garth here was due to bring his dancing queen but she got a show so he had to leave her behind. So it's just the two of us."

"I'm really grateful you came. It means a lot, it really does."

"Wouldn't miss it for the world. Debbie looks lovely, and so happy."

I looked across at the girls' corner and smiled. She did, she looked beautiful.

"So tell me," Ziggy said, wrapping an arm around my shoulder, "how's the midlife crisis — oh sorry, the *thing!*"

"You're such a prick."

"That," he said, "Is a well-established fact, but does not answer the question."

Mimicking someone who I guessed was supposed to be me, but sounded nothing in the slightest like me at all, he said, "Oh tell me, great and all-knowing General, *dude*, what does it mean to grow old, oh wise one?"

Roaring with laughter and egged on by everyone else, Garth jumped in and, rubbing his chin in a pantomime of deep thought, added in a similar squeaky voice, "Oh, hang on, let me milk a goat while I consider that deep philosophical question."

"You," I said, "have been hanging around too much with him. And you're both idiots."

Chiming in, Stafford said, "One minute, I've just got to consult Ziggy's list . . ." and started unravelling an imaginary scroll. It looked really funny.

"Not you as well — you bunch of mongrels! And that was *nothing* like me at all," I said, even though I knew it was. There was no spite in what they were doing. Besides, it was hilarious. Oh well, if you can't beat them . . .

"You lot know nothing about me," I said, trying to look indignant. "Now, tell me, do my man-boobs look big in this?" I said, looking down and hooking up my pecs.

"Oh don't," Debbie said, coming over, and while the others kept laughing and taunting she put protective arms around me.

It kind of degenerated from there, and went on, and on, and on . . .

"How long are you going to keep this up?" I said.

Ziggy shrugged and said, "The sty's the limit." The groan could be heard from outer space, and someone, who might have been me, threw crisps at him.

I didn't mind being the butt of the jokes. I kind of liked it, although it was a bit of a shock to find out how transparent I obviously was, or maybe how perceptive they were. They really knew me, even some of the stuff I'd never voiced out loud — not knowingly, anyway. But most of the quips revolved around me and my bromance with the General. I could cope with that. Happily.

By early afternoon the house was packed. Debbie went and got two skirt hangers, the ones with crocodile clips at each end, and hung the quilt up in the corner of the lounge. It was funny to watch people go over to it just to search for their square. But everyone seemed to like it.

I left it, and left it, and left it, and left it, until I could leave it no longer. "I've got to go and do the animals," I said. That's the downside to having a smallholding, it's seven days a week, 365 days a year. No days off. Ever. Doesn't matter what's going on.

Ziggy and three others decided to come with me.

"So," I said, when we were clear of the party. "Tell all."

Deep Ziggy-style sigh. "It's like she wants me to change but every time I do she knocks me back for it. The thing is she knows my buttons because she put them there. It's all, 'grow up' and 'don't be such a child'. This time it was me who called it a day on us. We were in the middle of some stupid row, and I just thought, I can't do this anymore. This is not me, and it's not who I want to be. So I kissed her on the forehead, told her I'd support her and the baby as much as I could, wished her luck and walked out."

"Ouch!"

"Yeah, as you can imagine I'm extremely popular at the moment."

"I bet. Have you heard from her since?"

"That's the funny thing, she hasn't stopped calling and texting me. Look . . ." He brought out his phone, his new phone, and swished through the messages. They were all from her. "It's weird, it's as though she's gone back to the days when we first got together. She's flirty and fun and we're getting on brilliantly. When we're like this, makes me remember why we hit it off so amazingly in the first place. I've got to go home after the party tonight — I'm presuming because it's you it's not going to be a late one? Tucked up in bed at the same time as all good four-year-olds?"

I laughed.

"Me and Garth are booked on the last train. I know it'll be late, but I thought I might go around to her house when I get back. What do you think?"

There's a beauty in getting older

"Come here," I said, scrunching over onto Debbie's side of the bed. The party was over and almost everyone had left.

"I didn't know if you'd still want me now I'm fifty," she said.

I sat up. "Good. I wanted to talk to you about that. Now, seriously, I was watching an advert on the telly and apparently there's this over-fifties pension plan —"

"Simon!"

"You don't understand. Hear me out. You get a free Parker pen just for enquiring. That's not something to be sneezed at."

"*Simon!*"

I started laughing. "I'm going to have so much fun."

"Yeah, well not tonight you're not. My mother's in the next room." She lay back and on cue Solly got up on the bed and flopped down between us. Yes, even though he's a Great Dane and the size of a horse, he does sleep on our bed. In the middle. Taking up all he space. Bless him.

"Did you enjoy today?" I said.

"I loved it. Thank you. And thank you for my quilt. You didn't hear the comments, everyone thought it was amazing."

"As long as you thought it was amazing."

"Oh it is, it really is. It's incredible. I can't believe all the people you contacted, and that they all sent you something."

"One day I'll tell you how keen everyone was to get involved. You've no idea how popular you are. Did you know? You can be honest with me now, did you know what I was doing?"

She shook her head. "I swear I didn't."

She did. There's no way she didn't know. But it's done now. Over. Finished. No more secrets. No more packages. No more squares! Back on my side of the bed I snuggled into Solly and fell sleep.

For once I wasn't the first one up in the morning. Debbie's mum was. She was washing up the party stuff from last night when I walked into the kitchen, the drainer already crowded with clean glasses and mugs.

I helped for a bit until it was nearly all done then went out to start the morning rounds, which went without a hitch. Blimey, I'm getting good at this smallholding lark. Geese let out, including Angel Wings. Bertie Wooster and the ducks next. Stupid the cockerel and the rest of the chickens after that. Quail fed and watered. Turkeys fed and watered. Senorita . . .

small breakfast — you should see the size of her! Horses, Georgie Girl and Alfie checked on. Amber milked, Bee stroked, Curry cuddled — all fed and watered. Sheep and lambs watched, while fussing Dex. Then the pigs: Winnie, Pru, wife-of-right-now and the yobs. Saving the best until last, I crawled in with the General.

"Big boy," I said, slumping down next to him. "How's it going?"

It takes a lot of effort to have a *thing* going on, you know. Maintaining that much angst doesn't come cheap. It's only when you pass through it and make it to the other side you realise how much effort it all took. Freed from it, I felt lighter.

Look, I'm only forty-seven, which isn't old. It isn't old at all. But I guess trying to support ourselves and a whole load of animals on a remote smallholding is hard work and does abuse your body, and it's too easy to feel old before your time. Nicks, aches and pains don't heal quite as fast as they once had, and out here, doing what we do, that matters, and I suppose I do get more emotional than if I was an estate agent in London sitting behind a desk. But I don't know if that's more to do with living around animals than my age. I suppose that's one of the drawbacks of not having a parent's lead to follow. I do feel like I'm out on a limb with that, but then I don't think it has anything to do with hitting middle age. That's just one of those things. Debbie and I skipped out of the world into which we were born and did something different, so of course we're not going to have peers to copy. We're making our own way, stumble by stumble.

There are some things I still don't understand and probably never will. Things my younger self buried, and probably for good reason. I don't know why the childhood fear of death came back so strongly, but I do think that was the looming dark presence in my mind. It's weird how those fears never really go away, no matter how hard you try to bury them. But it's gone, for now.

"I should have brought a cup of coffee down with me," I said, resting against the General.

Clearly I don't have it all worked out, but living out here on Exmoor, on this self-sufficient little farm, I've managed to crack a lot of it. I know that hitting middle age is much more than simply your body ageing. Granted, the physical side of it is important, but perhaps it's not as important as I'd thought. The Well Man test proved that I was healthy, and the lifestyle keeps me fit. With any luck I won't even develop man boobs. Okay, I need reading glasses to shear a sheep, but I can live with that.

"So, middle age then, what do you reckon, General?" I gave him a nudge with my elbow. He didn't respond. Guess I'm on my own for this one.

The really interesting discovery I've made is that a lot of it is to do with living in the moment. Mindfulness — yeah, that's it! The really interesting "getting older" changes are happening to me on the inside, and the older I seem to get, the more interesting it feels to be as present and in the moment as I can. I'm not brilliant at it, but I'm getting better and working on it, and you'd be amazed when you're in the zone how easy it is to feel happy.

As for the rest of it, the body image stuff, the *"what have I got to show for my life?"* drama — even the worry that one day I'll find myself cooking lunch at one in the morning as opposed to one on the afternoon — it's not worth stressing over. And the less you stress, the less important it feels.

So no, I know I'm not old, but I am getting older, and the key thing is I'm no longer scared at that prospect. It's okay. There's a kind of beauty in getting older.

"Even in you, big boy," I said out loud to the General. "There's a beauty even in you getting older. Listen, I've got to go. Laters, yeah." And I went.

Up at the house Debbie and her mum were still clearing up. That's when you know you've had a good party, when it takes you a whole day to put everything straight afterwards. They had a CD on. I kicked off my wellies, took off my coat and joined them. When the chorus to the song came on, we all sang to it.

"At the Copa, Copacabana, the hottest spot north of Havana, yeah. At the Copa-aaaaa, the Copacabaaana-aaaaaaaa . . ."

Epilogue

Several months later . . .

My phone rang. I was halfway through morning rounds, surrounded by sheep, chickens, goats, Senorita and Dex.

It was Ziggy.

"Ziggy!"

Nothing. Silence. Then . . . a sob? *A sob?*

"Ziggy, are you okay?"

"Yeah." He was crying, sobbing his heart out. "I'm a dad. She had it. Just now. A girl. She had a little baby girl. *I'm a fucking dad!*"

"Oh Ziggy, that's unreal! Congratulations, man. Congratulations!"

"Thanks. Listen, you're still coming to the wedding, right? Nothing's going to die or give birth on you, is it? You've got it all under control, yeah?"

"You ask me that every time. Yes, you idiot. Now bugger off and go play with your daughter. Shake a rattle in her face or whatever you do with newborns. What's her name, by the way?"

But he was gone. Welcome to the world anyway, baby Ziggy. Your daddy may be a loony, but he's got a heart of gold and he's going to love you to bits.

She is not the only birth I can announce, either. A month or so ago wife-of-right-now had five bouncing baby piglets. That's right, wife-of-right-now. That's right! All hail the General. And she's not the only one he'd been fraternising with. Remember how Senorita was getting a proper thunder belly on her? Well it turns out there was a reason for it. One morning I came down and there were seven babies nuzzling at her. Seems she's not as scared of other pigs as she led me to believe. There was only that one occasion when I left her in with the General for a couple of hours. Quite a game girl on the quiet, our Senorita.

Other than that all the animals are fine. Angel Wings is still tottering about, as is Bertie Wooster, whom it seems has got himself waterproof again and can now go out and play in the rain with the others, lucky thing. The General's still handsome and Curry is still the world's most annoying goat.

My phone rang. Assuming it was Ziggy calling back I didn't bother looking at the screen, just answered it.

"You cut off before you told me her name," I said. "And aren't you supposed to give me a birth weight or something? It's all so different with piglets."

"It's me," Debbie said.

I told her Ziggy's news. I know I was stealing his thunder, but I couldn't help myself.

"Did he cry?"

"Sobbed so hard he could hardly speak. We'll have to send him something."

"Why don't you make a Babygro for the baby?"

I had a flashback to Ziggy sitting in front of me in the pub all those months ago, the night we made up the lists, and him saying, "Fashion, trust me, what you make is not fashion." The thought made me smile, because he's wrong, wrong, wrong.

Debbie continued, "There must be patterns you can look up online. You could even iron on a nice transfer photograph of one of the animals."

I'd walked along the path until I was standing in front of the General's enclosure. I could see him inside his house, lounging on the straw. Head on one side, tongue lolling out, he was looking at me, holding eye contact, listening to every word I said.

"A happy photograph," Debbie said.

"I think that's an excellent idea."

Author note

I'm sitting here in the warm glow of having finished writing this book. It's a good feeling. Half an hour ago Debbie and our Great Dane, Solomon, came in and watched me type "THE END" and we all cheered. I suspect tonight there'll be a celebratory meal and a glass or two of homemade plonk, because that's what you do when you reach the end of a project, no matter how much you've loved the process, and I have — believe me I've laughed, cried and blushed my way through every page — but it's done, and now there are some things I need to share with you.

While I've been as honest as I possibly can, and everything you read really did happen, I have played with the timings of some of the events for the sake of storytelling, and the characters of Ziggy, Garth and Stafford are amalgamations of people in my life and are not meant to represent any one individual person. The animals, however, are all their gorgeous, cantankerous, idiosyncratic, wonderful selves.

Quick shout outs to my long-suffering agent Jane Graham Maw, and the wonderful team at Orion, especially Emma Smith. To Debbie, I love you. To Solomon, leave your bits alone. To the General, yo dude. And to anyone who picks up this book and reads it, thank you.

Buy free-range.

Simon x

Other titles published by Ulverscroft:

PIGS IN CLOVER

Simon Dawson

A drunken misunderstanding changes Simon's life forever. Along with his wife and Great Dane, he moves to the wilds of Devon and takes up the challenge of leaving city life behind. Suddenly surrounded by pigs, chickens, goats and geese, it becomes a journey full of surprises — some funny, some tragic — leading Simon to question Mother Nature, himself, the food he eats, and his place in it all. Whether chasing turkeys, musing over life with the General (the resident alpha pig) or getting knee-deep in mud and mess, Simon learns what it takes to truly survive self-sufficiency and enjoy a slice of the good life.

I LEAP OVER THE WALL

Monica Baldwin

At the age of twenty-one, Monica Baldwin, daughter of Prime Minister Stanley Baldwin, entered one of the oldest and most strictly enclosed contemplative orders of the Roman Catholic Church. Twenty-eight years later, after a prolonged struggle with her vocation, she left the convent. But the world Monica had known in 1914 was very different to the world into which she emerged at the height of the Second World War. This is the account of one woman's two very different lives, with revealing descriptions of the world of a novice, the daily duties of a nun, and the spiritual aspects of convent life. Interwoven with these, as the author is confronted with fashions, politics and art totally unfamiliar to her, are the trials and tribulations of coping with a new and alien world.

THE REAL PEAKY BLINDERS

Carl Chinn

In the backstreets of Birmingham after the First World War, Billy Kimber was a feared fighter with an astute mind and magnetic personality. These attributes earned him the leadership of the Birmingham Gang that dominated the highly profitable protection rackets of the racecourses of England. The members of this gang had once been "sloggers" or "peaky blinders", and their rise to supremacy was attributable to their viciousness and to Kimber's shrewd alliances with other mobs. But they soon incurred the envy of the Sabini Gang of London, who fought violently to oust Kimber and his men and take over their rackets. The Birmingham Gang battled back fiercely in the infamous and bloodstained racecourse wars of the 1920s. These were the real Peaky Blinders, and this is their story.

MY LIFE IN HOUSES

Margaret Forster

Margaret Forster takes us on a journey through the houses she's lived in: from the council house in Carlisle where she was born in 1938, to her beloved London house of today — via the Lake District, Oxford, Hampstead, and a spell in the Mediterranean. This is not a book about bricks and mortar, but a book about what houses are to us, and the effect they have on the way we live our lives. It takes a backwards glance at the changing nature of our accommodation: from blacking grates and outside privies to cities dominated by bedsits and lodgings; and houses today being converted back into single dwellings, all open-plan spaces and bringing the outside in. It is also a very personal inquiry into the meaning of home.

THE BUCKET

Allan Ahlberg

In 1938 Allan Ahlberg was picked up in London by his new adoptive mother and taken back to Oldbury in the Black Country. Now one of the most successful children's book writers in the world, here Allan writes of an oddly enchanted childhood lived out in an industrial town; of a tough and fiercely protective mother; of fearsome bacon slicers; of "fugitive memories, the ones that shimmer on the edges of things: trapdoors in the grass, Dad's dancing overalls". Of "two mothers, two fathers and me like a parcel or a baton (or a hot potato!) passed between them". Using a mix of prose and poetry, supported by new drawings by his daughter Jessica and old photographs, *The Bucket* brings to life the childhood that inspired Allan's classic picture books.

BOBBY ON THE BEAT

Bob Dixon

Bob Dixon spent years "on the beat" as a police constable with the Metropolitan Police in the early 1960s, witnessing all manner of incidents, from the serious to the ludicrous. Spending the majority of his time in London's East End dealing with drunks, fatalities on the road, domestic disputes, and even suicides, as well as policing at major public events such as Guy Fawkes night, New Year's Eve, and anti-Vietnam War marches, life was colourful and varied, if not always safe. This memoir of a London copper charts Bob Dixon's experiences as a young police officer before he joined the CID, covering his life before signing up for the force, his rigorous training, and the vagaries of first patrolling the beat, as well as the lighter side of policing.